STORY
S-T-R-E-T-C-H-E-R-S
for the
Primary Grades:

Activities to Expand Children's Books, Revised Edition

Shirley C. Raines and Brian Scott Smith

Additional books in the STORY S-T-R-E-T-C-H-E-R-S series or written by Shirley Raines:

Raines, Shirley C., Karen Miller, and Leah Curry-Rood. 2002. *STORY S-T-R-E-T-C-H-E-R-S for infants, toddlers, and twos: Experiences, activities, and games for popular children's books*. Silver Spring, MD: Gryphon House, Inc.

Isbell, Rebecca and Shirley C. Raines. 2000. *Tell it again! 2: More easy-to-tell stories with activities for young children*. Silver Spring, MD: Gryphon House, Inc.

Raines, Shirley C. and Rebecca Isbell. 1999. *Tell it again!* Silver Spring, MD: Gryphon House, Inc.

Raines, Shirley C. 1994. *450 more STORY S-T-R-E-T-C-H-E-R-S for the primary grades: Activities to expand children's favorite books*. Silver Spring, MD: Gryphon House, Inc.

Raines, Shirley C. and Robert J. Canady. 1992. *STORY S-T-R-E-T-C-H-E-R-S for the primary grades: Activities to expand children's favorite books*. Silver Spring, MD: Gryphon House, Inc.

Raines, Shirley C. and Robert J. Canady. 1990. *More STORY S-T-R-E-T-C-H-E-R-S: More Activities to expand children's favorite books*. Silver Spring, MD: Gryphon House, Inc.

Raines, Shirley C. & Robert J. Canady. 1989. *STORY S-T-R-E-T-C-H-E-R-S: Activities to expand children's favorite books (Pre-K and K)*. Silver Spring, MD: Gryphon House, Inc.

STORY STRETCHERS

FOR THE
PRIMARY GRADES

Activities to Expand Children's Books
REVISED EDITION

SHIRLEY C. RAINES
and **BRIAN SCOTT SMITH**

Gryphon House
Silver Spring, MD

Library of Congress Cataloging-in-Publication Data
Raines, Shirley C.
 Story stretchers for the primary grades : activities to expand children's books / Shirley Raines and Brian Scott Smith. -- Rev. ed.
    p. cm.
   ISBN 978-0-87659-309-7 (pbk.)
1. Children's literature--Study and teaching (Primary)--United States. 2. Education, Primary--Activity programs--Handbooks, manuals, etc. 3. Children--Books and reading--Handbooks, manuals, etc. 4. Teaching--Aids and devices--Handbooks, manuals, etc. I. Smith, Brian Scott, 1966- II. Title.
 LB1527.R35 2011
 372.64'044--dc22

                                        2011011474

Bulk purchase
Gryphon House books are available for special premiums and sales promotions as well as for fund-raising use. Special editions or book excerpts also can be created to specification. For details, contact the Director of Sales at the address above.

Disclaimer
Gryphon House Inc. and the authors cannot be held responsible for damage, mishap, or injury incurred during the use of or because of activities in this book. Appropriate and reasonable caution and adult supervision of children involved in activities and corresponding to the age and capability of each child involved, is recommended at all times. Do not leave children unattended at any time. Observe safety and caution at all times.

Acknowledgments

Cover of ABOUT BIRDS: A GUIDE FOR CHILDREN by Cathryn Sill. Illustrated by John Sill. Copyright © 1997. Published by Peachtree. Used by permission.

Cover of AIRPLANES: SOARING! TURNING! DIVING! by Patricia Hubbell. Illustrated by Megan Halsey and Sean Addy. Text copyright © 2008 by Patricia Hubbell. Illustrations copyright © 2008 by Megan Halsey and Sean Addy. Published by Marshall Cavendish. Used by permission.

Cover of ALEXANDER AND THE TERRRIBLE, HORRIBLE, NO GOOD, VERY BAD DAY by Judith Viorst, illustrated by Ray Cruz. Text copyright © 1972 by Judith Viorst. Illustrations copyright renewed © 2000 by Ray Cruz. Preface copyright © 2009 by Judith Viorst and Ray Cruz. Reprinted with permission from Simon and Schuster.

Cover of ALL KINDS OF FAMILIES by Norma Simon. Illustrated by Joe Lasker. Text copyright © 1976 by Norma Simon. Illustrations copyright © 1976 by Joe Lasker. Published by Albert Whitman & Company. Used by permission.

Cover of ALWAYS GOT MY FEET by Laura Purdie Salas. Copyright © 2008. Published by Capstone Press. Used by permission.

Cover of AMAZING GRACE by Mary Hoffman, illustrated by Caroline Binch, used by permission: AMAZING GRACE by Mary Hoffman, illustrated by Caroline Binch. Text © 1991 by Mary Hoffman. Illustrations © by Caroline Binch. Used by permission of Dial Books for Young Readers, A Division of Penguin Young Readers Group, A Member of Penguin Group (USA) Inc., 345 Hudson Street, New York, NY 10014. All rights reserved.

Cover of AMELIA BEDELIA'S FAMILY ALBUM. Text copyright © 1988 by Peggy Parish. Illustrations copyright © 1988 by Lynn Sweat. Published by HarperCollins Publishers. Used by permission.

Cover of ANGELINA AND ALICE (ANGELINA BALLERINA) by Katharine Holabird, illustrated by Helen Craig, used by permission: ANGELINA AND ALICE (ANGELINA BALLERINA) by Katharine Holabird, illustrated by Helen Craig. Text © 1987 by Katharine Holabird. Illustrations © 1987 by Helen Craig. Used by permission of Viking Children's Books, A Division of Penguin Young Readers Group, A Member of Penguin Group (USA) Inc., 345 Hudson Street, New York, NY 10014. All rights reserved.

Cover of ARROWHAWK by Lola M. Schaefer. Illustrated by Gabi Swiatkowska.Text copyright © 2004 by Lola M. Schaefer. Illustrations copyright © 2004 by Gabi Swiatkowska. Published by Henry Holt and Company, LLC. Used by permission.

Cover of ARTHUR'S BIRTHDAY by Marc Tolon Brown. Copyright © 1991. Published by Little, Brown and Company, a division of Hachette Book Group, Inc. Used by permission.

Cover of ARTHUR'S TEACHER TROUBLE by Marc Tolon Brown. Copyright © 1986 by Marc Brown. Published by Little, Brown and Company, a division of Hachette Book Group, Inc. Used by permission.

Cover of BOOK FAIR DAY by Lynn Plourde, illustrated by Thor Wickstrom, used by permission: BOOK FAIR DAY by Lynn Plourde, illustrated by Thor Wickstrom. Text © 2006 by Lynn Plourde. Illustrations © 2006 by Thor Wickstrom. Used by permission of Dutton Children's Books, A Division of Penguin Young Readers Group, A Member of Penguin Group (USA) Inc., 345 Hudson Street, New York, NY 10014. All rights reserved.

Cover of BOX TURTLE AT LONG POND. Text copyright © 1989 by William Trimpi George. Illustrations copyright © 1989 by Lindsay Barrett George. Published by Greenwillow Books, a division of HarperCollins Publishers. Used by permission.

Cover of BUTTON UP! WRINKLED RHYMES by Alice Shertle. Pictures by Petra Mathers. Text copyright © 2009 by Alice Shertle. Illustrations copyright © 2009 by Petra Mathers. Published by Harcourt Children's Books, a division of Houghton Mifflin Harcourt Publishing Company. Used by permission.

Cover of A CHAIR FOR MY MOTHER by Vera B. Williams. Copyright © 1982 by Vera B. Williams. Published by HarperCollins Children's Books, a division of HarperCollins Publishers. Used by permission.

Cover of CHARLOTTE'S WEB. Copyright © 1952 by E. B. White. Text copyright renewed © 1980 by E. B. White. Illustrations copyright renewed © 1980 by Estate of Garth Williams. Published by HarperCollins Children's Books, a division of HarperCollins Publishers. Used by permission.

Cover of CHESTER'S WAY. Copyright © 1988 by Kevin Henkes. Published by HarperCollins Children's Books, a division of HarperCollins Publishers. Used by permission.

Cover of CHRYSANTHEMUM. Copyright © 1991 by Kevin Henkes. Published by HarperCollins Children's Books, a division of HarperCollins Publishers. Used by permission.

Cover of A COUPLE OF BOYS HAVE THE BEST WEEK EVER by Marla Frazee. Copyright © 2008 by Marla Frazee. Published by Harcourt. Used by permission.

Cover of DEWEY: THERE'S A CAT IN THE LIBRARY! by Vicki Myron. Copyright © 2009 by Vicki Myron. Published by Little, Brown and Company, a division of Hachette Book Group, Inc. Used by permission.

Cover of DINOSAURS GO GREEN! HOW TO PROTECT OUR PLANET by Marc Brown and Laurie Krasny Brown. Copyright © 1992, 2009 by Laurie Krasny Brown and Marc Brown. Published by Little, Brown and Company, a division of Hachette Book Group, Inc. Used by permission.

Cover of DIRT ON MY SHIRT by Jeff Foxworthy. Illustrations by Steve Bjorkman. Copyright © 2008 by Jeff Foxworthy. Published by HarperCollins Children's Books, a division of HarperCollins Publishers. Used by permission.

Cover of EIGHT ATE: A FEAST OF HOMONYM RIDDLES by Marvin Terban. Illustrated by Guilio Maestro. Text copyright © 1982 by Marvin Terban. Illustration copyright © 1982 by Guilio Maestro. First Clarion paper edition, 1982; reissued 2007. Published by Clarion Books, a Houghton Mifflin company imprint. Used by permission.

Cover of ENCYCLOPEDIA BROWN'S BOOK OF STRANGE BUT TRUE CRIMES by Donald J. Sobol and Rose Sobol, used by permission: Book cover from ENCYCLOPEDIA BROWN'S BOOK OF STRANGE BUT TRUE CRIMES by Donald J. Sobol, jacket painting by Mike Wimmer. Jacket painting copyright © 1991 by Mike Wimmer. Reprinted by permission of Scholastic Inc.

Cover of THE FANTASTIC UNDERSEA LIFE OF JACQUES COUSTEAU by Dan Yaccarino. Copyright © 2009 by Dan Yaccarino. Published by Alfred A. Knopf, an imprint of Random House Children's Books, a division of Random House, Inc. Used by permission.

Cover of FIRST GRADE, HERE I COME! by Nancy Carlson, used by permission: FIRST GRADE, HERE I COME by Nancy Carlson, copyright © 2006 by Nancy Carlson. Used by permission of Viking Children's Books, A Division of Penguin Young Readers Group, A Member of Penguin Group (USA) Inc., 345 Hudson Street, New York, NY 10014. All rights reserved.

Cover of FLAT STANLEY by Jeff Brown. Text copyright © 1964 by Jeff Brown. Copyright renewed © 1992 by Jeff Brown. Illustrations by Macky Pamintuan, copyright © 2009 by HarperCollins Publishers. Published by HarperCollins Children's Books, a division of HarperCollins Publishers. Used by permission.

Cover of FOR THE LOVE OF AUTUMN by Patricia Polacco, used by permission: FOR THE LOVE OF AUTUMN by Patricia Polacco, copyright © 2008 by Babushka, Inc. Used by permission of Philomel Books, A Division of Penguin Young Readers Group, A Member of Penguin Group (USA) Inc., 345 Hudson Street, New York, NY 10014. All rights reserved.

Cover of FROG AND TOAD ARE FRIENDS by Arnold Lobel. Copyright © 1970 by Arnold Lobel. Published by HarperCollins Children's Books, a division of HarperCollins Publishers. Used by permission.

Cover of FROGS by Nic Bishop, used by permission: Book cover from FROGS by Nic Bishop. Copyright © 2008 by Nic Bishop. Reprinted by permission of Scholastic Inc.

Cover of GEORGE AND MARTHA: RISE AND SHINE by James Marshall. Copyright © 1976 by James Marshall. Published by Houghton Mifflin Books for Children, a division of Houghton Mifflin Harcourt. Used by permission.

Cover of MY VISIT TO THE AQUARIUM by Aliki. Copyright © 1993 by Aliki Brandenberg. Published by HarperCollins Children's Books, a division of HarperCollins Publishers. Used by permission.

Cover of NATE THE GREAT GOES UNDERCOVER by Marjorie Weinman Sharmat. Illustrated by Marc Simont. Text copyright © 1974 by Marjorie Weinman Sharmat. Illustrations copyright © 1974 by Marc Simont. Extra Fun Activities copyright © 2006 by Emily Costello. Extra Fun Activities illustrations copyright © 2006 by Laura Hart. Published by Yearling Books, an imprint of Random House children's books, a division of Random House, Inc. Used by permission.

Cover of OFFICER BUCKLE AND GLORIA by Peggy Rathman, used by permission: OFFICER BUCKLE AND GLORIA by Peggy Rathman, copyright © 1995 by Peggy Rathman. Used by permission of G.P. Putnam's Sons, A Division of Penguin Young Readers Group, A Member of Penguin Group (USA) Inc., 345 Hudson Street, New York, NY 10014. All rights reserved.

Cover of OH, THE PLACES YOU'LL GO! by Dr. Seuss. TM and copyright © 1990 by Dr. Seuss Enterprises, L.P. Published by Random House Children's Books, a division of Random House, Inc. Used by permission.

Cover of ONCE UPON A COOL MOTORCYCLE DUDE by Kevin O'Malley. Illustrated by Carol Heyer and Scott Goto. Copyright © 2005. Published by Walker Books. Used by permission.

Cover of ONE FINE DAY by Nonny Hogrogian. Copyright © 1971 by Nonny Hogrogian. Reprinted with permission from Simon and Schuster.

Cover illustration from THE PAPER BAG PRINCESS, written by Robert N. Munsch, illustrated by Michael Martchenko, and published by Annick Press. © 1980 Used by permission.

Cover of PLANTING THE TREES OF KENYA: THE STORY OF WANGARI MAATHAI by Claire A. Nivola. Copyright © 2008 by Claire A. Nivola. Published by Farrar, Straus & Giroux. Used by permission.

Cover of RAINBOW CROW retold by Nancy Van Laan, illustrated by Beatriz Vidal. Text copyright © 1989 by Nancy Van Laan. Illustrations copyright © 1989 by Beatriz Vidal. Published by Alfred A. Knopf. Used by permission.

Cover of RAMONA QUIMBY, AGE 8 by Beverly Cleary. Copyright © 1991 by Beverly Cleary. Published by HarperCollins Children's Books, a division of HarperCollins Publishers. Used by permission.

Cover of RECYCLE! A HANDBOOK FOR KIDS by Gail Gibbons. Copyright © 1992 by Gail Gibbons. Published by Little, Brown and Company, a division of Hachette Book Group, Inc. Used by permission.

Cover of THE RELATIVES CAME by Cynthia Rylant, illustrated by Stephen Gammell. Text copyright © 1985 by Cynthia Rylant. Illustrations copyright © 1985 by Stephen Gammell. Reprinted with permission from Simon and Schuster.

Cover of RICHARD SCARRY'S CARS AND TRUCKS AND THINGS THAT GO by Richard Scarry. Copyright © 1974 by Richard Scarry. Copyright renewed 2002 by Richard Scarry II. Published by Golden Books, an imprint of Random House Children's Books, a division of Random House, Inc. Used by permission.

Cover of RIPTIDE by Frances Ward Weller, illustrated by Robert J. Blake, used by permission: RIPTIDE by Frances Ward Weller, illustrated by Robert J. Blake. Text © 1990 by Frances Ward Weller. Illustrations by Robert J. Blake. Used by permission of Philomel Books, A Division of Penguin Young Readers Group, A Member of Penguin Group (USA) Inc., 345 Hudson Street, New York, NY 10014. All rights reserved.

Cover of SAM THE SEA COW by Francine Jacobs. Illustrated by Laura Kelly. Copyright © 1979 by Francine Jacobs. Copyright © 1991 by Laura Kelly. Published by Walker Books. Used by permission.

Cover of SPARROWS by Hans Post and Kees Heij. Illustrated by Irene Goode. Copyright © 2008. Published by Boyds Mill Press. Used by permission.

Cover of THE STINKY CHEESE MAN AND OTHER FAIRLY STUPID TALES by Jon Scieszka, illustrated by Lane Smith used by permission: THE STINKY CHEESE MAN AND OTHER FAIRLY STUPID TALES by Jon Scieszka, illustrated by Lane Smith. Text © 1992 by Jon Scieszka. Illustrations © 1992 by Lane Smith. Used by permission of Viking Penguin, A Division of Penguin Young Readers Group, A Member of Penguin Group (USA) Inc., 345 Hudson Street, New York, NY 10014. All rights reserved.

Cover of STUFF!: REDUCE, REUSE, RECYLE by Steven Kroll. Illustrated by Steve Cox. Text copyright © 2009 by Steve Kroll. Illustrations copyright © 2009 by Steve Cox. Published by Marshall Cavendish. Used by permission.

Cover of SWISH! by Bill Martin Jr. and Michael Sampson. Illustrated by Michael Chesworth. Text copyright © 1997 by Bill Martin Jr. and Michael Sampson. Illustrations copyright © 1997 by Michael Chesworth. Published by Henry Holt and Company, LLC. Used by permission.

Cover of TEACH US, AMELIA BEDELIA by Peggy Parish. Illustrated by Lynn Sweat. Text copyright 1977 by Margaret Parish. Illustrations copyright 1977, 2003 by Lynn Sweat. Published by HarperCollins Children's Books, a division of HarperCollins Publishers. Used by permission.

Cover of THE TRUE STORY OF THE THREE LITTLE PIGS by Jon Scieszka, illustrated by Lane Smith, used by permission: THE TRUE STORY OF THE THREE LITTLE PIGS by Jon Scieszka, illustrated by Lane Smith. Text © 1989 by Jon Scieszka. Illustrations © 1989 by Lane Smith. Used by permission of Viking Penguin, A Division of Penguin Young Readers Group, A Member of Penguin Group (USA) Inc., 345 Hudson Street, New York, NY 10014. All rights reserved.

Contents

Preface

Selecting quality children's books, planning the thematic units, writing the STORY S-T-R-E-T-C-H-E-R-S, and finding the accompanying Internet references involved many people. While our colleagues are many, we want to thank a few special individuals.

Thank you to the authors, illustrators, and publishers who recognized the value of the STORY S-T-R-E-T-C-H-E-R-S series as a way to bring more children to their books. We also are grateful to the teachers, librarians, parents, after-school care providers, principals, and curriculum specialists who selected this resource book because you recognize the power of story to attract and to teach children.

To my husband, Robert J. Canady, who was instrumental in the writing of the first books, thanks for believing in this new writing partnership with my son, Brian Scott Smith.

To Kathy Charner, Editor Extraordinaire, for tracking down the permissions from publishers, authors, and illustrators, but most importantly, for helping us express our ideas more straightforwardly. We would be remiss, however, if we failed to give credit to Leah Curry-Rood, former publisher of Gryphon House, who helped us with previous selections of children's books and who kept pushing us to find "the best" children's books. She also was a co-author with Karen Miller and me of *STORY S-T-R-E-T-C-H-E-R-S for Infants, Toddlers, and Twos*. To Larry Rood, former president of Gryphon House, who believed in the concept of STORY S-T-R-E-T-C-H-E-R-S enough to publish the first book, which later led to the series of five books. Larry and Leah must be thanked by teachers, librarians, and parents for championing the cause of providing resource books of the highest quality at a reasonable cost. They also ran a company of the highest quality, whose employees were treated with dignity and valued for their contributions. I am pleased to have my name associated with Gryphon House.

To Lynda Kathryn Sharp, who co-taught a children's literature course with me at the University of Memphis and provided access to primary-grade teachers who excel in matching children's interests with quality children's literature. To Jean Rakow, who helped us discover the explosion of electronic materials now available to assist teachers and librarians. To Kelli Luebbe, who helped prepare the manuscript and to Shirl Sharpe and Autumn McGhee, who helped track down books for their availability; we could not have completed this book without you.

To the children—every teacher and teacher-educator must thank the children. We have come to count on you for the honesty, joy, and seriousness with which you tackle the world that we adults share with you. Thank you for the time we have spent together in your classrooms and libraries searching for books whose titles could not be remembered, but whose covers you knew you would recognize. You are the reason that we include illustrations of the book covers as part of *STORY S-T-R-E-T-C-H-E-R-S for the Primary Grades: Activities to Expand Children's Books, Revised Edition*.

Over the years, we were often asked if we had a book about literature-rich and print-rich environments that promote literacy learning and skills development, and that strengthen concepts. Now, we can say, "Yes, six books, including the latest: *STORY S-T-R-E-T-C-H-E-R-S for the Primary Grades: Activities to Expand Children's Books, Revised Edition*. This revised book includes many new children's books and the best book selections from the two previous STORY S-T-R-E-T-C-H-E-R books for the primary grades.

Shirley C. Raines

and

Brian Scott Smith

Introduction

STORY S-T-R-E-T-C-H-E-R-S for the Primary Grades: Activities to Expand Children's Books, Revised Edition is the sixth in this series of resource books for teachers, librarians and teachers. In this revised edition, we added new children's books and combined them with the best children's books from the two previous STORY S-T-R-E-T-C-H-E-R books written for the primary grades. We kept many of your favorite children's books, such as *Alexander and the Terrible, Horrible, No Good, Very Bad Day; The Magic School Bus;* and *Frog and Toad*. We added more Caldecott Honor and Medal winners, such as *A Couple of Boys Have the Best Week Ever, The Stinky Cheese Man,* and *The Hello, Goodbye Window*.

About the Format of the Book

For teachers, parents, and librarians new to the STORY S-T-R-E-T-C-H-E-R-S series, a few words about this resource book for you. We devised STORY S-T-R-E-T-C-H-E-R-S because first-, second-, and third-grade children love a good story. We grouped children's favorite books around curriculum themes and selected 18 different curriculum themes for this book. For each theme, we feature five children's books.

The themes are ones often found in social studies, science, and language arts curriculum in the primary grades. For example, among the social studies units, we included families; for science, endangered animals; and for language arts, folktales, fables, and legends.

For each children's book in the 18 curriculum themes, we have written five STORY S-T-R-E-T-C-H-E-R-S or activities that connect to the book and are appropriate for primary-grade children. These 450 activities s-t-r-e-t-c-h the 90 children's books and also support the curriculum. For each book, there is a story line or story summary that includes information about the illustrations. Suggestions for the read-aloud presentation of each book are provided to make the story or factual information come alive for the listeners.

Among the 90 children's books are old favorites, classics that have stood the test of time, and some new favorites that teachers, librarians, bookstore owners, and children have called to our attention. From the hundreds of new books on the market, we selected ones that appeal to children, and we tested their appeal by asking teachers to read them to their classes and gauge the children's interest. This is the reason for the subtitle: *Activities to Expand Children's Books*. We also verified that the books featured are currently in print or readily available.

Some of your students' favorites may not have been selected because the topics were of a very sensitive nature that did not lend themselves to being stretched easily or extended into other areas of the curriculum. For example, a book about the death of a pet may be an excellent selection as a part of a unit on caring for pets, but the sensitivity of the topic may not lend itself to related activities. Likewise, some family books about divorce or books about disabilities are excellent read-aloud suggestions and can be included in units, but may not be appropriate for extension activities or STORY S-T-R-E-T-C-H-E-R-S.

Integrated Thematic Units

While an integrated unit by its nature includes activities across the curriculum, the social studies, science, and language arts themes in this book are based on strong concepts. The conceptual understandings are developed through the shared experience of the story and reinforced by the recommended STORY S-T-R-E-T-C-H-E-R-S. Collectively, each thematic unit contains five read-aloud suggestions and 25 STORY S-T-R-E-T-C-H-E-R-S inspired by the five focus books. As with all STORY S-T-R-E-T-C-H-E-R activities, and indeed all good instruction, the teacher or parent will make the associations and connections that best fit the developmental needs of the age and the individual interests of each child. Concepts are built through the themes and connections to excellent stories. Using the books, the stories, and their main ideas throughout the curriculum gives children more exposure to the main ideas and reinforces the concepts in interesting ways.

In *STORY S-T-R-E-T-C-H-E-R-S for the Primary Grades: Activities to Expand Children's Books, Revised Edition*, some very pertinent, new, integrated thematic units are included. Some examples are the environmental unit of "Recycle, Reuse, Repurpose"; "Endangered Animals"; "Birds"; and "Trees and Rain Forests." While often thought of as science units, because of the social studies aspects of the human interaction around each of these concerns, they also are rich social studies units, exploring geography, behaviors, and individual and community responsibilities. We have also kept the favorite social studies units "Friends," "Families," "Dogs and Cats" and "Transportation."

For the essential reading and language arts units, we have "Folktales, Fables, and Legends"; "Poetry Children Want to Read"; and "Favorite Characters in a Series." We developed two units often requested by teachers and librarians and very popular with primary-grade children: "Jokes, Riddles, and Fun with Words" and "Fractured Fairy Tales and Stories with a Twist."

References, Additional References, and Websites

At the end of each thematic unit, there is reference information for the five focus books, an annotated bibliography for three additional references, and a selection of websites, which are excellent resources. For example, in the first unit, "Look What I Can Do!" we include websites that help teachers and parents support children's character development and engender a genuine sense of pride based on what they are learning. In the unit "Endangered Animals," websites with audio and visual resources are included to help teachers and parents increase children's understanding of the plight of these animals. For some books, there are additional materials, such as bird posters from the Audubon Society. Whenever possible, we provide websites from the publisher, author, or illustrator for the book. These references, additional references, and websites provide the teacher, parent, or librarian with more resources to enrich the thematic unit.

Read-Aloud, the Reading Process, and Concept Development

Teachers are like great musicians. To become a great musician one must know the music and then use one's skills and knowledge to make the music come to life. Teachers know children's books and can make them come to life for children by using what they know about different concepts and about children's interests and abilities. In *STORY S-T-R-E-T-C-H-E-R-S for the Primary Grades: Activities to Expand Children's Books, Revised Edition*, we help teachers bring books to life by presenting the story line for the book, including a note about illustrations. Just as music has notations to guide the musician about how to play it, the notations in the Read-Aloud Presentations in this book suggest how to present the story.

In the Read-Aloud Presentations, the reading is presented as an interactive thought/language process. The suggestions are based on relating the children's prior knowledge and experiences to the main ideas of the story, asking the children to offer predictions, and confirming information drawn from their own experiences. The students also integrate the concepts and new information by using them in the STORY S-T-R-E-T-C-H-E-R-S activities. Through the activities, the students build more connections to the concepts and main ideas for each unit.

After the read-aloud suggestions, we offer five ways to "orchestrate" the curriculum to take advantage of the story's underlying concepts, illustrations, and associations that are easy for children to make. These activities that connect the book, the concepts, the theme, and the areas of the curriculum are the STORY S-T-R-E-T-C-H-E-R-S.

Often the children are asked to revisit the book to read the text and look at the illustrations again. In the STORY S-T-R-E-T-C-H-E-R-S for the classroom library, we suggest many individual and guided reading activities. Rich listening, speaking, and drama possibilities help children to develop a strong sense of story.

In addition to the read-aloud presentations and other language arts activities, we assume that teachers who use children's literature will also provide blocks of time for children to read books of their own choosing. In addition to the focus books for each unit, the classroom library or display areas should include a variety of other books on the theme that the children can choose to read. A diverse collection of books from different genres is needed in the classroom library to allow children to follow their own reading interests. Of course, some of the children's favorite books should also be a part of the permanent classroom collection.

The Writing Process

There are many STORY S-T-R-E-T-C-H-E-R-S that offer opportunities for children to write. A core concept in classrooms where children are active language users is the belief that children's writing is as natural a response to stories as are listening to stories and dramatizing and discussing stories. The suggestions for writing are based on a developmental view of children's writing. Children's thinking about a story or about a concept naturally leads to writing about what they know, what they observe, and what they can imagine.

Writing is a "constructivist" process. Children construct their writing from the printed symbols they know, whether it is the invented spelling of the first grader or the uncertain sentence structure of the third grader writing his or her own book. Children should be encouraged to use whatever they know and to construct language in print and speech, while growing in their abilities to write and to spell.

Throughout the book, we suggest that children read their writing to an editing or a listening group. Whether the writing is constructed on a sheet of paper or on a computer screen or describes a drawing, it helps children to understand that they can improve their own writing by editing it. For many children in the primary grades, prewriting may mean drawing a picture or talking with a writing partner. The second step is writing a draft. If a child gets stuck and needs more ideas, the child can call for a writing partner or a writing conference with the teacher or an editing group.

First graders who are just learning to edit for content will usually add sentences to the ends of their stories, rather than rearranging the stories. Second and third graders can rewrite drafts by rearranging and inserting new content. After one or more drafts, the teacher and the child can decide whether to edit the piece for classroom publication.

Writing is meant to be read; therefore, we suggest providing many opportunities for children to share their compositions. Whether this means setting aside a regular time each day for individual children to sit in a special chair (an "author's chair") and read his or her writing to the audience, or dramatize her or his writing with puppets, or present a particular piece of writing with musical accompaniment, the ways of sharing one's writing are as rich and diverse as the children's imaginations. From prewriting to publication, the amount of editing and rewriting depends upon the children's abilities and interests. Children should not be expected to edit everything they write for classroom publication. As they refine their understanding of what makes a good story or a good informational piece, they can select those pieces of writing with the most potential and edit them to the classroom publication stage.

Teachers often ask when they should give instruction in writing. Certainly, the teacher is a role model and many of the STORY S-T-R-E-T-C-H-E-R-S suggest that teachers brainstorm with children about possible content, compose group stories, and model the editing process with the teacher's own writing. By connecting great children's books with the writing process, the teacher helps focus the students' attention on specific aspects of story structure. From quality children's books, teachers can provide examples that help children develop attention-getters for the beginning sections of their stories, use more descriptive words, write dialogue, connect episodes, and find just the right point at which to end the story for an effective climax.

By assisting children throughout the writing process, the teacher can assess and then provide the specific help each child needs. We suggest keeping a portfolio, letting the students select pieces for the portfolio that they enjoyed writing or ones that reflect their best writing. The writing portfolios can be shared with parents and used to help the children see their own progress throughout the year.

Choice Is a Powerful Motivator

Choice is integral to the operation of a classroom that uses children's literature as an organizing structure. In addition to the obvious choices of which books they read from well-stocked school and classroom libraries, there are other choices children can make throughout the day and throughout the curriculum. Children who exercise choice become more creative, expressive, and motivated. Provide a balance of child-choice and teacher-directed activities so children can choose which STORY S-T-R-E-T-C-H-E-R-S they will complete, which topics they will write about, how they will share their writing, and which science and nature problems they will investigate in more depth, including how to display their findings in mathematical terms.

Representational Competence and the Problem-Solving Process: Science and Mathematical Understanding

Although children are active learners who are capable of choosing from a variety of possible activities, there must be the expectation that they also will develop their representational competence—the ability to represent what they have learned. Whether they use a calendar to keep track of the weather for a month, a balance to compare weights, or a graph to chart preferences, children are asked to solve problems by collecting data, summarizing or demonstrating their findings, and selecting ways to represent their solutions. While rather simple by adult standards, this systematic observation, conscious record keeping, and discovery of ways to share findings with others are the basics of science and mathematical problem solving. Children can generate problems and explanations that employ sound scientific and mathematical understandings. In addition to becoming more competent in reading and writing, children who perform science and mathematics STORY S-T-R-E-T-C-H-E-R-S also demonstrate their knowledge of the vocabulary and the skills of science and mathematics. They come to know the concepts and use the appropriate terms, phrases, and vocabulary by representing what they have learned.

Literature Is the Experience

Quality children's literature is central to expanding students' ever-widening view of the world. In addition to the thousands of ways hearing and reading the story and information books make the curriculum more interesting, we know that the literature itself is the experience. The primary-school child who confidently says, "I can read that book," and plunges into *Frog and Toad Are Friends* does so because the author tells a predictable but interesting story. While savoring the content of the story, he also is relishing the style of the writing. The girl who pores over *My Visit to the Aquarium*, then rushes over to proclaim that a skate is a fish and not just something you put on your feet has learned a valuable concept, but the fact that the literature is written factually yet rhythmically makes the child return to the text to read it again. Aliki's beautiful illustrations also draw her back to connect with the words, the beauty of the text. The child who discovers other Aliki books and announces, "I like books by this author," is stating preferences, a major milestone for children becoming accomplished readers and thinkers. When children identify favorite characters and favorite authors and seek certain types of stories, then literature has become the experience.

Art appreciation is also part of the children's literature experience. Someone said that children's books are the last source of inexpensive, great art. Illustrations give children the opportunity to observe closely and appreciate great drawings, paintings, pastels, and watercolors. We have included the full names of authors and illustrators, so that adults can become familiar with them and request other books by these authors and illustrators.

How to Use the Book

Teachers, librarians, and parents have told us that they use STORY S-T-R-E-T-C-H-E-R books as they are written, or by adapting, revising, and writing their own variations. As authors of *STORY S-T-R-E-T-C-H-E-R-S for the Primary Grades: Activities to Expand Children's Books, Revised Edition*, we help you by identifying quality children's literature, promoting active learning, and strengthening the curriculum. The power of story, the enticement of beautiful illustrations, and the fascination of factual information is paired with children's natural curiosity to provide a powerful teaching tool, the STORY S-T-R-E-T-C-H-E-R-S resource books.

Some teachers, especially beginning teachers, use all of the books and STORY S-T-R-E-T-C-H-E-R-S in a unit, using one focus book per day. Other teachers read the five focus books during the time they have set aside for reading aloud to the children and complete some of the STORY S-T-R-E-T-C-H-E-R-S, selecting one or two activities for each day of the week. Some librarians read one or two of the focus books and coordinate with teachers to conduct the STORY S-T-R-E-T-C-H-E-R-S in various areas of the curriculum. Some art and music teachers coordinate their art and music activities as STORY S-T-R-E-T-C-H-E-R-S so they relate to the themes the children are studying in their classrooms. Likewise, some specialty science teachers in elementary schools focus only on the science themes and the related STORY S-T-R-E-T-C-H-E-R-S to support the science concepts that the children are learning and to develop their problem-solving skills. Most important, these adults are adopting, adapting, revising, and devising STORY S-T-R-E-T-C-H-E-R-S with their students in mind.

Whether they are used by a student teacher, beginning teacher, or seasoned veteran, the goal of these STORY S-T-R-E-T-C-H-E-R-S is to connect children, stories, and the curriculum through good books. Librarians; reading specialists; scout leaders; specialty art, music, and science teachers; after-school care providers; principals; and curriculum directors have found many inventive ways to incorporate STORY S-T-R-E-T-C-H-E-R-S into their classrooms, organizations, centers, schools, and libraries.

Over these many years, we appreciate the reception the STORY S-T-R-E-T-C-H-E-R-S series of books has received. The success stories you have shared with us at state conferences, national conventions, and local school visits were the driving force for another STORY S-T-R-E-T-C-H-E-R-S book. This revised edition combines the best of the two former books written for the primary grades with new children's books and STORY S-T-R-E-T-C-H-E-R-S. We eagerly await your responses.

References

Gardner, Howard. 2006. *Multiple Intelligences: New Horizons in Theory and Practice.* New York: Basic Books.

Isbell, Rebecca T. and Shirley C. Raines. 2007. *Creativity and the Arts with Young Children.* Clifton Park, NY: Thomson Delmar Learning.

Jalongo, M.R. 2003, Summer. A position paper of the Association for Childhood Education International: the child's right to creative thought and expression. *Childhood Education.* 79(4), 218-228.

Look What I Can Do!

The Little Engine That Could

By Watty Piper
Illustrated by Loren Long

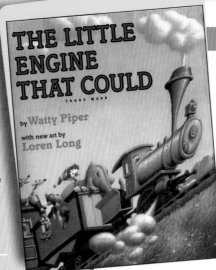

Story Line

When the little train breaks down and cannot deliver the Christmas toys, good food, and treats to the children on the other side of the mountain, she needs help. The shiny new engine, used to pulling passenger cars, will not help. The big, black freight engine will not help. The rusty old engine is too tired to help. When it seems like the boys and girls on the other side of the mountain will have no toys or good food or treats, along comes the little, blue roundhouse engine who tries. "I think I can. I think I can. I think I can," became one of the most memorable phrases in children's literature and motivation for trying.

Read-Aloud Presentation

Begin with repeating the phrase, "I think I can. I think I can. I think I can." Ask the children to recall a time when they tried very hard to learn something new, such as riding a bike or hitting a baseball or kicking a soccer goal. Ask who has said, "I think I can. I think I can. I think I can." Recall with the children the story of *The Little Engine That Could*, read the book, and note the sequence of the different engines and the ending, "I thought I could. I thought I could. I thought I could." Ask them to chant the phrase with you.

STORY S-T-R-E-T-C-H-E-R

Art: I Tried and I Could Pictures

What the children will learn

To compare early attempts at learning to do something well (before) and (later on), the pleasure of being successful

Materials you will need

Newsprint or construction paper, crayons or markers

What to do

1. Recall with the children their earlier discussion of all the things they once did not know how to do and now they do, such as riding a bike, hitting a ball, kicking a soccer ball, or skateboarding.
2. Have the children fold their art paper in half and on one side write, "I think I can. I think I can. I think I can." On the other side write, "I thought I could. I thought I could. I thought I could."
3. Let the students draw their failed attempts to learn a skill on one side of the paper and their success in learning that skill on the other side.

Something to think about

Discuss new things the students are learning in school, such as new math problems. Point out how it seems hard at first, but soon you are telling them, "I thought you could."

STORY S-T-R-E-T-C-H-E-R

Mathematics: How Many Toys Fit?

What the children will learn

To estimate size and amount of space

Materials you will need

Different sizes of boxes, toys, and games

What to do

1. Stack toys and games from around the classroom on a table.
2. Select a few children and have them estimate the number of toys that will fit in the different sizes of boxes, like the boxcars in *The Little Engine That Could*.
3. Let the children try packing each box; others can look on and say whether or not they think more toys and games will fit in the box.

Something to think about

Discuss how, when traveling, it is often difficult to get everything into our suitcases. Relate *that* to wanting to fit everything in a backpack, just like they wanted to put more toys in the boxcars.

STORY S-T-R-E-T-C-H-E-R

Music: "She'll Be Comin' 'Round the Mountain When She Comes"

What the children will learn

To adapt an old folk song to fit a story

Materials you will need

Chart paper or whiteboard, markers

What to do

1. Recall the words to "She'll Be Comin' 'Round the Mountain When She Comes" (see Appendix page 235).
2. Rewrite the lyrics to fit the story of *The Little Engine That Could*.

   For example, the verses could begin:
   > She'll be on the little blue engine when she comes. Ya-hoo!
   > She'll be chugging round the mountain, when she comes.

   > She'll be puffing I think I can, I think I can, I think I can.
   > She'll be shouting, I thought I could, I thought I could, I thought I could!

Something to think about

Substitute the other engines—passenger, freight, and rusty old train—and make up lyrics for them. For example, the passenger train could say, "I'm too fancy for toys and things, I'm too fancy for toys and things, I'm too fancy for toys and things, so I'm gone."

STORY S-T-R-E-T-C-H-E-R

Science: Tug of War: How Much Can We Pull?

What the children will learn

To consider the energy and force needed to counteract another force

Materials you will need

A long rope or long jump rope, bandana, stake or some other marker

What to do

1. Tie the bandana around the middle of the rope. Place the middle of the rope on the ground over the stake or marker.
2. Line up the children by height. Direct every other child to opposite sides of the rope, with the tallest children at the ends of the rope.
3. Tell the children that they are to pull against each other as in a tug of war.
4. Give a signal and have the children shout, "I think I can! I think I can! I think I can!"
5. Place a different set of children together, mix them up, and play the game again.
6. Discuss force and resistance.

Something to think about

If you have an odd number of children or a child who is not able to participate, let that child be the referee who signals the beginning and the end of the game, as well as declares the winning side.

STORY S-T-R-E-T-C-H-E-R

Writing: Next Scene—The Other Side of the Mountain

What the children will learn

To use their imaginations to write in the context of the story

Materials you will need

Writing journals or paper, pens, or computers

What to do

1. Form small groups or work with writing partners and talk through what it must have been like when *The Little Engine That Could* arrived with the toys on the other side of the mountain.
2. Ask the students to write the scene that they visualized with their group or writing partner.
3. Share some of the "next scenes" at the end of the class.

Something to think about

Some children may want to draw their scenes. If they do, consider cutting pages the same size as those in the book. Let the children add their pages to the copy of the book and leave it in the classroom library or writing corner for other children to read the story additions on their own.

Koala Lou

By Mem Fox
Illustrated by Pamela Lofts

Story Line

Koala Lou is a delight to her mother, who often tells Koala Lou, "Koala Lou, I DO love you." But when Koala Lou's mother has other babies, she is too busy to notice every little thing that Koala Lou does. Koala Lou decides the one best way to get her mother's attention is to win one of the games in the Bush Olympics. Despite her long training and practicing, Koala Lou loses the gum-tree-climbing contest to Koala Klaws. She is so upset that she runs away and hides. That evening she returns home and is greeted by the words she most wants to hear, "Koala Lou, I DO love you." Pamela Lofts's colorful illustrations are endearing and so animated that the story can be told by just looking at the illustrations. She has included a number of other bush animals in addition to the ones mentioned in the story.

Read-Aloud Presentation

Talk with the children about special skills they have developed that require a lot of practice, such as kicking a soccer ball or hitting a t-ball. Tell them that in this story Koala Lou was practicing for the Bush Olympics. Have the children listen for what *Koala Lou* was learning to do. Discuss how much she wanted her mother to see her win a medal in the Bush Olympics. Also, let the children talk about how sometimes they miss a kick for a goal in soccer or miss hitting the ball, and discuss their their parents' reactions when they win and when they do not. At the end of the story, let the children join you in reading the phrase, "Koala Lou, I do love you."

STORY S-T-R-E-T-C-H-E-R

Art: Olympic Decoration

What the children will learn
To plan and decorate the classroom

Materials you will need
Construction paper, poster board, markers, crepe paper, tape, paper and pen

What to do
1. Have the children look at the decorations for the Bush Olympics in *Koala Lou*.
2. Ask the children to look around the room for materials they could use to decorate for "Our Bush Olympics." For example, a jump rope could be the finish line, clipped edges of construction paper could decorate booths for games, and crepe paper streamers could divide areas.
3. Note the possibilities and then divide the class into decorating teams, each with a captain who is responsible for checking with other teams so that the teams' decorations do not overlap.

Something to think about
Often children in today's society are accustomed to buying party decorations. Encourage the children to recycle materials and use items in unusual ways.

STORY S-T-R-E-T-C-H-E-R

Games: Our Version of the Bush Olympics

What the children will learn
To improvise cooperative games

Materials you will need
Ropes, balls, chairs, boxes, hoops

What to do
1. Read *Koala Lou* again, and pause for the children to think of variations on the games played in the Bush Olympics. Also invent team games that require cooperation; for example, create scavenger hunts, obstacle courses, and team relays.
2. Let the children divide into teams. Each team is responsible for assembling the materials needed for the game, diagramming how to set up the game, and leading the rest of the class in playing the game.
3. Emphasize the inventiveness of each game.

4. Continue to play the games, and notice how the children improve with practice.

Something to think about
Play games that depend on cooperation for the players to succeed, rather than emphasizing competition for its own sake. (This STORY S-T-R-E-T-C-H-E-R was adapted from an idea by Kathryn Castle.) See www.australianfauna.com for names of Australian animals to use to name the teams.

Language Arts: Koala Lou, I DO Love You

What the children will learn
To read the recurring phrases on cue

Materials you will need
CD or cassette tape, CD or tape recorder, xylophone and mallet, listening station, headphones

What to do
1. With a small group of children in a quiet area in the classroom, make a recording of *Koala Lou*. Have the children recall the phrase that is repeated throughout the book, "Koala Lou, I DO love you!"
2. Assign one child to make the page-turning signal, gently tapping a xylophone.
3. Decide on a hand signal or cue so that the children will know when to say their line.
4. Record the story, with you or a proficient reader reading the story.
5. Place the recording and book at the listening station.

Something to think about
Young children profit from repeated readings of books. Encourage children who are less proficient readers to select a favorite story to hear again and again, and then let them read it to you.

Science: Koala and Other Bush Animals

What the children will learn
To identify the koala, emu, platypus, kookaburra, and other bush animals

Materials you will need
Reference books and websites containing pictures of Australian animals, large index cards, pencils

What to do
1. Let the children compare the illustrator's animated versions of the animals in *Koala Lou* with photographs of the real animals in the reference books or on the Australian fauna website.
2. Spend time talking with the children about the animals featured in *Koala Lou*, but also discuss other animals that might have come to the Bush Olympics.
3. Let each child write facts he or she would like to remember about the animals on the index cards. Ask for at least one card from each student.

Something to think about
Create a display about Australian animals from pictures drawn by the children.

Writing: Journal of Feelings About Winning and Losing

What the children will learn
To use journals to write about their feelings

Materials you will need
Notebooks or journals for each child, pencils, pens

What to do
1. Talk with the children about journals and diaries.
2. Explain to the children they can choose to share their journals, or they can choose not to share them. Discuss with the children how it sometimes helps to have someone read about our feelings. They can empathize with us if they have had similar experiences.
3. Ask the children to write about a time when they won a game, a time when they lost a game, and how they felt each time.
4. Let each child decide whether or not she or he wants you to read the journal entry.
5. If you read a child's journal entry, then write a few lines of reply.

Something to think about
Other writing experiences that can be prompted by *Koala Lou* include writing about an Olympics that is held in a different country and describing the animals that might be there.

Look What I Can Do

Amazing Grace

By Mary Hoffman
Illustrated by
Caroline Binch

by *Mary Hoffman* illustrated by *Caroline Binch*

Amazing
Grace

Story Line

Grace loves acting out stories. She dresses up in costumes, dramatizes fairy tales, and imagines all the different things she might be when she grows up. One day, Grace's teacher announces that the class will put on a play. Grace volunteers to be Peter Pan, but some of the children say she cannot be Peter Pan because Grace is a girl and Peter Pan is a boy. They also tell Grace she cannot be Peter Pan because she is black and Peter Pan is white. Grace is upset, so she talks with her mother and grandmother. They tell her she can be anything she wants to be and encourage her to try out for the part. Grace tries and wins the part. She is a terrific Peter Pan and believes again in her abilities. Caroline Binch's illustrations are beautiful, full color, and many are full page. Grace and her family are painted in beautiful, realistic, African-American skin tones.

Read-Aloud Presentation

Tell the children about an incident in your life when someone said you could not do something and you proved otherwise. For example, when you were a child your big brother might have said you were too little to ride a bicycle, but you learned. Talk with the children about how it feels to be told you cannot do something when you know you are capable. Let some children share examples from their lives. Discuss how Grace, the little girl in the story, was told she could not do something, and it was not because of ability. Read *Amazing Grace* and let the children talk about Grace's feelings and how she showed the other students that she was capable. Talk with the children about how skin color is not a reason to think someone cannot do something that others do.

STORY S-T-R-E-T-C-H-E-R

Art: The Real Me and the Pretend Me

What the children will learn
To portray themselves realistically and imaginatively

Materials you will need
Drawing paper, stapler, crayons, markers, index cards

What to do
1. Give each child two sheets of drawing paper stapled together at the top. On the top sheet of paper, ask the children to draw a self-portrait.
2. Ask the children to lift the sheet of paper and draw another picture on the second sheet. This time ask them to draw a picture of themselves pretending to be a famous person they would like to be like, from stories, movies, sports, or the news.
3. To create captions, ask each child to write on an index card a riddle describing the famous person he or she is pretending to be.
4. Post the drawings and cards on a bulletin board. Bulletin board readers will read the riddles, try to guess who the student is pretending to be, then lift the outside page to see the drawing underneath.

Something to think about
Older children can create a series of "pretend me" pictures.

STORY S-T-R-E-T-C-H-E-R

Creative Dramatics: Pretending, Make-Believe, and Just Playing

What the children will learn
To enjoy the natural pleasures of playing together

Materials you will need
Variety of dress-up clothes, uniforms, hats, shoes

What to do
1. Invite parents to bring in discarded clothes, uniforms, and party dresses with which the children could have fun improvising roles.
2. Leave the clothes out in the classroom, and let the children play different roles as they are inspired.

Something to think about

Play is one of the most creative and critical thinking activities by which we learn. Young children use more sophisticated language, solve more elaborate problems, and improvise using a higher-level thought process when allowed to play on their own.

Creative Dramatics: Parade of Grace's Favorite Characters

What the children will learn
To develop costumes that portray characters

Materials you will need
Chart paper, marker, dress-up clothes

What to do
1. Look through *Amazing Grace,* and make a list of all the characters Grace likes to play. They include Joan of Arc, Anansi the Spider, the wooden horse of Troy, a pirate, Hiawatha, Mowgli, Aladdin, Doctor Grace, and Peter Pan.
2. Let the children decide which characters they want to be.
3. Plan a parade of Grace's favorite characters. Let the children devise their own costumes. (It is all right for more than one child to select the same character.)

Something to think about
Schedule the parade to go to another classroom where the children have read *Amazing Grace*, and let these children guess who the characters are. If possible, videotape the children's parade to show families and to document the students' abilities and interests.

Language Arts: Reading and Predicting *Peter Pan*

What the children will learn
To listen while a book is read, and predict the next events

Materials you will need
Copy of *Peter Pan*, chart tablet, marker, CD and CD player or tape and tape recorder

What to do
1. Read Barrie's *Peter Pan*, one chapter at each reading session.

2. At the end of each chapter, invite the children to predict what they think will happen next.
3. At the beginning of the next reading session, review the children's predictions. Read on, contrasting the children's predictions with what actually happens.
4. Alternate printing the children's predictions on chart paper with recording their predictions on tape or CD.

Something to think about
Read about the other characters Grace enjoyed pretending to be: Joan of Arc, Anansi the Spider, Hiawatha, and Mowgli.

Writing: Expressing Feelings, "Look What I Can Do"

What the children will learn
To express their feelings in writing

Materials you will need
Diaries or personal journals, pencils or pens

What to do
1. With small groups of children at the writing center, read *Amazing Grace* again.
2. Discuss how Grace feels when the children tell her that she cannot play Peter Pan because she is a girl and because she is African American.
3. Ask the children to talk about times when they were told they could not do something. Perhaps older brothers or sisters said that they could not play a game because they were too young. Children might remember a time when they felt misunderstood.
4. If the students want to write about a time like this in their lives, encourage them to write it in their diaries.

Something to think about
As an alternative, ask the children to pretend that they are Grace and to write about how they would feel if they had her experience.

Chrysanthemum

By Kevin Henkes

Story Line

Chrysanthemum is a wonderfully happy child who loves her name, until she starts school. There the children make fun of her name, and she longs for a shorter name of only a few letters. Plagued by insults, Chrysanthemum dreams that her name is Jane. It is only after meeting the music teacher, Delphinium Twinkle, that Chrysanthemum grows to love her name again. On every page, the line drawings with watercolor washes by Henkes wonderfully express the personalities of the characters. The details of the illustrations show life at school and home as a celebratory frenzy of activity and emotion. Even though Henkes draws the characters as mouse children, he gives them human qualities.

Read-Aloud Presentation

Ask the children to think of people's names that are also flowers, like Daisy, Rose, and Iris. Show the cover of *Chrysanthemum* and talk about the significance of the little girl mouse holding onto the stem of the large golden flower. Discuss with the children some of the problems a child named Chrysanthemum might have. Read the book and discuss whether the problems the children mentioned are those that Chrysanthemum encounters. End the read-aloud session by announcing some of the STORY S-T-R-E-T-C-H-E-R-S for the day.

Art: Decorative Name Plaques

What the children will learn
To create their own interpretations of their names

Materials you will need
Large index cards, markers

What to do
1. Show the illustrations of Chrysanthemum's name written in icing on a cake and in her own handwriting, decorated with hearts.
2. Fold a large index card in half. Instruct the children to write their names expressively on one side and then decorate the card with symbols they like, such as butterflies, rainbows, baseballs, and so on.
3. As the children move from center to center throughout the day, ask them to place the personal name plaques they made at their work stations.

Something to think about
Laminate the name cards for extended use. So they can be folded after laminating, cut a straight line through the plastic at the fold.

Creative Dramatics: Mrs. Twinkle's Play

What the children will learn
To take the seed of an idea and develop it into a script

Materials you will need
Writing supplies, pencils, paper

What to do
1. Read *Chrysanthemum* again, and discuss the play Mrs. Twinkle might have organized.
2. Let the children who are interested create a script for the play.
3. After the children have written the script, ask them to draw storyboards or major scenes to help them decide how to stage the play.
4. After the script writers and the storyboard artists have finished, encourage other children to help with props and staging.
5. Choose the actors for the play from among the script writers.
6. Continue the play by rotating roles. On different days, other children can act in the play.

Something to think about
With younger children, dramatize the book *Chrysanthemum* itself. Assign the roles, making sure to include some of the less-popular children. Let some of the children improvise the actions as you read the book aloud.

Mathematics: Ordering from Flower and Seed Catalogs

What the children will learn
To read catalogs, select flowers, and calculate costs

Materials you will need
Flower and seed catalogs, scrap paper, photocopies of the blank order forms, pretend money, calculators

What to do
1. Begin by looking through the catalogs for flowers named after people.
2. Compare the pictures of chrysanthemums in the catalogs to Kevin Henkes's illustration of a chrysanthemum on the book cover.
3. Ask the children to find flowers whose names they would like to have.
4. Give each child ten dollars of pretend money with which to order seeds.
5. Work with the children as they read and complete the order forms, helping them understand that they must save money for shipping and handling costs.
6. Help the children become good consumers by finding ways to make their dollars go further, by placing orders together, for example.

Something to think about
If your budget allows, let the children order packages of real seeds. Vary the activity according to the mathematical abilities of the students.

Special Project: Field Trip to a Florist

What the children will learn
To identify different greenhouse flowers and plants and appreciate a florist's artistry and services

Materials you will need
None

What to do
1. Determine if any parents or grandparents of the children are in the floral business. Contact either these relatives or a local florist, and plan a field trip to see real chrysanthemums and other flowers.
2. Visit the florist ahead of time, and explain that the inspiration for this STORY S-T-R-E-T-C-H-E-R field trip was the book *Chrysanthemum*. Discuss the ages of the children who will be coming, and plan as active and educational a field trip as possible.
3. Arrange for parent volunteers.
4. Tour the florist shop and the delivery van to see how flowers are transported.
5. Watch the florist make a beautiful arrangement.

Something to think about
This special project STORY S-T-R-E-T-C-H-E-R is both a science and social studies activity. Learning about caring for flowers and plants involves science, and learning about running a florist shop is social studies.

Writing: Acrostic of Names

What the children will learn
To write descriptive words and phrases

Materials you will need
Heavy typing paper or construction paper, markers, crayons

What to do
1. Ask the children to write the letters of their names vertically down the left margin of a sheet of paper.
2. Then ask them to write words or phrases beginning with those letters to describe themselves. for example:.

C is for Coloring my name
H is for Happy
R is for Radiant
Y is for Young
S is for Starting school
A is for Another name
N is for Nice teacher
T is for Teased
H is for Hungry for special dessert
E is for Envying people with short names
M is for Macaroni and cheese, favorite dinner
U is for Understanding
M is for Me
CHRYSANTHEMUM!

3. Display the name acrostics on a bulletin board.

Something to think about
Ask the children to do acrostics of their favorite book characters or of their last names.

Oh, The Places You'll Go!

By Dr. Seuss

Story Line

Dr. Seuss succeeds in speaking both to the child and to the adult in this celebration of life in verse. *Oh, The Places You'll Go!* resounds with confidence as the character strides through life making choices. The twists and turns and "waiting places" feel familiar to adults and like new adventures to young readers. With rhyme and reasoning, Dr. Seuss reassures the traveler that the road ahead, while filled with some scary, lonely, and unexpected lurches, is worth the journey, because we learn to balance our lives and succeed, "98 and ¾ percent guaranteed." In classic Seuss style, the wacky illustrations, colors, lines, patterns, and print propel the reader through the book as magically as do his words of wisdom.

Read-Aloud Presentation

Shield the author's name on the book cover, and ask the children to guess who the author is. The instantly recognizable Seuss illustrations help to create an air of anticipation. Ask the children to recall some of their favorite Dr. Seuss books. Look at the character on the first page of the book, and ask the children where they think he might be going. Then read the book from cover to cover without stopping. (The rhyming pattern will be interrupted if you pause for discussion.) After you have finished, ask the children what they think the author wants us to know or to do. Select a few key pages to read again. For example, show the illustrations of the elephants carrying banners as the character walks along. Discuss what this might mean. Explain that this is a book that offers advice, and discuss what advice means. See the Dr. Seuss website at www.seussville.com.

STORY S-T-R-E-T-C-H-E-R

Art: Celebration Banners

What the children will learn
To interpret their interests and personalities in graphic designs

Materials you will need
Poster board in a variety of colors or large sheets of construction paper, markers, crayons, hole puncher, collage materials

What to do
1. Look at the illustration of elephants parading down the street carrying pink banners on long sticks. Talk about the celebratory mood of a parade.
2. Ask the children to imagine that the parade is for them and that the banners announce who they are and what they like to do.
3. Brainstorm with the children about what their own personal banners might look like. For example, Riley's banner might have a tent because she likes to camp, and a violin because she takes music lessons.
4. Cut a shape for the banners similar to those in the Seuss illustrations.
5. Let the children decorate their banners however they choose.

Something to think about
Fly the banners by hanging them from the ceiling with fishing wire or by punching holes in the top of each banner and threading yarn through the holes to hang them from the ceiling.

STORY S-T-R-E-T-C-H-E-R

Language Arts: Congratulations Chanters

What the children will learn
To read with expression

Materials you will need
CDs and CD player or tapes and tape recorder, index cards, pencils or pens, stapler

What to do
1. Select four or five interested children, and prepare a recording of *Oh, The Places You'll Go!*
2. Ask the children to print the first four lines of the book on their index cards. This is phrase one.

3. On the other side of the card, print the title of the book, *Oh, The Places You'll Go!* This is phrase two.
4. Ask the children to rehearse, reading the phrases with enthusiasm.
5. Request a volunteer to make the page-turning signal by snapping the stapler.
6. Hold up one finger as the signal for the chanters to read in unison phrase one.
7. Read the rest of the book. Whenever the text repeats the title of the book, hold up two fingers as the signal for the children to chant, "Oh, the places you'll go!"
8. Place the recording and the book at the listening station so that the rest of the class can listen to the recording and read the book.

Something to think about
With older children, select pages for individuals to read. Play marching music in the background, and ask the children to clap in time to the rhythm of the music and the book.

STORY S-T-R-E-T-C-H-E-R

Music and Movement: Marching in a Parade

What the children will learn
To march in time to music

Materials you will need
A march recorded on tape or CD; tape or CD player

What to do
1. Seat the children in a semicircle.
2. Read the passage in the Dr. Seuss book about playing in a band.
3. Play a booming recording of marching music.
4. March around the room, pretending to play a sliding trombone.
5. Invite two children to join you and pretend to be playing drums.
6. Continue adding children until everyone is up and marching as you snake around the room.
7. As the music nears its end, bring the students back into a semicircle. Continue clapping hands and slapping knees in time to the music.

Something to think about
On another day, add rhythm band instruments.

STORY S-T-R-E-T-C-H-E-R

Special Project: Star of the Week

What the children will learn
To get to know their classmates and appreciate each other

Materials you will need
Bulletin board, slips of paper, calendar, index cards, markers, push pins

What to do
1. Create a bulletin board highlighting a different child each week.
2. Draw names and write the names onto the school calendar in order as they are drawn. (Avoid weeks with holidays.)
3. Ask the child who is star of the week to bring in baby pictures or photographs of her family, as well as favorite toys or games.
4. Help the child create an interesting bulletin board display about herself. Ask her to write captions for the photographs.
5. At the bottom of the bulletin board, print "Oh, The Places You'll Go!"

Something to think about
Ask older students to interview the children, and record or videotape the interviews. Place the recordings on a bookshelf under the "Star of the Week" bulletin board.

STORY S-T-R-E-T-C-H-E-R

Writing: Congratulations Cards

What the children will learn
To write a rhyming verse or sentiments of congratulation

Materials you will need
Index cards, heavy typing paper or construction paper, markers, crayons, pastel chalks, hair spray

What to do
1. With small groups of children, prepare congratulations cards or thank-you cards to recognize an achievement. For example, if a child has just earned a merit badge in the Girl Scouts or Boy Scouts, make a card to celebrate the success, or make a card when a child writes a story for the classroom collection.
2. Brainstorm a special congratulations card for every child in the room. Before doing this with the children, think about those children whom the class may have difficulty

Look What I Can Do

seeing as successful, and prepare a few statements about them in advance.

3. Write each child's name on an index card.

4. While the small group brainstorms, record key phrases on the cards until every child is mentioned.

5. Shuffle the index cards and ask the children to each draw a card.

6. The children design a surprise congratulations card for the class member whose name they have drawn. Remind the children to keep the card a surprise until they are ready to present the card.

Something to think about

As an alternative, design thank-you cards for the librarian, cafeteria workers, secretarial and custodial staffs, thanking them for their service to the school.

References

Fox, Mem. 1989. *Koala Lou*. Illustrated by Pamela Lofts. Boston: Houghton Mifflin Harcourt.

Henkes, Kevin. 1991. *Chrysanthemum*. New York: HarperCollins.

Hoffman, Mary. 1991. *Amazing Grace*. Illustrated by Caroline Binch. New York: Penguin.

Piper, Watty. 2005. *The Little Engine That Could*. Illustrated by Loren Long. New York: Penguin.

Seuss, Dr. 1990. *Oh, The Places You'll Go!*. New York: Random House.

Additional References

Barrie, J. M. 2003. *Peter Pan*. Illustrated by Michael Hague. New York: Henry Holt.

Greenfield, Eloise. 1988. *Nathaniel Talking*. Illustrated by Jan Spivey Gilchrist. New York: Writers & Readers. *A nine-year-old says what he thinks in raps, chants, and poems.*

Lionni, Leo. 1995. *Matthew's Dream*. New York: Dragonfly Books. *A visit to an art museum inspires a young mouse to become a painter.*

McCully, Emily Arnold. 1997. *Mirette on the High Wire*. New York: Putnam. *Mirette learns tightrope walking from Monsieur Bellini, a guest in her mother's boarding house, not knowing that he is a celebrated tightrope artist who has withdrawn from performing because of fear.*

Websites

1. Seussville: www.seussville.com
   - Biography
   - NEA's Dr. Seuss Day and other events
   - Games based on books
2. HumanityQuest.com: www.humanityquest.com/index.asp
   - Self-esteem themed links page
   - Lesson plans
   - Numerous self-esteem activities
3. Australian Fauna: www.australianfauna.com
   - Alphabetical list of all native animals
   - Clip-art of animal pictures
   - Amazing animal facts

Families

All Kinds of Families

By Norma Simon
Illustrated by Joe Lasker

Story Line

Simon's book is an excellent beginning for a unit on families, because it warmly and affectionately portrays many different types of families and family life. The text and illustrations help children to think of themselves as family members and to see what changes in families and what remains the same. The book celebrates family special events, holidays, stories, and feelings at both happy and sad times. Lasker alternates pages of black line drawings with soft, warmly colored illustrations.

Read-Aloud Presentation

Tell the children about your family—the family you were a part of growing up and the family you are a part of now. Select several children, and ask them to tell who their family members are. Continue by asking the children to tell how their families have changed.

Draw out comments about extended families—grandparents, uncles, aunts, cousins. Have one child describe a time when the greatest number of people from his or her family came together for a special event. Read *All Kinds of Families*. After the reading, relate the earlier discussion of families to the illustrations in the book. Ask some children to tell about family gatherings they were reminded of by the pictures in the book. End the session by announcing the books you will read aloud for the unit. Encourage children to find library books about families as well as to read the ones you have collected for the classroom.

STORY S-T-R-E-T-C-H-E-R

Art: My Family Portrait

What the children will learn
To illustrate their immediate family

Materials you will need
Construction paper or art paper, crayons, markers, colored pens, glue

What to do
1. Talk with the children about the bulletin board you would like to make for the unit, one that shows all their families.
2. Have the children draw their family portraits. Then let the children choose a contrasting color of construction paper and make a mat or a border for their family portraits.
3. Ask the children to title their portraits using their names such as "Marty's Family" or "Christy's Family."
4. Arrange the bulletin board.

Something to think about
After the drawings have been up for a few days, have the children bring in family photographs to add to the bulletin board. Place them near the children's drawings, and let the children add captions.

STORY S-T-R-E-T-C-H-E-R
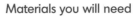

Classroom Library: My Name Comes From

What the children will learn
To associate their names with family members or meanings of names

Materials you will need
Name books, such as baby-name books or reference books about the meanings of names; chart tablet or poster board; markers

What to do
1. Display the reference books on names.
2. Ask the students if they were named after people in their families.
3. Look up the meaning of the child's name in a reference book and write this information on the chart tablet.
4. Let the class add to the name charts until the charts include information about everyone's names.

Something to think about
Include reference materials that reflect a variety of cultures, ask the children to provide information about their names, or invite parents or older students from a variety of cultures to come to class and talk about their names. Younger children can talk about family members'

nicknames. Older children can trace name changes over time and family moves to this country, or changed spellings of names over time. In some Native American cultures, special names are sacred and are used only in ceremonies. Do not ask these children their Indian names; use the names they use at school.

Cooking: Our Family Recipes

What the children will learn
To read recipes and to associate them with family times

Materials you will need
Materials for parent newsletter, sample recipe

What to do

1. In a parent newsletter, ask for copies of favorite family recipes for a class recipe book. Include a sample recipe from your family, and ask the families to write their recipes in the same format. For example, list the ingredients and steps for preparing the recipe "Granny Irene's Pineapple Upside-Down Cake."
2. Encourage the families to include simple recipes for snacks as well.
3. Collect the recipes and review them.
4. Select recipes that would make good snacks.
5. Invite family members to come to class and help small groups of children prepare the snack recipes, or ask the families to send enough of the snack for the entire class to sample.

Something to think about
Duplicate copies of the recipes and bind them into a book for the students to give to their families. Younger children can write a sentence about why they like a certain food or what they remember about a family event where the recipe was served. Older children can interview the relative to whom the recipe belongs and write a brief history of the recipe to include in the book.

Music and Movement: Music My Family Enjoys

What the children will learn
To recognize a variety of family music preferences

Materials you will need
CDs and CD player or tapes and tape player, chart tablet or poster board, markers

What to do

1. Find out what types of music the children's families enjoy.
2. Ask several of the children whose families have strong musical interests to bring a recording of the music their families play at family gatherings.
3. Listen to different selections on different days of the week.
4. Make a list of the main instruments that are used in the recordings.
5. Emphasize how music is a part of family life and family celebrations

Something to think about
If any of the families of your children include professional musicians, ask them to play for the class. Invite amateur musicians who are members of family groups to play for the class.

Writing: Writing to Someone in My Family

What the children will learn
To express their feelings in letter form

Materials you will need
Stationery or paper, scrap paper, envelopes, pencils, pens, and stamps

What to do

1. With the small group of children who come to the writing center, read a few family letters you have received.
2. Let the children talk about letters and greeting cards they have received in the mail.
3. Discuss relatives to whom the children would like to write. Ask them what special message they would like to communicate.
4. Let the children write a practice letter on scrap paper, help them edit it, then ask them to copy the letter onto the stationery they want to use.

Something to think about
Children who do not know their extended families can write a letter to a member of their immediate family. See the Teacher Vision website (www.teachervision.fen.com) for activities related to extended families.

Julius, the Baby of the World

By Kevin Henkes

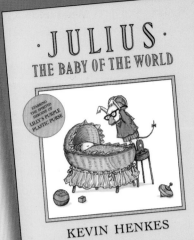

Story Line

Lilly thinks her new baby brother is disgusting. She has to share her room with him and keep her voice down while he sleeps. She cannot understand why her parents think he is the most beautiful baby in the world. When Lilly tries some of the things Julius does, like screaming and crying, she is sent to the uncooperative chair. Lilly runs away from home seven times in one morning. All of her parents' attempts to help Lilly like Julius fail until the day when Cousin Garland says she thinks Julius is disgusting. Lilly doesn't like her cousin talking about Julius like that; after all, Julius is her brother. Henkes's drawings are black ink and full-color art with lots of lavender backgrounds but splashed with brighter pastels as well as reds and pinks. The pictures are rich in pattern and detail. The humor in the story and illustrations are sure to make this selection a favorite one.

Read-Aloud Presentation

Ask children who have baby brothers or sisters to tell the class what they do to help take care of the baby. Show the cover of *Julius, the Baby of the World*. If you have already read books by Kevin Henkes, the children may recognize Lilly. She is introduced in *Chester's Way*, a book covered in the "Friends" unit. Ask the children what Lilly is doing on the cover—trying to scare Julius with one of her disguises. Read the book, and at the end discuss how Lilly feels at the beginning of the book, her funny antics, and how she feels at the end of the story.

STORY S-T-R-E-T-C-H-E-R

Art: Lavender and Pastel Family Pictures

What the children will learn
To use pastels and chalks for drawing

Materials you will need
Pastels or chalks, scraps of construction paper, art paper, lavender construction paper, hair spray **(adult use only)**

What to do
1. With the children who choose to come to the art center during choice time, look at Henkes's use of lavender throughout the book, on the endpapers, and as background for important scenes.
2. Have the children find the lavender in every picture.
3. Let the children experiment with the pastels on scraps of construction paper.
4. Allow the children to choose whether they want to make pastel pictures on the lavender construction paper or use chalk, including lavender chalk, on art paper.
5. After the children finish their drawings, spray the drawings lightly with hair spray to make the pastels adhere to the paper without smudging. **(Spray the drawings when the children are out of the classroom.)**

Something to think about
Keep the pastels and chalks available throughout the week. It takes time for children to explore the possibilities of a medium and to gain some sense of control over the materials.

STORY S-T-R-E-T-C-H-E-R

Classroom Library: Story Retelling Tapes

What the children will learn
To retell stories using pictures

Materials you will need
CDs and CD player or tapes and tape player, stapler

What to do
1. Make a recording of *Julius, the Baby of the World*. Be sure to provide a page-turning signal, such as clicking a stapler.
2. Turn over the tape or make another recording on a CD. Ask the children who have babies in their families to

retell the story of *Julius, the Baby of the World* by looking at the pictures. Again, be sure to record a page-turning signal.

3. Mark one recording with a drawing of a book and the other with a drawing of a child's face.
4. Place the recording at the listening station in the classroom library.

Something to think about
Older children can form story retelling groups and take turns telling the story in a round-robin fashion. Younger children can alternate, with the teacher telling the story on one page and the child on the next page.

STORY S-T-R-E-T-C-H-E-R

Creative Dramatics: A Parade of Lilly Disguises

What the children will learn
To improvise costumes

Materials you will need
An assortment of old clothes, construction paper crowns, boots, hats, old costume jewelry, optional—dolls, baby clothes

What to do
1. With the children who are interested, look at the illustrations of Lilly in her many disguises, including her yellow crown and red boots.
2. Let the children talk about how they like to play dress-up at home with their brothers, sisters, or friends.
3. Have the children dress up in a variety of Lilly disguises.
4. Later on in the day, have a Lilly parade of disguises and read *Julius, the Baby of the World* again.

Something to think about
On another day, show the picture at the end of the book of Lilly and Julius playing together in their disguises. Add dolls and baby clothes, and let the children dress up the dolls as if they were Julius in his disguises.

STORY S-T-R-E-T-C-H-E-R

Music and Movement: Lullabies from Our Families

What the children will learn
To sing a variety of lullabies

Materials you will need
CDs or tapes of lullabies, CD or tape player, chart tablet, marker

What to do
1. Copy the words from several famous lullabies onto sheets of chart tablet paper. Selections could include, "Hush, Little Baby"; "Lullaby and Good Night" (Brahms's Lullaby); or "Rock-a-bye Baby." (See Appendix page XX for the words to these lullabies. If you do not know the melodies, simply chant the songs or use an Internet site such as www.kididdles.com to hear the song.)
2. Teach the songs to the children.
3. Have the children sing the lullabies that their families sang to them when the children were babies.
4. Include lullabies from a variety of cultures and ones that families improvised.

Something to think about
Invite the music teacher to sing and play lullabies. Older children can write lullabies with a modern twist.

STORY S-T-R-E-T-C-H-E-R

Writing: Signs for My Room

What the children will learn
To write poster messages to their families

Materials you will need
Scraps of poster board or construction paper, markers, crayons

What to do
1. Look through the illustrations of *Julius, the Baby of the World*. Find all the signs and posters Lilly writes to describe her feelings about Julius and about the property in her room.
2. Ask the children what messages they would like to write to communicate with their brothers, sisters, or other family members.
3. Provide the materials and let the children make the signs as well as write the messages.
4. Have the group brainstorm some messages that might make their class function better, such as signs telling where to place homework, labels for the art center shelves, or reminders about keeping the game and puzzle pieces organized.

Something to think about
Use as much humor as possible to get across rules for class operation. Let the children think of funny ways to communicate the messages on the posters.

The Hello, Goodbye Window

By Norton Juster
Illustrated by Chris Raschka

Story Line

A Caldecott Medal winner, *The Hello, Goodbye Window*, celebrates the relationships of grandparents, Nanna and Poppy, and their granddaughter. The magic of a special window that can be a door appeals to young children, but the antics of the hellos, goodbyes, games, and reflections frame the many activities that the little girl enjoys with her grandparents. The window-door opens up into the old-fashioned kitchen. Readers are entertained by a harmonica-playing Poppy, by Nanna's gardening while an imaginary tiger is hiding in the bushes, and by the little girl's own imagination. Lovingly depicted in childlike drawings of wet pastels, watercolors, and crayon resist, the etched patterns and the illustrations capture the warmth of the relationship between the grandparents and their granddaughter.

Read-Aloud Suggestions

Discuss who has grandparents living nearby and the names the children call their grandparents. Let volunteers describe the ways they say goodbye to grandparents, with hugs, throwing kisses, smacking kisses over the telephone. Show the children the cover of the book and discuss the title, *The Hello, Goodbye Window*. See if the children have a special viewing place for their goodbyes. Discuss the meaning of the Caldecott Medal, the most prestigious award for an illustrator. Have the children discuss what they like about the cover illustration, and ask them to decide if the cover fits the story, which is one of the criteria for the Caldecott Medal.

Art: Our Own Hello, Goodbye Window

What the children will learn
To depict two-dimensional art

Materials you will need
White construction paper or drawing paper, brightly colored construction paper, scissors, crayons, plastic knives

What to do
1. Have the children draw a large window in their brightly colored construction paper and cut around three of the four sides, leaving a flap at the top or on a side.
2. Close the flap and let the children color a picture of themselves looking through the window.
3. Demonstrate how to layer colors and then, using a plastic knife, scrape away the top layer to create a pattern. Look at some of the patterns Raschka created for the little girl's leggings and jumper.
4. Trace around the cut-out window for the second piece of paper. In the space created by tracing around the cutout from the first sheet of paper, ask the children to color a picture of their grandparents or other older adults who are close to them.
5. Glue the two pieces of paper together around the edges and let the art dry.
6. After the edges are dry, let the children fold their flap on the first page so that they can look under it and see the grandparents they drew inside.

Something to think about
For younger children, have them experiment with two-layer coloring and scraping patterns. Older children could try wet pastels over crayon patterns or crayon-resist techniques. For additional arts and crafts, see A to Z Teacher Stuff at www.atozteacherstuff.com/Themes/Family.

STORY S-T-R-E-T-C-H-E-R

Music and Movement: Poppy's "O, Susanna"

What the children will learn
To sing a traditional American folk song

Materials you will need
A traditional or folk songbook, chart paper *or* computer with whiteboard and projecting capabilities, markers

What to do

1. Write or project the words to "O, Susanna" (see page 236 for the lyrics to this song) on the chart tablet or whiteboard. (To hear the melody of "O, Susanna," use an Internet search engine, or websites such as www.songsforteaching.com.)
2. Sing the song through once for the children to learn the words. Invite them to sing along with you.
3. Reread the pages in the book where Poppy could play "O, Susanna" fast or slow. Have the children sing it fast, sing it slow, sing it sitting down or standing up.

Something to think about

Since Poppy played "O, Susanna" on the harmonica, invite a harmonica player to come to class and play the song.

STORY S-T-R-E-T-C-H-E-R

Cooking and Snack Time: Poppy's Oatmeal with Bananas and Raisins

What the children will learn

To follow directions to prepare a simple breakfast

Materials you will need

Instant oatmeal, hot water, bananas, raisins, bowls, spoons, plastic knives, liquid-measuring cup

What to do

1. Make a poster board or write on whiteboard the directions for making instant oatmeal: "Empty packet into bowl. Add up to ½ cup hot water. Stir. **(Caution: Only an adult should add the hot water.)**
2. Help children peel and slice bananas, using one-half banana per child.
3. Add bananas to the oatmeal and sprinkle with raisins.
4. Enjoy Poppy's oatmeal with the children.

Something to think about

Ask the cafeteria staff to prepare homemade oatmeal. Let the children compare instant oatmeal to homemade oatmeal.

STORY S-T-R-E-T-C-H-E-R

Science: Mirrors and Window Reflections

What the children will learn

To experiment and compare reflections

Materials you will need

Handheld mirrors, full-length mirror, and black-out curtain or dark paper to darken the window(s) in the room

What to do

1. Read the part of the story where the little girl compares looking out of the hello, goodbye window at night and how the window reflects like a mirror in the bathroom.
2. Have the children examine themselves in the handheld mirrors or in a full-length classroom mirror. Ask the children how to notice how distinctly they can see individual hairs on their heads, individual eyebrows, or eyelashes.
3. Darken the classroom and place a black-out curtain or shade over the windows. See if the children can still see their reflections; notice if it is harder to see their distinct features.

Something to think about

Older children can view a YouTube video about how mirrors are made.

STORY S-T-R-E-T-C-H-E-R

Writing: A Thank-You Letter to Grandparents, Nanna and Poppy

What the children will learn

To express their feelings and appreciation in writing

Materials you will need

Chart tablet, marker, notepaper or heavy paper that is easy to fold, envelopes, stamps

Materials you will need

Chart tablet, marker, notepaper or heavy paper that is easy to fold, envelopes, stamps

What to do

1. Discuss with the children what their grandparents do for them that is special.
2. List the activities on chart tablet paper. Compare what Nanna and Poppy do with the little girl with what the children's grandparents do with them.
3. Discuss why we write thank-you notes and how special it makes people feel to receive thank-you notes, even if they live nearby and can be told "thank you" in person.
4. Distribute the notepaper and let children draw a small picture of what they appreciate their grandparents doing or how they feel about their grandparents.

Something to think about

Consider having a grandparents' day or week at your school, much like parents' day. If children do not have grandparents nearby, they may invite other relatives or older friends of the family.

Amelia Bedelia's Family Album

By Peggy Parish
Illustrated by Lynn Sweat

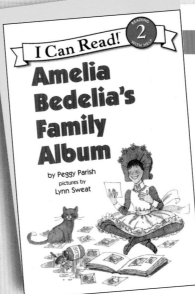

Story Line

The Rogers family is so happy with Amelia Bedelia's work that they want to give her a party and invite her friends. To plan the party, Mrs. Rogers asks Amelia who should be invited. Amelia Bedelia takes down the family picture album and tells Mrs. Rogers about all of her relatives. In usual Amelia Bedelia fashion, there are funny interpretations of what each family member does. For example, when Amelia Bedelia describes her mother as a "loafer," Mrs. Rogers thinks that means that she is lazy, but oh, no, Amelia Bedelia says that means she bakes loaves of bread. The story ends with another Amelia Bedelia surprise when Mrs. Rogers tells her to invite everybody. So Amelia goes into the street and invites *everybody* to come to her party. Lynn Sweat's drawings of Amelia Bedelia have become as familiar as Peggy Parish's clever characterization of the mixed-up maid.

Read-Aloud Presentation

If the children already know about Amelia Bedelia books, simply telling them you will be reading an Amelia Bedelia story will bring on cheers and claps. Ask the children why they like these stories. Read *Amelia Bedelia's Family Album*. Pause after reading about Amelia Bedelia's mother being a loafer, and let the children predict what Amelia Bedelia will say in response to Mrs. Rogers's questions about each family member who follows. Show some pictures of your family members, and make up Amelia Bedelia descriptions of them. Let the children think of other descriptions they might write. For example, show a picture of a man who is a tax collector. Then let the children draw a picture of him going along picking up thumbtacks. See www.kidsreads.com/series/series-amelia-titles.asp for additional Amelia Bedelia books that may interest the students.

Classroom Library: Our Amelia Bedelia Family Album

What the children will learn
To predict Amelia Bedelia meanings of words

Materials you will need
Children's writings from the writing center activity

What to do
1. Place the children's illustrated writings (from the writing center activity) of their Amelia Bedelia family members in the classroom library.
2. Encourage the children to go in pairs to the classroom library and share the guessing. The two children look at the pictures on the outside of the cards then guess what Amelia Bedelia would say. Then one child reads the Amelia Bedelia definition.

Something to think about
To make the Amelia Bedelia pictures into a more permanent book for the library, place the pictures on large index cards and slip them into the plastic sleeves in a photo album. The children can then read one side of the picture and turn the page to read the funny definition.

Creative Dramatics: Which Amelia Bedelia Family Member Am I?

What the children will learn
To pantomime actions

Materials you will need
Scraps of paper, pen or pencil, box

What to do
1. Read *Amelia Bedelia's Family Album* again.
2. Write the names of Amelia Bedelia's family members on scraps of paper and place them in a box.
3. At random, let each child draw the name of a family member from the box.
4. Let the children take turns pantomiming the different relatives while the audience guesses their identities.

Something to think about

Young children can use props and dress-up clothes to dramatize their actions. Older children can pantomime the Amelia Bedelia family members from the book and the descriptions the class wrote in the writing center.

STORY S-T-R-E-T-C-H-E-R

Creative Dramatics: Amelia Bedelia's Family at Our School

What the children will learn

To interpret the meaning of words

Materials you will need

None needed

What to do

1. Invite members of the school staff, such as the secretary, principal, librarian, reading specialist, cafeteria workers, or others to come to your classroom on different days of the week and announce themselves as members of Amelia Bedelia's family.
2. Pretend to be Mrs. Rogers and ask the family members what they do. Then let the actors give their Amelia Bedelia-style descriptions of what they do.
3. Ask all the Amelia Bedelia family actors to join the class for the party (see the special event STORY S-T-R-E-T-C-H-E-R).

Something to think about

Take photographs of the school staff who come as Amelia Bedelia's family, and add them to the family album in the class library.

STORY S-T-R-E-T-C-H-E-R

Special Event: An Amelia Bedelia Mixed-Up Family Portrait

What the children will learn

To plan a party

Materials you will need

Chart tablet, markers, paper, pencils, decorations, food, party games

What to do

1. Talk about the kind of party Amelia Bedelia might have, because she seems to get everything mixed up.
2. Brainstorm some ideas for party games. Write all the ideas on a chart tablet. For example, instead of Pin the

Tail on the Donkey, the game might be Pin the Head on the Donkey.
3. Think about some mixed-up party food, such as pineapple upside-down cake or party mix with pretzels and nuts. Everything served at the party should be mixed-up.
4. Plan the party decorations with giant drawings from *Amelia Bedelia's Family Album*.
5. Write party invitations and address them to the family members.
6. Let children choose the invitations for Amelia Bedelia family members at random, and come to the party dressed like that family member.

Something to think about

Write a parent newsletter explaining the special party and the use of Peggy Parish's Amelia Bedelia stories to help children understand that words can have different meanings.

STORY S-T-R-E-T-C-H-E-R

Writing: Funny Families

What the children will learn

To write funny meanings for words instead of usual meanings

Materials you will need

Old magazines or catalogs, scissors, glue, construction paper or drawing paper, colored pencils, crayons or markers

What to do

1. Let the students cut out pictures from magazines or catalogs and pretend the people pictured are members of their families.
2. Fold the sheets of construction paper or drawing paper into halves vertically, like greeting cards.
3. Glue the picture of the person on the outside.
4. Write the name of the person and what he or she does on the outside.
5. On the inside, draw a picture illustrating what the person does, and write the Amelia Bedelia interpretation of the person's job.
6. Place the individual Amelia Bedelia family pictures in the classroom library.

Something to think about

Younger children may have difficulty coming up with Amelia Bedelia definitions. They can draw one of their own family members and then work with you to come up with a funny description.

The Relatives Came

By Cynthia Rylant
Illustrated by
Stephen Gammell

Story Line

This warm, delightful story is told with jaunty, funny pictures of the relatives' trip from the mountains of Virginia to the home of the child telling the story. Each scene shows how the family's daily life is changed because the relative are there. Rylant tells of bountiful tables filled with food, cramped sleeping, extra breathing in the house, and music and games. The sadness yet relief when the visitors go home is a feeling many children understand. The passing of time is represented by the grapes—just turning purple when the relatives leave Virginia; deep purple when they return home. Gammell's colored-pencil illustrations are rich in detail without being cluttered, featuring expressive faces and humorously exaggerated actions. *The Relatives Came* is a Caldecott Honor Book.

Read-Aloud Presentation

Discuss a long family trip you have taken. Talk about all the preparations that were needed. Mention some of the food you took and games and activities you did to keep yourselves entertained across the miles. Solicit some comments from the children. Read *The Relatives Came*. Stop occasionally to enjoy the funny expressions and to point out the actions in the pictures. After the reading, let the children tell about some of the visits they have had from relatives and how they felt when the relatives left. Announce the STORY S-T-R-E-T-C-H-E-R activities associated with the book.

Art: Colored-Pencil Sketches of Family Visits

What the children will learn
To use different techniques to create shading and emphasis in a picture

Materials you will need
Colored pencils, sharpeners, papers in a variety of textures

What to do
1. Look again at Stephen Gammell's illustrations in *The Relatives Came*. Discuss the fact that the book is a Caldecott Honor book, which means that the artist was given an award for his effective illustrations.
2. Examine how Gammell created the shading and shadows and how he used bright colors to outline some shapes to create emphasis.
3. Ask the children to draw pictures of relatives' visits or their own family's visits using the colored pencils. Encourage them to try some of Gammell's shading, shadowing, and emphasis techniques.
4. Let the children experiment with the effects of different textures of paper on the colored-pencil shading.
5. Display the children's family drawings in the class library with the book jacket of *The Relatives Came*.

Something to think about
Older children can illustrate their own versions of family visits to accompany the stories they write in the writing center. Younger children may enjoy doing a colored-pencil mural of the book and dividing the scenes.

STORY S-T-R-E-T-C-H-E-R

Art: Sculpting Funny Station Wagons and Cars

What the children will learn
To sculpt using simple tools

Materials you will need
Playdough or modeling clay, coffee stirrers or straws, Popsicle sticks, pencils, metal spatula, meat trays

What to do
1. Look at the funny illustrations of the multicolored station wagon in *The Relatives Came*.

2. Ask a volunteer to sculpt the station wagon, and encourage the other children to make other funny cars.
3. Demonstrate how to use a variety of simple tools—straws, Popsicle sticks, pencils—to create lines.
4. After the children finish making their sculptures, gently lift the sculptures from the table by sliding a metal spatula around the edges. Place the sculptures on meat trays so they are easy to move.
5. Display the station wagon in the class library and the other funny cars around the room.

Something to think about
Do not emphasize the end product too soon. Let the children experiment over the course of the week. All art media require several sessions before the artists can gain enough control to use the material creatively.

Classroom Library: Verbal Renditions of Our Pictures

What the children will learn
To use words to describe what they have expressed in drawings

Materials you will need
CD and CD player or tapes and tape player, stapler, construction paper

What to do
1. In small groups, ask the children to come to the classroom library and talk about their colored-pencil drawings from the art STORY S-T-R-E-T-C-H-E-R.
2. Have the children tell what happened before the scene they drew, what happened in the scene they drew, and what happened next.
3. Record the children's verbal renditions.
4. Place the recordings in the library area, and staple the children's pictures together in the order that the children's stories are heard on the recording.
5. Make a construction-paper cover for the children's drawings.

Something to think about
It is not necessary to record all of the sessions of children telling stories. Some should be savored just for the moment. However, recording often motivates the children to work on their oral language and to plan their stories.

Creative Dramatics: Dramatizing the Two Families' Preparations

What the children will learn
To improvise scenes, feelings, dialogue

Materials you will need
None needed

What to do
1. Read *The Relatives Came* again.
2. Talk about how much preparation is needed for the one family to get ready for the trip.
3. Brainstorm a list of things that a family would have to do to prepare for a trip, such as deciding which clothes to pack, selecting toys and games to take, preparing the food for the trip, packing the car, and other preparations.
4. Invite one child to be the organizer of the trip, and assign other volunteers to the remaining roles. Improvise the scenes.
5. With another group of actors, improvise the preparations necessary for the family who receives the relatives in their home for the long visit.

Something to think about
It is best to work in small groups for improvisations. If you have a reluctant group of actors, take on the role of mother or father, and the children will usually join you.

Writing: Family Trips and Visits

What the children will learn
To write, edit, and publish family stories

Materials you will need
Paper, pencils, markers, contact paper, tape, stapler

What to do
1. Tell the children you would like to publish some family stories for the class library to go along with the focus books for the unit.
2. Discuss the steps in the writing process: prewriting—getting ideas and planning their stories; writing and rewriting; editing; and, finally, publishing the books.
3. Model the steps by writing family stories with small groups.

Families

4. Encourage the children to add their own individual stories, and assist in the editing until they are ready for published book form.

Something to think about

Some schools have volunteers who can type the children's stories on the computer or help older children type, and volunteers who work in publishing centers where children can go to select covers and format their books. While these volunteers are a wonderful support for a class or a school where children write often, it is still important for the teacher to model the steps and go through the entire process several times before turning these final steps over to the volunteers.

References

Henkes, Kevin. 1990. *Julius, The Baby of the World*. New York: HarperCollins.

Juster, Norton. 2005. *The Hello, Goodbye Window*. Illustrated by Chris Raschka. New York: HarperCollins.

Parish, Peggy. 1988. *Amelia Bedelia's Family Album*. Illustrated by Lynn Sweat. New York: HarperCollins.

Rylant, Cynthia. 1985. *The Relatives Came*. Illustrated by Stephen Gammell. New York: Simon and Schuster.

Simon, Norma. 1976. *All Kinds of Families*. Illustrated by Joe Lasker. Niles, IL: Albert Whitman and Company.

Additional References

Crews, Donald. 1998. *Bigmama's*. New York: Greenwillow Books. *Visiting Bigmama's house in the country, young Donald Crews finds his relatives full of news, and the old place and its surroundings just the same as the year before.*

Rosenberry, Vera. 2000. *Vera Runs Away*. New York: Henry Holt. *After no one pays attention to her, even when she has a great report card, Vera runs away. When she begins to feel hungry, she wonders what her family is doing while she is running away.*

Sweeney, Joan. 2000. *Me and My Family Tree*. Illustrated by Annette Cable. New York: Dragonfly Books. *A child uses a family tree to explain how the members of her extended family are related.*

Websites

1. A to Z Teacher Stuff: www.atozteacherstuff.com/Themes/Family
   - Links to family-themed sites
   - Arts and crafts
   - Lesson plans and activities
2. Teacher Vision: www.teachervision.fen.com
   - Family-themed links sorted by grade level
   - Slideshows
   - Printable articles and activities
3. Embracing the Child: www.embracingthechild.org/caldecott.html
   - Titles of winners of Caldecott Medal and Honor winners
   - Book reviews
   - Connections to other major children's book awards
4. Mirrors-How its made. Rvd4always. November 18, 2008 www.YouTube.com. Excellent source for additional references on how things are made. **Caution** as there are advertisements that also appear on YouTube.
5. Kididdles: www.kididdles.com
   - Free downloads of lullabies
6. Kidsread.com: www.kidsreads.com/series/series-amelia-titles.asp
   - Titles
   - Book reviews
   - Frequently asked questions

Friends

Frog and Toad Are Friends

By Arnold Lobel

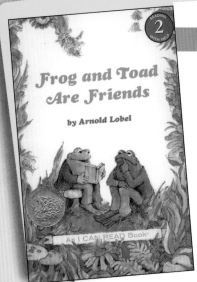

Story Line

Frog and Toad Are Friends, a Caldecott Honor Book, contains five stories about these incomparable friends who enjoy each other's company even when faced with life's little inconveniences, such as awakening after hibernation, trying to think of a story to tell, losing a button, wearing a new bathing suit, and waiting for a letter. First and second graders have adopted this wonderful pair of friends. Even though Frog must forgive Toad's moodiness and sometimes his lack of understanding, they endure, friends to the end. Arnold Lobel's famous friends are instantly recognizable.

Read-Aloud Presentation

Before announcing the read-aloud selection for the day, ask the children to talk about things they like to do with their friends. (The Live Wire Media website has some friendship discussion questions. See www.goodcharacter.com/YCC/BeingFriends.html.) Then show the cover of *Frog and Toad Are Friends*. Undoubtedly some of your students will have read Frog and Toad stories. Ask them not to tell any of the secrets of the story, and tell them you will have a special STORY S-T-R-E-T-C-H-E-R for them later in the library. Since there are five Frog and Toad stories, read one per day. Each story is very different and should be savored on its own. Discuss with the children what very good friends Frog and Toad are. Look at the cover of the book. Tell the children that sometimes Toad likes to read stories to Frog, but they each also love to tell stories. Then read, "The Story."

Art: Lost Button Pictures

What the children will learn
To create a picture inspired by a book

Materials you will need
Thick construction paper, poster board, buttons, glue, markers, crayons

What to do
1. Let the children select a button they like and glue it anywhere on their paper.
2. Ask the children to imagine the place where this button is.
3. Pretend they are walking along and find Toad's lost button.
4. Encourage the children to draw a scene where they find Toad's button.
5. Help the artists imagine many alternatives. One student might find Toad's button on a cloud as she parachutes to the ground. Another student could discover Toad's button underwater while he snorkels.

Something to think about
Younger children enjoy the act of gluing buttons onto paper. They also like creating patterns with buttons. Consider letting each child sew a favorite button onto an old jacket. Wear the jacket each time you read a Frog and Toad story.

STORY S-T-R-E-T-C-H-E-R

Classroom Library: Frog and Toad Recording

What the children will learn
To read with expression

Materials you will need
CDs and CD player or tapes and tape recorder, stapler

What to do
1. Ask the children who have already read Frog and Toad books to join you in the classroom library. Have them decide which Frog and Toad story they would like to record.
2. Select four children to work together.
3. One child will read Frog's lines in each story; one will read Toad's lines; one will read the narrator's lines; and one will operate the recorder.

4. During the recording, the operator should also be responsible for creating a page-turning signal, such as clicking a stapler.
5. Encourage the children to rehearse their reading and taping signals.
6. Label and store the recording at the classroom listening station, with copies of the Frog and Toad books.

Something to think about
Videotape children reading Frog and Toad stories. Use the camera to scan the pages of the book while the children read.

STORY S-T-R-E-T-C-H-E-R

Creative Dramatics: Dramatizing "A Lost Button"

What the children will learn
To extend a script and act out the parts

Materials you will need
Chalkboard, chalk, poster board, markers

What to do
1. Read the story "A Lost Button" again.
2. Ask the students to recall other characters (a snail, sparrow, raccoon, turtle, field mouse, lizards, and dragonflies) that are in the Frog and Toad books.
3. Ask the students to imagine that all of these characters are part of "A Lost Button."
4. Let the students imagine what Frog and Toad might say to each of these characters as they look for the button.
5. Cut pieces of poster board and print the name of a character on each piece. Punch a hole in the upper left and right corners of the poster board. Insert a length of string and tie it so that the poster board sign identifying the character can hang around a child's neck.
6. Distribute the signs and begin the drama.
7. Encourage the children to act and sound like their characters. For example, the sparrow might say, "Chirp, chirp. Excuse me, did you lose a button?" The snake might say, "Hiss, hiss. Excuse me, did you lose a button?"

Something to think about
With younger students, read the story and let them act out the motions. Limit the characters to Frog, Toad, sparrow, and raccoon.

STORY S-T-R-E-T-C-H-E-R

Mathematics: Totaling Toad's Calendar

What the children will learn
To count months and days, to do simple addition

Materials you will need
Commercial calendars, pencils or markers

What to do
1. Read "Spring" from *Frog and Toad Are Friends*.
2. Distribute the calendars and try to decide during which months Frog talks about the snow melting.
3. Read "Spring" again and encourage the students to listen for more clues in the story (until they hear April mentioned).
4. Find out how long Toad has been asleep. (The story says he has been asleep since November.)
5. Ask the students to look at their calendars and count how many months Frog has slept.
6. Write down the number of days in each month.
7. Later in the story, Toad says to wake him at "half past May." Let the students decide when half past May would be. Determine how many more days they should add to Toad's total.

Something to think about
Younger students can simply count the days and mark them on their calendars. Older students can add the numbers of days, noting that different months have different numbers of days.

STORY S-T-R-E-T-C-H-E-R

Writing: Writing a Letter to Toad

What the children will learn
To communicate with a friend through a letter

Materials you will need
Writing paper, pens, pencils, mailbox, stamps

What to do
1. Bring a letter from a friend to the classroom, and discuss how pleased you were to receive the letter.
2. Read, or let a volunteer read, "The Letter" story from *Frog and Toad Are Friends*.
3. Ask the children to write letters to Toad.
4. Send these letters to reading and writing partners from other classrooms, who will write back to the children.

Something to think about
Older children may prefer writing a letter to a friend or to a classmate who has moved away.

Arthur's Birthday

By Marc Brown

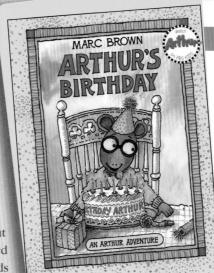

Story Line

Arthur delivers his birthday party invitations to his friends only to find that his party and Muffy's party are scheduled on the same day. For a week, their friends are upset, not knowing which party to attend. Finally, the boys decide to stick together and go to Arthur's party, while the girls plan to go to Muffy's. Then Arthur comes up with an ingenious plan that makes it possible for them to attend both. Marc Brown's humor, cartoonlike drawings, and plot are as ingenious as Arthur's plan.

Read–Aloud Presentation

Ask the children what their favorite day of the year is. Invariably, someone will answer, "My birthday!" Show the children the cover of *Arthur's Birthday,* and let them predict who will come to Arthur's party. If you have read other Arthur stories, they will recall the names of his best friends, Buster, the Brain, Binky Barnes, and Francine. Let the children who have birthdays this month tell their favorite flavors of birthday cake, their favorite party games, and how their families celebrate birthdays. Tell them that Arthur has planned his birthday party, but it looks like some of the friends may not come. Read *Arthur's Birthday*. Pause after the scene in which Arthur delivers his party invitation to Muffy, when she finds out Saturday afternoon is his birthday party as well as hers. Let the children try to decide what Arthur and Muffy can do so that all their friends can attend their parties. Continue reading, and stop before the scene where Francine and Arthur hide in the tree house writing notes to their friends. Have the children guess what Arthur and Francine are plotting. Finish the story and announce all the "friends" STORY S-T-R-E-T-C-H-E-R-S based on *Arthur's Birthday*.

Art: Friends Decorate for Arthur's Party

What the children will learn
To recycle throwaways or "trashables"; to make party decorations

Materials you will need
Plastic bottles, egg cartons, paper towel tubes, milk cartons, plastic hosiery containers shaped like eggs, construction paper, tape, scissors

What to do
1. Begin the art project by asking pairs of children to work together and make party decorations.
2. In small groups, have the children brainstorm possible uses for the materials at hand.
3. Set a date for the projects to be finished.
4. Plan a display of the projects, and invite other classes to see the students' inventive uses of recyclable materials.

Something to think about
While Arthur's story merits making birthday party decorations, this activity can be scheduled at any time of the year. The children can make recycled decorations for a harvest celebration in the fall, Valentine's Day in the winter, or St. Patrick's Day in the spring.

Cooking: Decorating Arthur's and Muffy's Cakes

What the children will learn
To decorate a cake

Materials you will need
Unfrosted cakes, contrasting colors of cake frosting, knives or spatulas, margarine tubs with warm water, optional—sprinkles, raisins or small candies, powdered sugar, doilies

What to do
1. Either bake two cakes in class or ask a parent or class volunteer to bake the cakes ahead of time.
2. Demonstrate how to spread the frosting by dipping the knife or spatula in warm water, then into the frosting before spreading on the cake.

3. Working in small groups, let the children decorate the cakes, starting with the sides.
4. Decorate the cakes with different colors of frosting and sprinkles, raisins, or small candies.
5. Decorate one of the cakes without frosting the top. Place a doily on the top and sprinkle powdered sugar over it, then remove the doily to reveal a pretty pattern.

Something to think about
Encourage parents to bring their child's birthday cake or cupcakes to the class unfrosted, and let the children decorate them.

STORY S-T-R-E-T-C-H-E-R

Games: Birthday Party Games

What the children will learn
To play party games and practice their good manners

Materials you will need
Several party games—Pin the Tail on the Donkey, a piñata, Hide-and-Go-Seek, and other party games the children recommend

What to do
1. Mention the gift Francine gives Arthur, a bottle marked "Francine's Spin the Bottle Game." Explain that this is not the "kissing" game of Spin the Bottle, but a Take a Walk with a Friend game. The spinners have to walk around the room together.
2. Ask the children about other games they like to play at their parties.
3. Collect all the game materials.
4. On the following day, play the games throughout the day inside or outside or at the end of the day.

Something to think about
For a cross-cultural perspective, have children from different cultures plan the party activities.

STORY S-T-R-E-T-C-H-E-R

Mathematics: Birthday Calendar Math

What the children will learn
To use calendars as devices to record important events

Materials you will need
Calendars collected from home or photocopied, markers and chart tablet or chalkboard and chalk

What to do
1. Distribute the calendars, or have the children bring one from home.
2. Let the children mark their classmates' birthdays in each month.
3. Make a chart listing all the months of the year, beginning with the present month.
4. With the children, count the number of children who have birthdays in each month.
5. Write the names of the months and the number of children who have birthdays each month. Add the number of birthdays for each month to get a total for the entire 12 months.
6. Ask the children to tell you how they know if the answer is correct. They should say that the total number of birthdays equals the number of children in the class.

Something to think about
For first graders, mark the birthdays for this month only. Let them place a mark on birthdays and on today's date and count the number of days in between.

STORY S-T-R-E-T-C-H-E-R

Writing: Party Invitations

What the children will learn
To write formal invitations that include all the important information

Materials you will need
Party invitations you have received, stationery or paper, construction paper, glue, crayons, markers, old envelopes

What to do
1. Discuss with the children the important information to include in a good invitation. Let the children generate the list of important points.
2. If possible, show the children a party invitation you have received. Read it to them and see if the invitation covers all the points the children mentioned.
3. As a group, list the information necessary for the children to host a party for Arthur in the classroom.
4. Divide the children into four groups.
5. Let each group use the information to compose their own invitations to the school staff to come to Arthur's party.

Something to think about
Keep writing experiences as authentic as possible. Writing real invitations and receiving replies helps the children appreciate the importance of writing in their daily lives.

Chester's Way

By Kevin Henkes

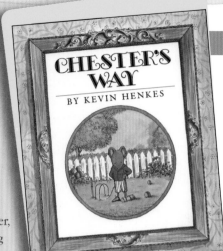

Story Line

Chester and Wilson, Wilson and Chester, are always together and always doing things just alike. They cut their sandwiches in diagonals just alike, double-knot their shoes just alike, even play croquet and baseball just alike. Then when Lilly arrives in the neighborhood, they notice she has her own way of doing things. Chester and Wilson avoid her until that fateful day when Lilly comes to the rescue and scares away some bigger guys with her scary cat disguise and squirt gun. After that, the three are inseparable—until Victor moves into the neighborhood. Henkes's delightful illustrations are black-line drawings washed with cheerful watercolors.

Read-Aloud Presentation

Select some well-known best friends from the classroom. Describe some of the ways in which they are just alike and some of the things that they like to do together. If you have new children in the classroom, ask them what things they like to do with a best friend from their old neighborhood. After a brief discussion, read *Chester's Way*. Pause after the scene that first introduces Lilly, and ask the children to predict what will happen next. Keep the predictions brief; stop after only two or three. Ask for predictions after the scene where Chester and Wilson are hiding behind the tree, watching Lilly in her funny disguises, and after Lilly rescues Chester and Wilson. Finally, at the end of the book, ask each child to silently imagine what might happen to the friends now that Victor has moved to the neighborhood. Give each child a sheet of paper to draw the next scene or write a new story about Chester, Wilson, Lilly, and Victor.

Art: Lilly's Disguises

What the children will learn
To make paper bag disguises or costumes

Materials you will need
Brown paper bags, markers, scissors, tape or glue or staples, optional—yarn, funny masks, Groucho Marx moustaches and glasses

What to do
1. Look again at Kevin Henkes's illustrations of Lilly and her disguises.
2. Let the children try on some of the disguises you have collected.
3. Point out the illustration of Lilly in her paper bag mask.
4. Brainstorm with the children some disguises they could make.
5. Help to cut out eyes and make slits in the sides of the bags so they will fall down over the children's shoulders.
6. Let the children wear their disguises and sit with their friends while you read the story again.

Something to think about
Ask parents or children to contribute funny old masks.

Mathematics and Snack Time: The Shapes of Lilly's Sandwiches

What the children will learn
To recognize the shapes created from the sandwich bread and the snacks

Materials you will need
Milk, plastic knives, plates, napkins, whole wheat bread, peanut butter, jelly, cookie cutters, optional—apples, oranges, strawberries, raisins

What to do
1. Prepare an area for snacks.
2. Help the children recognize the different shapes of the cookie cutters and foods. Bread could be a rectangle or a square. Peel an orange and notice the curved shape of the orange slice; cut apples in eighths to create similar shapes, or cut apples horizontally for a star shape in the center.

3. Allow children to cut different shapes of bread, apples, and orange wedges and then spread them with peanut butter. They can decorate their sandwiches using slices of strawberries and raisins, like Lilly did in *Chester's Way*.
4. Serve with milk and enjoy the "shape sandwiches."

Something to think about

If any of your students have allergies to peanuts, substitute a cheese spread or cheese slices.

STORY S-T-R-E-T-C-H-E-R

Music and Movement: Bicycle Hand Signals

What the children will learn

To recognize signals and practice bike safety

Materials you will need

Chart tablet, poster board, marker

What to do

1. If you have children whose brothers or sisters are members of the school safety patrol, invite them to the classroom to show the hand signals they use to direct pedestrians.
2. Ask the safety patrol to discuss special problems with bicyclers and pedestrians.
3. Ask them to demonstrate hand signals they give to bicyclers.
4. Demonstrate hand signals bicyclers can use to inform walkers, drivers, and other bike riders before they turn.
5. Practice the signals patrollers use, and ask pairs of friends to use bicycle hand signals throughout the day.

Something to think about

This STORY S-T-R-E-T-C-H-E-R emphasizes both a movement activity and a social studies activity: learning to obey signals and rules.

STORY S-T-R-E-T-C-H-E-R

Games: Chester and Wilson's Game— Croquet

What the children will learn

To play croquet with friends

Materials you will need

Croquet set with mallet, balls, wickets, scraps of paper, pencil, hat or fishbowl

What to do

1. Briefly explain the object of the game: to move one's ball through the series of wickets (hoops). Demonstrate how to hit the ball.
2. Let a few children begin playing. Soon they will be confronted with the problem of how to get their ball through the wicket when another player's ball is in the way.
3. After they seem to have the knack of playing, assign the different colored balls to characters in the story. For example, the red-striped ball is Chester's; the green, Wilson's; the blue, Lilly's; and the yellow, Victor's.
4. Draw names from a hat or a fishbowl to determine who will be Chester, Wilson, Lilly, and Victor for the day.
5. Play croquet every day for at least a week.

Something to think about

Consult with the physical education teacher in your school and plan instruction in the finer points of croquet.

STORY S-T-R-E-T-C-H-E-R

Writing: Writing with a Friend, the Next Episode

What the children will learn

To confer with a friend and extend the story

Materials you will need

Writing paper, pencils

What to do

1. Pair the children into writing partners, friends who will write the next episodes of the Chester, Wilson, Lilly, and Victor story together.
2. Some children will begin writing immediately from ideas prompted by your reading the book aloud. Assist those children who are having difficulty getting started by letting them look at Henkes's last illustration.
3. Suggest that they draw what might happen next.
4. Brainstorm what would happen if a new neighbor, just their age, moved in next door to them.
5. Let the writers who are interested continue their writing and rewriting until they are ready to read their "next episode" stories to the class.

Something to think about

Give children a choice of writing a story about Chester, Wilson, Lilly, and Victor, continuing a project they are presently working on, or starting a new project.

Angelina and Alice

By Katharine Holabird
Illustrated by Helen Craig

Story Line

Primary-grade children worry about making friends and learning how to do physical activities, such as cartwheels, swinging high, and doing somersaults. A favorite character among primary-grade children is Angelina, who faces some of the same worries. These two mouse characters, Angelina and Alice, like doing tricks together, but Alice can do perfect handstands. Angelina tries but falls and is laughed at by everyone, including Alice. When the gym teacher has them find a partner to learn new tricks, Angelina is sure no one will want to be with her, but Alice does. With the friendship mended, they go on to star in a village gymnastics festival, performing on the parallel bars and rings, and dancing with colored ribbons. The Craig illustrations match the text wonderfully with pastels and sparkles on the cover and characteristic Alice colors throughout.

Read-Aloud Presentation

Angelina is a favorite animated television character as well as a favorite book character. Ask the children who have seen Angelina on television to tell what they know about her. If some boys say the story is for girls, help them see that the story is about friendships. Also, have the children remember when they were trying to learn something new. Let them talk about learning to ride a bike or a skateboard or to play soccer or hockey. Ask if anyone teased them when they were learning, or if they were embarrassed to let their friends see them learning. Recall an event from your childhood, if needed. Read *Angelina and Alice*, and ask the children to listen for what Angelina is trying to learn to do, for who teases her, and how she feels. After the read-aloud presentation, announce the art STORY S-T-R-E-T-C-H-E-R.

Art: Before and After Learning Something New

What the children will learn
To use art to recall learning something new

Materials you will need
Choice of colored pencils, markers or crayons, construction paper or drawing paper

What to do
1. Have the children recall the story of Angelina and how she tries and tries to learn how to do handstands. Ask the children what task they had a hard time learning to do, such as tumbling, riding a bike, or doing flips on a trampoline.
2. Have the students fold a piece of construction paper in half.
3. On the cover write the word *Before*. On the inside write the word *After*.
4. Ask the children to draw pictures of themselves on the cover before they learned to ride a bike or some other difficult skill.
5. Have the students draw a picture inside of themselves now that they can do their activity.

Something to think about
Second and third graders could write a sentence or two about how they felt when they were learning and how they feel now that they have mastered their new skills.

Music and Movement: Dancing with Ribbons

What the children will learn
To move in response to the rhythm of the music and in coordination with their team

Materials you will need
Recording of waltz music, scarves, ribbons or crepe paper, scissors, stapler, wooden dowels or paper towel rolls

What to do
1. Show the students the pictures of the gymnastics festival where Angelina and Alice are dancing with the ribbons.
2. Distribute scarves and let the children move in response to the waltz music, twirling their scarves in long, flowing, and circular motions.

3. Demonstrate how to make a baton of ribbons for dancing by using either wooden dowels to which you staple the ribbons or using paper towel rolls and stapling on strips of crepe paper.

Something to think about
First graders will probably do well with the scarves. Second and third graders should be able to handle the ribbons or crepe paper streamers. The longer the ribbon or streamer, the more difficult it is to control.

Social Development: Name-Calling Hurts

What the children will learn
To express their feelings about name-calling and to discuss how to handle a situation where one experiences name-calling

Materials you will need
Copy of *Angelina and Alice*

What to do
1. Reread the section of the book where Angelina is called "Angelina Thumbelina" and ask how we know how she feels.
2. Look at the illustrations showing how Angelina is feeling when Alice leaves her.
3. Discuss an experience you had as a child when someone called you a name that you did not like.
4. Decide what the students should do when their feelings are hurt.
5. Role-play some situations where the hurt child says how she or he feels. Rehearse the sentence, "Please do not call me that name. I do not like it."

Something to think about
Discuss that anyone who is called a name over and over again should tell the teacher. It is an early sign of bullying if children gang up on one child and call that child a name.

Special Project: Class Gymnastics Festival

What the children will learn
To demonstrate the gymnastics they have learned

Materials you will need
Gym equipment (If gym equipment is not available, use tumbling mats, jump ropes, rhythm ribbons, and trampoline.)

What to do
1. Working with the physical education or gymnastics teacher, decide on some routines your class could perform for the school, parents, and community.
2. Assist with the planning of the teams, much like Mr. Hopper in *Angelina and Alice*.
3. During a group time, plan the schedule of events and chart out who will perform which routines.
4. Distribute brochures to the school, parents, and community announcing the Class Gymnastics Festival (see next STORY S-T-R-E-T-C-H-E-R).

Something to think about
Plan awards for all of the children for teamwork, for specialty acts, for best handstands, for best tumbling, for fastest climbers, for highest vaults, and for other events.

Writing and Art: Posters for the Class Gymnastics Festival

What the children will learn
To include the necessary information and the extra–appealing information to entice people to come to the festival

Materials you will need
Sample of brochures announcing events, chart tablet or whiteboard, markers, art or construction paper and a selection of markers, colored pencils, and crayons

What to do
1. Display a sample of brochures for various school and community events. Point out the essential information—who, what, when, where, costs.
2. Read some of the enticing phrases that make people want to attend: "future Olympians," "everyone participates," "door prizes," "special awards," "Come see what we have learned."
3. Fold the art or construction paper in half. On the outside, let the children make a colorful drawing; write the essential information on the inside.
4. Encourage the students to use some of the enticing phrases to try and capture the attention of the people they want to attend the festival.

Something to think about
For older second graders and third graders, let them make a video with an announcer using some of the enticing phrases, like a salesperson.

A Couple of Boys Have the Best Week Ever

By Marla Frazee

Story Line

A Caldecott Medal Honor Book, *A Couple of Boys Have the Best Week Ever* is both a friendship book and a book about relationships with grandparents. Humorously told and illustrated, James's and Eamon's thoughts are sidebars in a few thought balloons that capture the boys' true feelings. They want to go to nature camp in Antarctica and see penguins. Instead, they find themselves having adventures on side trips, traveling with Eamon's grandparents, Bill and Pam, who live at the beach. They enjoy eating banana waffles, sleeping on an air mattress, using binoculars, collecting rocks and shells on the beach at night, and arranging them to look like penguins and whales. From their secret handshake to their identical penguin walks, the boys charm Bill and Pam and, in turn, the boys enjoy the best week ever at their version of nature camp.

Read-Aloud Presentation

Discuss that a Caldecott Honor Book Award is given for illustrations and for the match between the story and the illustrations. Show the cover of the book, and see what the children can find out from the T-shirts the boys are wearing, where the story takes place, and what the boys' names are. Ask if anyone has grandparents living in Florida or near the beach. What would you do if you visited them? Then read the book through without stopping. Ask the children to describe some of the surprises in the book. Point out the balloons for the boys' secret thoughts. If time permits, allow the children to tell about their "Best Week Ever."

STORY S-T-R-E-T-C-H-E-R

Art: Decorating Camp T-Shirts

What the children will learn

To design a logo and transfer it with fabric paint to a T-shirt

Materials you will need

Paper, colored pencils or crayons, fabric paint, white T-shirts

What to do

1. Look at the illustration of James and Eamon on the cover of the book. Discuss the "nature camp" design on their T-shirts, an oval with a green leaf and the words *nature* above and *camp* below the oval.
2. Ask the children what symbol of nature they would like to use—a plant, an animal, a rowboat, or some other camping activity or equipment. Let the children experiment with designs on paper.
3. Teach them how to draw with tubes of fabric paint.
4. Insert plastic garbage bags between the front and back of the T-shirts, so that the fabric paint will not bleed through to the other side.
5. Leave the T-shirts lying flat to dry overnight.
6. Invite the children to wear the shirts for the indoor camping adventure.

Something to think about

Keep the children's experiments with designs, and use them on brown paper bags to identify their camping lunches.

STORY S-T-R-E-T-C-H-E-R

Art: Diorama of Antarctica or Favorite Nature Spot

What the children will learn

To use found objects in nature to depict a scene

Materials you will need

Seashells, mussel shells, rocks, pine cones, twigs, camera

What to do

1. Read the section of the book again where the boys show Eamon's grandparents their creative interpretation of Antarctica with the white rocks representing icebergs and the brown rocks being whales and the mussel shells representing penguins.

2. Place an assortment of natural objects on a table, and let teams of children take turns creating their own special diorama of a place they would like to visit.

3. Keep the displays or dioramas up for a day, and take pictures with the teams of children. Tell them that tomorrow the dioramas will go back to being pieces of nature, and new teams will make designs.

Something to think about

E-mail the pictures of the children to their parents (or grandparents), or place the photos on a classroom website. For children whose parents may not have computers, print a paper copy of the picture.

STORY S-T-R-E-T-C-H-E-R

Cooking: Waffles with Bananas for Snack

What the children will learn

To follow simple cooking directions and make measurements

Materials you will need

Frozen waffles, toaster, maple syrup, butter or margarine, bananas, plates, forks, knives, wooden tongs to remove the waffles from the toaster

What to do

1. Read the parts of the books that contain references to banana waffles with maple syrup.

2. Read the directions for toasting the waffles in the toaster. Make children aware of safety precautions when removing the waffles from the toaster.

3. Serve the waffles with butter and maple syrup, and let the children slice bananas for the tops of their waffles.

Something to think about

For older children, use a packaged waffle or pancake mix. Third graders can handle the addition of fractions in their measurements. If using waffle mix with younger children, mark the levels with masking tape around the measuring cup.

STORY S-T-R-E-T-C-H-E-R

Science: Discoveries with Binoculars

What the children will learn

To focus binoculars and to write down their observations

Materials you will need

Several pairs of binoculars

What to do

1. After the students experiment with the binoculars and learn to focus them, have the students use the binoculars to examine objects in the classroom.

2. Record those observations on a whiteboard or chart tablet. Call them *observations,* and discuss that this is what naturalists do, record their observations.

3. Allow the students to take the binoculars out on the playground and practice bringing sights into view and making observations of tiny specimens and of large specimens.

4. Consider designating an area of the playground that is most natural as an exploration area. Older children can use twine to mark off areas for a team to record all the objects found in a square foot. Children can take turns looking through the binoculars to see what other students are discovering, then they can write the names of things and record them in a journal.

Something to think about

For children with glasses, it is often difficult to use binoculars. Let them experiment with and without their glasses.

STORY S-T-R-E-T-C-H-E-R

Special Project: Indoor Nature Camp

What the children will learn

To plan an afternoon of indoor camping and organize themselves to assemble all of the necessary equipment

Materials you will need

Chart tablet or projector and whiteboard, markers, air mattresses, simple tents, sleeping bags, camp lunches or snacks

What to do

1. Read again the section of the book where James and Eamon create an indoor nature camp downstairs from the grandparents, complete with air mattresses, sleeping bags, games, and snacks.

2. Let the children brainstorm what they would want if they turned the classroom into an indoor nature camp. Write their brainstorming ideas on a chart tablet or whiteboard.

3. Have volunteers name the camping equipment they have at home that they might be able to bring to school.

4. Designate a day at the end of the week and have an afternoon of air mattresses, simple tents, sleeping bags, games, and camp lunches or snacks.

Friends

Something to think about

Ask some grandparents to assist with the afternoon. Consider having grandparents bring the snacks or perform different duties, such as air-mattress pumping, popping corn, or just playing games with the children in small groups. Also, consider singing some camping songs.

References

Brown, Marc. 1989. *Arthur's Birthday*. New York: Hachette.

Frazee, Marla. 2008. *A Couple of Boys Have the Best Week Ever*. New York: Houghton Mifflin Harcourt.

Henkes, Kevin. 1988. *Chester's Way*. New York: HarperCollins.

Holabird, Katherine. 2001. *Angelina and Alice*. Illustrated by Helen Craig. New York: Penguin.

Lobel, Arnold. 1970. *Frog and Toad Are Friends*. New York: HarperCollins.

Additional References

Cooper, Helen. 2005. *Pumpkin Soup*. New York: Farrar, Straus, and Giroux. *The Cat and the Squirrel come to blows with the Duck in arguing about who will perform what duty in preparing their pumpkin soup, and they almost lose the Duck's friendship when he decides to leave them.*

Fox, Mem. 1989. *Wilfrid Gordon McDonald Partridge*. Illustrated by Julie Vivas. Brooklyn, NY: Kane/Miller. *A small boy tries to discover the meaning of memory so he can restore that of an elderly friend.*

Lobel, Arnold. 1971. *Frog and Toad Together*. New York: HarperCollins. *Best friends Frog and Toad are always together. This book contains five wonderful stories about flowers, cookies, bravery, dreams, and, most of all, friendship.*

Websites

1. Angelina Ballerina: www.angelinaballerina.com
2. Live Wire Media: www.goodcharacter.com/YCC/BeingFriends.html
   - Discussion questions
   - Group activities
   - Writing and home assignments
3. Lesson Planet: The Search Engine for Teachers: www.lessonplanet.com/search?grade=All&keywords=friendship&rating=0&search_type=related
   - Great links page
   - Friendship themed poems and letters
   - Arts and crafts
   - Friendship lessons and activities

Feelings

Ira Says Goodbye

By Bernard Waber

Story Line

Ira's sister breaks the news that his best
friend, Reggie, is moving to Greendale.
The following days are filled with sadness
and excitement. Ira is sad and feels
betrayed that Reggie is excited about the
move. Reggie brags about his new house, new people
he will meet, and new fun things he can do when he
moves to Greendale. Ira thinks about all the things he
and Reggie like to do together: trading baseball cards,
playing hide-and-seek, performing magic tricks, taking
care of their pets. How the children express their
feelings as well as how they plan to keep in touch are
meaningful to primary-age children, whose friends
move often. Waber's illustrations of Ira and Reggie as
well as their families are the ones readers got to know
in *Ira Sleeps Over*.

Read-Aloud Presentation

Talk to the children about one of your friends who
moved away, including how much you miss your
friend. Tell the children about where your friend
moved and how happy your friend is living in the new
place. Talk about the fact that Ira and Reggie are very
good friends, good enough friends to admit that each
sleeps with a teddy bear. Read *Ira Says Goodbye*. Do
not pause during the reading, as the dialogue in the
story can be too easily interrupted. Read Ira's dialogue
very sadly and Reggie's quite excitedly. At the end of
the story, tell what you and your friend who moved
away do to stay in touch. Let children with friends
who have moved away describe how they keep in
touch. See Kids Health from Nemours
http://kidshealth.org/kid/feeling/index.html for other
discussions of feelings.

Creative Dramatics:
Friends' Magic Show

What the children will learn
To perform simple tricks with a partner

Materials you will need
Top hat, wand, magician's cape, card
table, simple reference books on
magic

What to do
1. Survey the students and find those
    who know how to do magic tricks.
2. With the magicians, plan their stage names and
    introductions, and let them chose assistants.
3. Choose an MC (Master or Mistress of Ceremonies).
4. Advertise the magic show for several days in advance.
5. Practice the magic show several times before the
    performance behind a curtain or in another room in the
    school.

Something to think about
Older children can organize a magic show for
kindergarteners.

Mathematics: Sorting Baseball Cards

What the children will learn
To sort by more than one attribute

Materials you will need
A collection of baseball cards, chart tablet and marker or
chalkboard and chalk, two to five small boxes

What to do
1. With the group of children who chose the mathematics
    area, brainstorm as many different ways as possible to
    sort the baseball cards.
2. Write the categories for sorting on the board or chart
    tablet. For example, by league, by team, by position, by
    home state, by home runs, by runs batted in, by years
    of playing, by rookie, by veteran.
3. Divide the cards among the children.
4. Sort the cards from the two most popular teams into
    two boxes. Set the rest of the cards aside.
5. Re-sort the cards several times into different categories.

Something to think about

First graders will probably sort by team. The third graders can sort the cards by the more advanced categories and use a Venn diagram of overlapping circles to sort cards that fit in two categories.

STORY S-T-R-E-T-C-H-E-R

Music and Movement: Friends Looking for Friends

What the children will learn

To interpret and identify distance by signals

Materials you will need

None needed

What to do

1. Arrange ahead of time for two friends to hide together somewhere in the classroom.
2. With all the children seated, tell them that two students from class pretending to be Ira and Reggie are in a secret hiding place.
3. Whisper in one child's ear the place where the two friends are hiding. Designate that child as the "signaler."
4. Select another child to be the "seeker." As the seeker looks for the two friends who are hiding, the signaler says, "getting warmer," when the seeker is near their hiding place, or "getting colder," when the seeker is moving away from the hiding place.
5. Continue playing the game, designating a new Ira and Reggie to hide while everyone closes their eyes. The seeker gets to be the next signaler.

Something to think about

Begin the game of hide-and-seek with the children in the classroom who do not get as much attention or who may not be as popular as other children.

STORY S-T-R-E-T-C-H-E-R

Special Project: Our Town

What the children will learn

To discover interesting activities in their community

Materials you will need

Bulletin board, community tourist brochures, construction paper, glue, scissors, stapler

What to do

1. Read again the part of the story where Reggie brags about all the things that are special about Greendale, the new town where he will be living.
2. Discuss with the children all the interesting activities that new people moving in would like to know about their town or community.
3. If possible, collect an assortment of tourist brochures and use them as reminders of special places and events.
4. Ask the children what they do on the weekend that would be helpful for newcomers to know.
5. Let the children make a kids' bulletin board of what children should know about their new town.

Something to think about

Invite children who are new to the school and the community to come and see the displays.

STORY S-T-R-E-T-C-H-E-R

Writing: Letter to a Classmate Who Has Moved

What the children will learn

To write a letter to a friend

Materials you will need

Stationery, envelopes, stamps

What to do

1. With the small group who chose the writing area during choice time, compose letters to a friend who has moved.
2. Talk about missing a child who has moved. If no one from the class has moved yet, then find the name of a child who moved last year.
3. Discuss some of the changes that have taken place since the child moved away. Samantha lost her two front teeth. Michael can ride a bike. Mrs. Andres, the teacher from last year, has a baby girl.
4. Have the children try to think of some activities that the child who moved away liked.
5. Compose a group letter.
6. Let all the children sign the letter.

Something to think about

Younger children may want to draw pictures to include in the letter. Divide the writing assignment so that each child is writing about a different activity that the child who moved away enjoyed.

Feelings

A Chair for My Mother

By Vera B. Williams

Story Line

A young girl tells the story of buying a new chair for her hardworking mother, a waitress at the Blue Tile Diner. Buying the chair is a big event, because she and her mother, grandmother, uncle, and aunt have all been saving their money for the purchase. The chair is the first furniture to be bought after a fire destroys their apartment. Kind relatives and neighbors provide all the other furnishings. The child earns money by helping her mother at the diner. The colorful illustrations by Vera B. Williams capture the lively spirit and warmth of a family and a community. *A Chair for My Mother* was a Caldecott Honor Book for 1983.

Read-Aloud Presentation

Ask the children to recall a special item they saved up their money to purchase. List these items on the chalkboard. Show the cover of the book, and let the children guess what the girl is saving her money to buy. Read the book and pause after the scene when the apartment burns to ask the children what they think the family will do. Turn the page, but before beginning to read, let the children seated near you tell the group what is happening in that illustration, which shows everyone in the neighborhood bringing something to the family. After reading the book, ask a few volunteers to describe how they felt, what they liked about the book, or something memorable from their own family life. (This book is an appropriate selection for this feelings unit and also for a unit about families.) See www.goodcharacter.com/YCC/Feelings.html for ideas to foster discussion about feelings with primary-grade students.

Art: Border Prints

What the children will learn
To adapt a style of painting to their own creative work

Materials you will need
Construction paper, scissors, glue, crayons, markers, watercolors, brushes, empty margarine tubs, water

What to do
1. Call attention to the illustrations in *A Chair for My Mother*, noting their unique style.
2. Show the children the different border prints and how they relate to the illustrations. For example, the kitchen illustration is bordered with teapots and cups and saucers.
3. Ask the children to draw or paint a memorable event from the lives of their families.
4. Demonstrate how to cut the paper to make border prints. After the brief demonstration, let the children work independently. Trim about one-half inch off several sheets of construction paper.
5. Place a contrasting color of construction paper beneath a trimmed sheet.
6. Glue the top sheet into place, leaving a one-half inch border exposed.
7. Display the prints around the classroom.

Something to think about
Let the children write or dictate captions for the backs of their pictures describing the family events they depicted.

Art and Creative Dramatics: Blue Tile Diner in Our Class

What the children will learn
To decorate the classroom

Materials you will need
Butcher paper, crayons, markers, stapler, construction paper, scissors, tape, laminating film or clear contact paper

What to do
1. Show the children the cover of *A Chair for My Mother*. Remind the children that this is the diner where the girl's mother works, and where Josephine, the boss, sometimes pays the little girl for doing extra jobs.

2. Ask the children to decorate part of the classroom like the Blue Tile Diner. Make a large mural on butcher paper showing different elements of the diner.
3. Edge the mural with blue construction paper.
4. Make a sign that says, "Blue Tile Diner."
5. Staple the Blue Tile Diner mural onto a bulletin board.
6. Push some of the class tables and chairs under the bulletin board.
7. Let each child make and decorate a place mat on a piece of construction paper by drawing an outline of a place setting on the paper. Laminate the place mats.
8. Serve snacks at the Blue Tile Diner.

Something to think about
Add a waitress uniform, aprons, chef's hat, name tags, menus, and signs announcing specials.

STORY S-T-R-E-T-C-H-E-R

Mathematics: "Guesstimate" the Amount of Money

What the children will learn
To estimate an amount of money and then count it

Materials you will need
Large, clear plastic jar with slit cut in the lid, pennies, index card, marker, scraps of paper, pencils, large envelope

What to do
1. Place a few pennies and other loose change into the jar, the "money jar."
2. On an index card, print the following: "Guess how much money is in this jar. Write your answer and your name on a piece of paper and put it in the envelope." Tape this sign to the side of the jar.
3. After a day or two, count the money, and find out who came closest to the correct amount.
4. Make the closest guesser the class accountant for the "Payment in Pennies" STORY S-T-R-E-T-C-H-E-R.

Something to think about
Continue this activity after the children start earning money in the social studies STORY S-T-R-E-T-C-H-E-R.

STORY S-T-R-E-T-C-H-E-R

Mathematics and Social Studies: Purchasing Power—Shopping for a Chair

What the children will learn
To comparison shop

Materials you will need
Newspaper ads, want ads, community bulletin boards, catalogs

What to do
1. Talk with the children about the big purchase in *A Chair for My Mother.*
2. Collect a few newspaper ads from furniture stores, community bulletin boards, catalogs, and other places.
3. Ask the entire class to decide what kind of chair they would like to purchase if they could buy a chair.
4. Let small groups of children scour the ads and decide where to find the best bargains.

Something to think about
If possible, take a field trip to a furniture store. Let the children see the whole operation, from ordering, loading, shipping, and unpacking to sales.

STORY S-T-R-E-T-C-H-E-R

Social Studies: Payment in Pennies

What the children will learn
To earn money for doing class jobs

Materials you will need
Large, clear plastic jar with slit cut in the lid, chart paper, marker, scraps of paper, coins

What to do
1. Collect about five dollars in pennies.
2. Mound the pennies on a table. Tell the children that this is the money they can earn and contribute to the class money jar.
3. With the children's help, write up a list of class jobs and the payment for each job.
4. Let the children rotate the jobs among themselves so that each has an opportunity to earn pennies.
5. At the end of the week, count the pennies in the jar, and decide whether or not to continue the project.

Something to think about
Let the class decide what they want to do with the money they earn.

Charlotte's Web

By E. B. White
Illustrated by Garth Williams

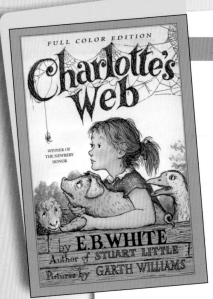

Story Line

This classic story has become a childhood favorite. E. B. White's *Charlotte's Web* is an excellent chapter book to read aloud because there are natural breaks in the story. Wilbur the pig, lovingly raised by Fern, is a barnyard animal whose plight captures the heart of the young listener. In danger of being butchered, Wilbur is saved from his fate by the inventive thinking of Charlotte the spider, who has helped him endure the scorn and teasing of the other barnyard animals. With tears and giggles, young children, particularly third graders, find Fern, Wilbur, Charlotte, Templeton the rat, and the other barnyard animals as appealing today as they were when the story was written in 1952. Garth Williams's scant pen-and-ink sketches highlight one or two of the main scenes in each chapter.

Read-Aloud Presentation

Many of the children may have already heard *Charlotte's Web* read to them by their parents or in a child-care setting, or they may have seen the animated movie version. Ask these children not to tell what is going to happen in the story, but to enjoy it again because good stories can be enjoyed more than once. Decide ahead of time how many chapters to read each day. If you read four or five of the short chapters a day, the book can be read in one week. Each day, before reading the next chapters, have the children recall what happened the day before. At the end of the book, be sure to allow time for the children to talk about their feelings. Tell the children how you feel so that they know it is all right for them to be open with their emotions.

Art: Spiderweb Prints

What the children will learn
To make an abstract representation

Materials you will need
Pictures of spiderwebs, scrap paper, pencils, black construction paper or poster board, white tempera paint, white glue, measuring cups and spoons, empty margarine tubs, cotton swabs

What to do
1. Look at the picture of the spiderweb at the beginning of chapter thirteen in *Charlotte's Web*. Find photographs of real orb spiderwebs on Internet websites. Notice the way many webs begin with a tightly spun core, with long lines radiating out to the edges and connecting lines around the perimeter.
2. Let the children describe the patterns they see.
3. Give them scraps of paper to practice drawing lines that look like an orb spiderweb.
4. Mix about a half-cup of white tempera paint and about a teaspoon of white glue in a margarine tub.
5. Demonstrate how to dip a cotton swab in the paint mixture and use it like a pencil to draw white spiderwebs onto black paper.
6. Dry overnight and display.

Something to think about
If you have shrubbery near your school, go out in the early morning and look for orb spiderwebs extending across the tops of the shrubs. The morning dew helps make the spiderwebs easier to see. The children's webs will be more interesting after observing real spiderwebs.

Art: Charlotte's Portrait Gallery

What the children will learn
To draw or paint from their imaginations

Materials you will need
Choice of art media: tempera paints, pastels, crayons, markers, collage materials, glue, construction paper or heavy texture paper, scissors, old picture frames, hammer, picture-hanging wire, and nails

What to do

1. Ask for volunteers to make portraits of the main characters in *Charlotte's Web*. Tell the volunteers to use their imaginations without regard for Garth Williams's versions of the characters.
2. Let the children volunteer to draw an animal or human of their choice.
3. Help the artists decide which media and frames best fit the portraits of their characters.
4. Cut the paper or poster board to fit the frame.
5. After the artists draw and paint the portraits, let the children frame and hang the portraits in the library.

Something to think about

If framing is not possible, mount the pictures onto heavy construction paper or poster board.

STORY S-T-R-E-T-C-H-E-R

Classroom Library: Voices for *Charlotte's Web*

What the children will learn

To modulate their voices

Materials you will need

CDs and CD player or tapes and tape recorder, stapler, paper, pencil or pen

What to do

1. Have the children recall the main events of the chapters read that day. Look at Garth Williams's illustrations, and ask the children to recall your voice as you were reading that part. Describe your voice as excited, somber, hurried, slow, or soft-spoken.
2. Make a list of what happens in the chapters, and let the children take turns telling about the events in a voice that reflects the mood of that part of the story.
3. Let the children practice retelling the chapters, then record them. Be sure to record an introduction that includes the chapter titles.
4. Ask a parent or friend to also read the chapters.
5. Place the recordings in the library collection for the listening station.

Something to think about

Use different children each day until all the students have been involved in recording their story retellings. Let younger children mimic the voices of individual characters without having to retell whole scenes with multiple characters.

STORY S-T-R-E-T-C-H-E-R

Writing: Reading Response Log

What the children will learn

To summarize what happens and predict events

Materials you will need

Notebooks or loose sheets of writing paper, pencils

What to do

1. Have the children make a date column down the left side of the page.
2. After the read-aloud time each day, ask the children to note the date in the left column and write in their own words what happened in the story in the right column.
3. Have the students write at least one prediction for what will happen the next day.

Something to think about

Let older children predict what Fern, Wilbur, and Charlotte will do in the following chapters.

STORY S-T-R-E-T-C-H-E-R

Writing: Attention Getters, Good Beginnings

What the children will learn

To write intriguing opening lines for their stories

Materials you will need

Paper and pencils

What to do

1. After you have read the entire book, read the opening sentences from several chapters.
2. Discuss with the students how E. B. White helps the reader see the sights, smell the smells, and feel the suspense of the story from the very first opening lines. Read again the first three or four sentences from chapter three that help the reader sense the barnyard through sight, smell, and mood.
3. Select a few of the students' writings that begin with good attention getters.
4. Ask the students to select one or two pieces of their writing and rewrite the opening lines with attention getters.

Something to think about

As an alternative, have the students write catchy captions for drawings from *Charlotte's Web*.

The Classic Tale of the Velveteen Rabbit or How Toys Become Real

By Margery Williams
Illustrated by Michael Hague

Story Line

This famous story is available from many publishers, but Hague's illustrations will help the children grasp the little bunny's longing to become real. The other nursery animals look down on the Velveteen Rabbit, all except the Skin Horse, who gives him sage advice. It is only when the little boy loves the little bunny for a long time that the bunny becomes real. A genuinely touching, classic story that no young child should miss and no teacher should miss sharing. It is a tale to be savored and loved again and again.

Read-Aloud Presentation

Hold a toy bunny rabbit on your lap. Show the children the cover of the book and have them compare the two bunnies, the toy bunny on your lap and the stuffed velveteen rabbit on the cover of the book. If some children have heard the book, ask them to save their comments until you have finished reading. Divide the book into at least three sections—the arrival of the toy bunny and the discussion with the Skin Horse about what it means to be real; the section where the little boy starts sleeping with the bunny and plays with him out in the garden all summer; and the final section in which the boy becomes ill and the little bunny is thrown away only to find some special magic. After reading the first section, have the children remember the story to that point. The next day, read the second section and, at the end of that reading, have the children recall the story. On another day or late on the same day, read the final part of the story, and let the children tell you the parts that made them happy, sad, and surprised.

Art: Tri-Fold Pictures— Beginning, Middle, End Pictures

What the children will learn
To identify main events at key points in the story

Materials you will need
Large sheets of drawing paper or butcher paper, colored pencils

What to do
1. Have the children fold their papers, accordion style, so there are three sections, each with the same width.
2. On the outside fold, ask the children to draw something that reminds them of the beginning of the story.
3. Open the paper up to the second fold and illustrate something from the middle of the story.
4. Open both folds and expose the center of the paper. Draw a scene from the end of the story.

Something to think about
Ask the children to take some of their favorite pieces of writing and make tri-fold illustrations of their own stories.

Art: Decorating the Nursery Fairy

What the children will learn
To use collage materials for decorations

Materials you will need
Scraps of satin, velveteen, aluminum foil, gift-wrap paper, ribbon, sequins or glitter, glue, construction paper or poster board, scissors, colored pencils

What to do
1. Read the description of the nursery fairy who makes the toys become real.
2. Ask the children to imagine what she might look like.
3. Show the artists the collage materials and ask them to draw and decorate the magic fairy.
4. Display the collages in the class library area with a copy of the book.

Something to think about
Some children may want to make poster board fairies that stand up like paper dolls and then dress the fairies in the sparkling collage dresses.

Classroom Library: Puppet Show

What the children will learn

To follow the sequence of the story and know when to enter the scene

Materials you will need

Stuffed animals and toys to represent the story's characters, table

What to do

1. Ask children to bring in stuffed animals and toys to represent all the characters in the story of *The Velveteen Rabbit*.
2. Identify the human characters. You can be the nurse. Let a child be the little boy and another be the doctor.
3. Select two very verbal children to pretend to be the Velveteen Rabbit and the Skin Horse.
4. Make a puppet stage from an overturned table. Turn a table over on its side, and seat the puppeteers behind the table in the order that they appear in the story.
5. Read the story and let each animal appear as it is mentioned. Have the children move the animals from side to side as if speaking.
6. Let the human characters appear in front of the puppet stage and pantomime the actions implied by the story.
7. On other days, let different children become different characters.

Something to think about

Older children may write dialogue and act out the story.

Music and Movement: Nursery Toys Dance

What the children will learn

To move like toys

Materials you will need

Recording of music from *The Nutcracker,* CD or tape player

What to do

1. Tell the children about *The Nutcracker* ballet, including the part where the toys come to life.
2. Ask the children to imagine how the toys in the nursery of *The Velveteen Rabbit* might move. Let the children improvise movements for the toy train, the wind-up mouse, the model boat, the jointed wooden lion, the skin horse, and the soft velveteen rabbit.
3. Let the children choose which toy they want to be.
4. Play the recording of *The Nutcracker* when the toys dance. This track is sometimes called "The Dance of the Toys" or "The Dance of the Flutes." Let the children pretend they are toys that are becoming real.
5. You can be the lovely fairy, and as you tap the "toys" with your "magic wand," the children begin to dance.

Something to think about

Do the activity on several different days so the children get to pretend to be different toys.

Writing: What Would Happen If One of My Toys Became Real?

What the children will learn

To imagine a similar plot with different characters

Materials you will need

Drawing paper, colored pencils, writing paper, pencils

What to do

1. Hold the bunny from read-aloud time. As a prewriting activity, improvise some dialogue, and begin telling a story about what might happen if the bunny became real.
2. Collect some stuffed animals from the classroom, and let the children think of other stories about them.
3. Have the children identify their favorite toys, and ask the children to imagine what might happen if these toys became real.
4. Let the children begin sketching main scenes from the stories they are imagining.
5. After they have a sense of the story they want to tell, ask the children to write the story.

Something to think about

Children can write individual stories but still work as writing partners. At intervals in the writing process, they can stop and read to their partners what they have written so far. The partners can listen and ask questions about any part they do not understand.

Alexander and the Terrible, Horrible, No Good, Very Bad Day

By Judith Viorst
Illustrated by Ray Cruz

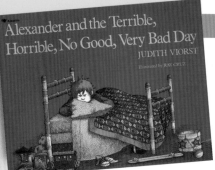

Story Line

Alexander's terrible day begins with him waking up with chewing gum in his hair and continues with so many irritating happenings that he thinks the only way to survive is to move to Australia. The common childhood mishaps, the bickering, the misunderstandings, and the out-of-sorts feelings are ones with which both adults and children can identify. Finally, Alexander realizes that everyone has bad days, "even in Australia." Ray Cruz's illustrations are detailed black-line drawings with textures, patterns, and shading that set just the right tone for the story.

Read-Aloud Presentation

Write on the chalkboard, "I'm having an Australia day," but do not tell the children what it means. Describe one of your mornings when everything seemed to go wrong. Let the children join in the discussion and describe some mornings when they know it is going to be a difficult day. Read *Alexander and the Terrible, Horrible, No Good, Very Bad Day.* Do not interrupt the reading for discussion because each scene adds to the frustration Alexander is feeling. After finishing the book, ask the children if they have ever had an "Alexander day" or an "Australia day." Reverse the mood and ask what Alexander's story might be like if he were having a "wonderful, marvelous, terrific, very good day." (Some of the suggestions for the read-aloud session and the STORY S-T-R-E-T-C-H-E-R-S were first published by Shirley Raines in *Ideas and Insights: Activities for Elementary Language Arts.* They are modified for this book.)

Art: Adding Details to Drawings

What the children will learn
To use dots, crosshatching strokes, patterns, and shading to make details in drawings

Materials you will need
Smooth typing paper or drawing paper, pencils, pencil sharpeners

What to do
1. Have the children look closely at the illustrator's drawings in *Alexander and the Terrible, Horrible, No Good, Very Bad Day.* Help them notice the many different ways Ray Cruz added details to the pictures—points or dots, patterns and stripes in clothing, crosshatching to show grains in the wood, and many, tiny lines to add texture to hair and faces.
2. Let the children experiment with drawing a variety of lines. Sharpen the pencils often to add the fine detail.
3. Ask the children to draw a picture about one of their "Alexander days" and to choose at least one of the techniques Cruz used to add detail to their drawings.
4. Display some of the drawings in the class library area with the copy of the book. Also display the drawings in the writing center.

Something to think about
Some teachers are concerned that teaching children drawing techniques will somehow interfere with their creativity. If children are taught techniques and are encouraged to observe the ways other artists use lines or colors, the students will begin to incorporate these techniques into their work in inventive ways.

Cooking: Alexander's Cupcakes

What the children will learn
To decorate cupcakes

Materials you will need
Cupcakes, individual-serving cartons of milk, canned frosting, raisins, sprinkles, little candies, mixing bowl, spatula, knives, empty margarine tubs, warm water

What to do

1. One of the scenes that gets a lot of laughs in *Alexander and the Terrible, Horrible, No Good, Very Bad Day* occurs at lunchtime when Alexander discovers that his mother forgot to put dessert in his lunch bag. Remind the children of that scene, and tell them that for a snack today they can decorate cupcakes for Alexander (and for themselves, of course).
2. Bake the cupcakes ahead of time.
3. Set up all the decorating materials on a separate table.
4. Demonstrate how to spread the frosting with a knife or spatula dipped in warm water.
5. Serve the cupcakes with cartons of cold milk.

Something to think about

Let the children plan a variety of nutritious lunch menus. Make copies to take home to their parents. Title the menus, "If My Lunch Box Could Talk."

STORY S-T-R-E-T-C-H-E-R

Creative Dramatics: Scenes from an Alexander Day

What the children will learn

To use movement to communicate scenes from the story

Materials you will need

Notepad, pencil, chalkboard, chalk

What to do

1. On a notepad, list all the scenes from the book and the number of children required to pantomime each scene.
2. Go to individuals and groups of two and three children and, in secret, sign them up for a scene from the book that they would like to act out.
3. Have the individuals and groups describe to you what they will do, and give them any hints that might make their miming more effective.
4. On the chalkboard, list the names of the children in the order that they will pantomime the scenes.
5. The children pantomime, and the audience guesses what scene the students are acting.

Something to think about

For younger children, provide a few simple props, and allow the audience to ask questions such as, "Did it happen at the beginning of the book or the end of the book?"

STORY S-T-R-E-T-C-H-E-R

Mathematics: Shoes, Shoes, and More Shoes

What the children will learn

To represent quantities with numerals, symbols, and graphs

Materials you will need

The children's shoes, paper, pencils, shoeboxes, poster board, markers, construction paper, scissors, tape, optional—play money, cash register

What to do

1. Assign jobs for the shoe store, such as inventory takers, clerks, customers, and cashier.
2. The inventory takers collect all the shoes in the class and list them by writing down descriptions of the shoes: for example, sneakers with red stripes and Velcro, white leather high-tops, canvas with leather strings.
3. After all the descriptions are written, have the children categorize the shoes in groups, such as high-top sneakers, low-top sneakers, canvas slip-ons.
4. Make a graph showing all the different categories of shoes. On a sheet of poster board, write the categories of shoes at the top, then count and write down the number of shoes in that category.
5. Cut out little shoes from construction paper. Let each child put a symbol on the chart to represent her or his shoes.
6. Have the clerks decide on prices for the shoes and mark the boxes or tag the shoes.
7. Let the customers come in and "buy" their own shoes.
8. The inventory takers remove a shoe symbol from the chart each time a pair of shoes is "sold."
9. The cashier takes their "money" and makes "change."

Something to think about

This activity works well as described, but it also can have a open-ended format: simply assemble the materials, let the children play shoe store, and observe what happens.

STORY S-T-R-E-T-C-H-E-R

Writing: Our Terrible, Horrible, No Good, Very Bad Days and Our Wonderful, Marvelous, Terrific, Very Good Days

What the children will learn

To create moods in their writing

Materials you will need

Paper, pencils

What to do

1. Recall the brainstorming during the read-aloud session when the children described some terrible days they had and what happens when they are having wonderful, marvelous, terrific, very good days.
2. Ask the children who are interested to write and illustrate one or both types of stories.
3. Help the children edit their writing by working with writing partners, listening groups, or editing groups (see a more detailed description of these writing activities on pages 14 and 15).
4. Publish the children's stories in book form (see page 234 of the Appendix for directions).
5. Place the books on display in the class library. Add library cards, and let the children check them out to read.

Something to think about

The degree of editing one does of children's writing is a matter of teacher and school preference.

References

Viorst, Judith. 1972. *Alexander and the Terrible, Horrible, No Good, Very Bad Day*. Illustrated by Ray Cruz. New York: Simon and Schuster.

Waber, Bernard. 1988. *Ira Says Goodbye*. New York: Houghton Mifflin Harcourt.

White, E. B. 1952. *Charlotte's Web*. Illustrated by Garth Willams. New York: HarperCollins.

Williams, Margery. 1981. *The Velveteen Rabbit or How Toys Become Real*. Illustrated by Michael Hague. New York: Macmillan.

Williams, Vera. 1982. *A Chair for My Mother*. New York: HarperCollins.

Additional References

Katz, Karen. 2002. *The Colors of Us*. New York: Henry Holt. *Seven-year-old Lena and her mother observe the variations in the color of their friends' skin, viewed in terms of foods and things found in nature.*

Modell, Frank. 1987. *One Zillion Valentines*. New York: Greenwillow. *When Marvin shows Milton how to make valentines, they decide to make one for each person in their neighborhood.*

Ringgold, Faith. 1996. *Tar Beach*. New York: Dragonfly Books. *A young girl dreams of flying above her Harlem home, claiming all she sees for herself and her family. This book is based on the author's quilt painting of the same name.*

Websites

1. Character Education:
   www.goodcharacter.com/YCC/Feelings.html
   • Teaching guides for K–12 Character Education
   • Character principles
   • Materials on a variety of feelings
2. Kids Health from Nemours:
   http://kidshealth.org/kid/feeling/index.html
   • Coping skills and discussion topics categorized by situation/environment
3. Education.com: www.education.com
   • Articles for parents and teachers about feelings
   • Coping with various feelings
   • Listening to children
4. Wikipedia.com:
   http://en.wikipedia.org/wiki/Spider_web
   • Photos of spiderwebs
   • Descriptions of spiders from around the world

School

First Grade, Here I Come!

By Nancy Carlson

Story Line

Henry, the mouse main character, reflects on his first day in first grade and how it is like kindergarten and how it is different. While he misses some of his old friends, he has made some new ones. He misses his kindergarten teacher, Ms. Bradley, but Mr. McCarthy's classroom has a cool science center with a guinea pig named Curly. Henry compares recess, the library, and the school cafeteria. The book reassuringly addresses some of the childhood uncertainties about the unknown. Carlson's brightly colored illustrations appeal to children, and the illustrations and text are linked so well that children can tell the story after hearing it read.

Read-Aloud Presentation

Ask children to remember their first day at school this year. What were they worried about? What surprised them? Show the cover of *First Grade, Here I Come!* and introduce the children to Henry. Some may know the Henry character from *Look Out, Kindergarten, Here I Come!* and *Henry's 100 Days of Kindergarten,* two other popular Carlson books. Read the story and pause to let children insert the surprises they found out about their grade level. For example, learning that they had to go down the hall to the bathroom instead of having one in the classroom, learning to carry one's own tray in the cafeteria, and learning where the school office is for delivering notes.

Art: Last Year at the Beginning of School and This Year at the Beginning of School

What the children will learn

To make comparisons

Materials you will need

Art paper, markers

What to do

1. Recall the many ways Henry finds first grade different from kindergarten and some of the things that are different, such as friends, teachers, classroom centers, cafeteria, restroom locations, principal's office, games at recess, art class, snack break, and classroom pets.
2. Have each child fold a large sheet of art paper in half and then open it up. On one side of their sheets, the children write the grade they were in last year, and on the other side, they write the grade they are in now.
3. Ask the children to draw pictures showing something that is different from last year.

Something to think about

Divide the class into four groups to draw four different sets of pictures. Have one group focus on teachers, another on classroom arrangements, one on recess and playground games, and another group draw pictures of snack time and the cafeteria. See the Teacher Planet website (www.teacherplanet.com/resource/back2school.php) for additional back-to-school ideas.

Art: Decorating Name Plates

What the children will learn

To draw some symbols that represent themselves and to write their names

Materials you will need

Poster board, markers, laminate

What to do

1. Show the children the name plates on the desks in Carlson's illustrations of Mr. McCarthy's first grade.
2. Write *Henry* on a strip of poster board.
3. Help the children identify something that interests Henry, such as soccer, spiders, and the worms in the science center.

4. Draw these things to decorate Henry's name plate.
5. Have the children choose some symbols they like and decorate their own name plates.
6. Laminate the name plates for the children to place on their desks.

Something to think about

Early in the year as students go out of the classroom for special classes such as music and art, turn the name plates into name tags by punching holes in the top two corners and placing string through them.

STORY S-T-R-E-T-C-H-E-R

Physical Activity: Playing Kickball

What the children will learn
To follow the rules for a game

Materials you will need
Kickball or soccer ball, optional—bases

What to do
1. Play kickball like baseball. Designate the bases, which can be children standing at home, first, second, third.
2. Disperse the other students around the field.
3. Serve as the pitcher.
4. Roll the ball to the student designated as a kicker. Let the student have three tries at kicking, and when she kicks it to someone, she will run as fast as possible around the bases.
5. The other children try to catch the kicked ball and throw it to the child who is acting as the base and will try to get the kicker out, depending on whether the ball or the kicker reaches the base first. If someone in the infield or outfield gets the ball, they toss it to the person on the base.

Something to think about
For first graders, practicing kicking the ball is sufficient as a game. The adult can be the pitcher and roll the ball to the kicker, the children can practice kicking the ball as far as possible, and the receiver can kick the ball back to the adult.

STORY S-T-R-E-T-C-H-E-R

Reading: Reading Picture Stories

What the children will learn
To describe illustrations by telling actions and emotions

Materials you will need
Painter's tape

What to do
1. Use painter's tape to cover up the words at the bottom of each page of *First Grade, Here I Come!*
2. Discuss how good illustrations as well as words tell a story. Also, discuss how one can read a story through words and can read the pictures by the actions of the characters and by their facial expressions.
3. Without reading the story, tell the story based on the pictures for a few pages, then ask a child to continue to tell the story by looking at the next picture, then on to the next child while trying to keep the meaning flowing.
4. Remove the painter's tape and read the story from the text, comparing the two stories.

Something to think about
Consider transcribing the "told" story from the illustrations, and read the two stories to the children.

STORY S-T-R-E-T-C-H-E-R

Science: Caring for Curly and Other Classroom Pets

What the children will learn
To follow instructions for caring for pets

Materials you will need
Materials specific to your classroom pet for litter, food, water, and cleaning supplies, poster board, markers, laminate

What to do
1. Discuss Curly, the guinea pig in Mr. McCarthy's class, and how there were special rules about his care.
2. Write the special rules for the children to care for the classroom pet in your class.
3. Add rebus drawings for students who are not reading well yet.
4. Laminate the care cards, and place them near the pet's cage or the aquarium.

Something to think about
Invite a veterinarian or an assistant in a veterinarian's office to demonstrate how to handle the pet or provide helpful information about caring for the pet. Older children who have pets can give presentations about caring for pets to your primary-grade children.

Miss Nelson Is Missing!

By Harry Allard
Illustrated by James Marshall

Story Line

When Miss Nelson's students in room 207 misbehave, she decides to teach them a lesson by disappearing. She is replaced by a demanding substitute, witchlike Viola Swamp, who piles on the homework and takes away privileges like story hour. The children imagine what may have happened to Miss Nelson and even bring Detective McSmogg to look for her. After several days, Miss Nelson reappears to the excitement of the now well-behaved children. The surprise ending leaves children trying to sort out who was dressed in the black dress and teaching their class while Miss Nelson was away, as well as where Viola Swamp went. Humorously and creatively told and illustrated, the story's pictures capture the children's feelings and leave the reader and viewer with a bit of intrigue.

Read-Aloud Presentation

Present the book by reading it and pausing at the picture of the children going to the police station. Have the children say where they imagine Miss Nelson might be, whether good places she might be or bad things that may have happened. Read on and hear where the children in the story imagine Miss Nelson is. Pause after the page where the words are, "'Hello, children,' someone said in a sweet voice," and ask the children who this might be. At the end of the book, ask the children who they want as their teacher, Miss Nelson or Miss Swamp, and why.

Art: Where Is Miss Nelson?

What the children will learn

To represent what they are imagining through art

Materials you will need

Easel, brushes, tempera paints

What to do

1. In the art area of the classroom, set up easels, tempera paints, and brushes.
2. During choice time, have the children recall the story of *Miss Nelson Is Missing!* Ask them to paint what they imagined happened to Miss Nelson.
3. Write a caption for each painting using the child's words or have the children write a sentence telling about where they imagine Miss Nelson to be.
4. Display the paintings with a copy of the book.

Something to think about

Reread the book, and instead of reading what author Allard imagined for where Miss Nelson is, insert the paintings by several of the children, and read the captions for their pictures as if they are part of the book.

Creative Dramatics: Acting with Disguises

What the children will learn

To portray different people and the different emotions their disguises might represent

Materials you will need

Witch's mask and costume or long black dress, hat for a detective, Halloween costumes representing friendly characters

What to do

1. Place the costumes in an area of the classroom for creative dramatics.
2. The first day you read *Miss Nelson Is Missing!*, have a teacher friend or an older student from another class come to your classroom dressed like Viola Swamp.
3. After a few minutes, have someone dressed like Detective McSmogg enter the room and act out a scene or pretend to look for Miss Nelson.

4. At choice time, allow different children to wear the costumes and act like the characters in *Miss Nelson Is Missing!*

Something to think about

For young children, have the actors take off their disguises so that the children can see who they are. On other days, add other costumes and let the children have fun pretending.

STORY S-T-R-E-T-C-H-E-R

Mathematics: Who and How Many Are Missing?

What the children will learn

To solve problems and to represent the problems as mathematical equations

Materials you will need

Chart of all of the names of the students in class, paper and pencil, chalk and chalkboard

What to do

1. Prearrange with two children to quietly hide in the classroom when you give a signal.
2. Have the children count the number of students in the classroom by counting with you or counting off.
3. Ask everyone to march around the room and then close their eyes. Turn off the lights, which is the signal for two children to hide.
4. Switch the lights back on and ask, "Who is missing?" Then, show by a numerical equation the answer to how many children can they see in the classroom. For example, there are twenty-five children in class, but two are missing, so $25 - 2 = 23$.

Something to think about

Try various combinations of who is missing, and try different numbers of children in hiding. Play the mathematics game by keeping children hidden and hiding additional children with each round so that they have to start with a new equation each time.

STORY S-T-R-E-T-C-H-E-R

Social Studies: Classroom Rules

What the children will learn

To state and follow classroom rules

Materials you will need

Poster board or chart tablet and markers

What to do

1. Discuss the children's behavior in *Miss Nelson Is Missing!* Have the children say what they think the children were doing that they should not do.
2. Write the rules of the classroom positively instead of negatively. For instance, instead of saying, "Do not be rude," say, "Be polite."
3. Start with a list of five to ten rules, refine them down to three or four, and post the rules in the classroom.

Something to think about

Recognize that young children have a difficult time remembering a long list of rules. It is more important to have a few that teach concepts such as respect and responsibility than to have a long list of "thou shall nots." See www.theteacherscorner.net/seasonal/back-to-school for ideas about rules for classroom behavior.

STORY S-T-R-E-T-C-H-E-R

Writing: Written Apologies for Behavior

What the children will learn

To express their feelings in writing

Materials you will need

Blank note cards or folded typing paper, pencils, crayons or markers

What to do

1. Write an apology for something that occurred in your life. For example, write an apology to another teacher for accidentally spilling coffee on her desk.
2. Help the children hear apologetic words and phrases such as, "sorry," "please, forgive me," and "sincerely."
3. When something happens with your class for which they owe someone an apology, jointly compose a letter to the person. For example, a letter might be written to the librarian for failing to bring back a book when someone else was waiting to check it out, or to the physical education teacher for not returning the balls and ropes the class borrowed so that other classes could use them.

Something to think about

Young children may have difficulty with the concept of "accepting an apology," so it helps if the person who receives the note comes and tells the class that he or she accepts the apology.

Swish!

*By Bill Martin, Jr. and
Michael Sampson
Illustrated by
Michael Chesworth*

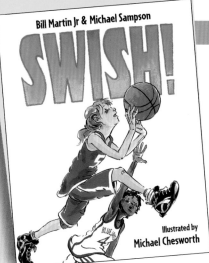

Story Line

The Cardinals and the Blue Jays are in a
tournament to decide the champions.
The tension builds as the clock ticks
away. The score is 44 to 44 with one
second left—who will win the game? The
authors use basketball terms such as *dribble, rim,
post,* and *swish.* The illustrator captures the motions of
the team members, their coaches, and the referees.
Written in a cadence that creates excitement, this
book engages listeners and beginning readers in a
story about sport in which many children participate.
The fact that these are girls' teams is exciting, as most
sports books are written for boys.

Read-Aloud Presentation

Find out which of the children play basketball with
brothers or sisters, for an after-school team, for a
church, or with a community organization. Have the
children discuss what they like about playing
basketball. Listen for some descriptive words they use
when they talk about the game, such as *dribble, pass,
rebound, score, basket, coach, steal,* and *net.* Have the
children think of a word that describes the sound the
ball makes when it goes through the net: *swish.* Show
the cover of the book to read the name, *Swish!* Ask the
children to listen to see which team wins, the
Cardinals or the Blue Jays.

STORY S-T-R-E-T-C-H-E-R

Art: Poster Announcing a Game

What the children will learn
To create a poster that captures action

Materials you will need
Paper, poster board, poster board
paints or acrylics, tape

What to do
1. Look at the illustration on the
cover of the book and discuss the fact that it shows the
action of one girl shooting and another girl guarding.
2. Ask the children to think of themselves playing
basketball. How would they want to be portrayed?
Shooting, guarding, dribbling, making a basket,
celebrating?
3. Distribute paper and let the children draw and paint
themselves playing basketball.
4. Group the children and let them create a poster from
their paintings that show different basketball actions.

Something to think about
If there are regularly scheduled after-school teams, even if
they are older students, use the posters to announce
games. When children see their artwork being given
prominence with a real event, they become more engaged
in art projects.

STORY S-T-R-E-T-C-H-E-R

Mathematics: Calculating Scores

What the children will learn
To relate addition to keeping score

What to do
1. Write the score on the board from the first time it is
mentioned in the book, 46 to 44, with the Blue Jays in
the lead. Have the children figure out how many points
the Cardinals need to make to win the game.
2. Probably, some child will know about three-point plays.
3. Write the score for a three-point play for the Blue Jays,
which would be 46 plus 3. Solve this math problem.
4. Write the score for a three-point play for the Cardinals,
which would be 44 plus 3. Solve this math problem.
5. Reread the ending of the book to see which problem
expresses what happened in the story.

Something to think about

Not all children are interested in sports, but being on a team can be a positive experience for a child, especially if it is a team that gives all children an opportunity to play—which is a sign of a good team.

Physical Activity: Learning to Dribble a Ball

What the children will learn
Eye-hand coordination and control of movement

Materials you will need
Basketballs or any other ball that bounces well, cones or chairs

What to do
1. Distribute balls. Ask some students to bounce the balls back and forth to one another. After a short time, move on to having the children pass the balls without bouncing.
2. Set up cones or chairs and have the students practice dribbling around the cones or chairs.
3. Make each stage—bouncing, passing, and dribbling—interesting by using quick change signals, like a whistle.

Something to think about
Parents are often eager for their children to excel physically, socially, and intellectually. Being able to do physical activities gives children confidence, helps them to relate to other children, and is intellectually stimulating as they keep track of instructions.

Reading: Reading with Expression

What the children will learn
To read with expression and emotion derived from the story

Materials you will need
CDs and CD player or tapes and tape recorder

What to do
1. Record yourself reading from the book.

2. Read the first part of the book *Swish!* and the last part of the book. Read each with a different cadence, slowly in the beginning, but still with excitement, because the first sentence is an exclamation. Read the last part with a higher voice and at a faster pace to show the thrill of a last-second, buzzer-beating score.
3. Select a few children to read from the book using the sentences you have modeled. After a practice session, record the children reading the story.

Something to think about
For children who are not yet proficient readers, rehearse a sentence or two with them several times until they feel comfortable reading aloud.

Writing: Using Action Words Associated with Basketball

What the children will learn
To use words that relate to basketball

Materials you will need
Chart tablet and markers or chalkboard and chalk, notepaper, scissors

What to do
1. Show the children the cover of the book and have them read the title, *Swish!*
2. Ask the children to think of other words that describe the action in basketball. On the board or chart tablet, write their words, such as *dribble, rebound, pass, jump, shoot, guard, score.*
3. Practice reading the words, and then number the words on the chart.
4. Write the numbers on small slips of notepaper, and let each child draw a number. When the children have drawn their numbers, tell them not to tell or show anyone their words.
5. Have the children pantomime their words, and let the other children guess the action words being pantomimed.

Something to think about
Think of some "cheer" words, such as *go, team, win, Cardinals, Blue Jays,* and *defense.* Make large cards and let the children practice their cheers, such as, "Go, Blue Jays, Go!" "Defense, Cardinals, Defense!" Divide the class in half and have different people hold up the cards for their side to cheer for the teams.

Arthur's Teacher Trouble

By Marc Brown

Story Line

Written and illustrated by one of the most recognized children's authors, Marc Brown manages to build on the suspense children feel when meeting their new teachers. Laced with the usual Arthur anxiety and the presence of his pesky sister, D.W., the story follows some trying weeks. Mr. Ratburn challenges his students to learn to spell well so they can compete in the school spellathon. Arthur studies hard, practices a lot, and learns to spell well enough to enter the contest. The teacher, rumored to be a vampire, announces at the end of the year that he is moving to kindergarten, where D.W. will be a student the next year.

Read-Aloud Presentation

Arthur is a familiar character to primary-aged children. Have the children recall some other Marc Brown Arthur stories. Discuss some of their anxieties before they knew you as their teacher. Were they worried about homework or rumors about how much you expected of them? Tell the children they are going to meet Arthur's new third grade teacher, Mr. Ratburn, in the story. Read *Arthur's Teacher Trouble*. Announce the STORY S-T-R-E-T-C-H-E-R-S to accompany the book.

Author Study: Marc Brown as Author

What the children will learn
To consider the main points of a biography

Materials you will need
Information from the website: www.lb-kids.com

What to do
1. Visit the Internet site and print a biography of Marc Brown. (There is an extensive Marc Brown biography is at www.kidsreads.com/authors/au-brown-marc.asp.)
2. With the children, generate a set of questions they would like answered about Marc Brown, such as, "How many Arthur books has he written?"
3. Read the biography from the website and find the answers to the children's questions.
4. In addition to answering their question about the number of Arthur books Brown has written, ask the children to tell you what other kinds of information they found out about Marc Brown, such as when he was born, where he lives, what his first book was, and other facts that make him an interesting person.

Something to think about
Authors and illustrators have websites that connect with their readers, as well as some that are based on their most famous characters, such as Arthur, at www.kidsreads.com.

Mathematics: Matching Mathematical Terms with Symbols

What the children will learn
To spell simple mathematical terms

Materials you will need
Strips of poster board, markers, magnetic tape

What to do
1. Write some simple mathematical terms and their accompanying mathematical symbols on separate strips of poster board. Some may include *add, addition* (+), *subtract, subtraction* (−), *multiply, multiplication* (x), *divide, division* (÷), *less than* (<), *greater* or *more than* (>).

2. During mathematics time, also work on the spelling of these terms and match them with the symbols. Let the children place the poster board strips over problems that are on the class whiteboard.

3. Stack the symbol strips of poster board together and select the children to draw from the stack then spell the appropriate word that goes with that symbol. For example, the first time (+) is drawn, the child spells *add*. The second child who draws (+) spells *addition*, and so on for the other words and symbols.

Something to think about
Print other math words and symbols, such as *equals* (=) and the words *difference, calculate, sum,* and *total*.

Music: Spelling Musical Words

What the children will learn
To spell words associated with music

Materials you will need
Sheets of music, poster board strips, optional—blank musical notation paper

What to do
1. On poster board strips, print the words *music, composer, note, treble, bass, higher, lower, clef, verse, stanza,* and *refrain*.
2. Show children the sheets of music, and point out the symbols and words that correspond to each other.
3. Before singing a favorite classroom song, place all of the spelling music words on the board, and point to them rather than saying them while you are singing, such as *higher* and *lower*.
4. Assign the musical words as the bonus spelling assignment for the week.

Something to think about
Ask a music teacher for additional phrases or words that she or he often uses with your class, and add those special phrases to the children's musical spelling list.

Reading: Readathon of Arthur Books

What the children will learn
To practice reading and gain in fluency and expressiveness

Materials you will need
Collection of Marc Brown's Arthur books

What to do
1. Form groups of at least four children to represent and read the parts of the narrator, Arthur, D.W., and Mr. Ratburn in the Arthur books.
2. In each group, the narrator reads aloud the parts of the story that are not words spoken by Arthur, D.W., or Mr. Ratburn. The other characters read their parts of the story.

Something to think about
Scan other Arthur books for characters and form reading groups around those books. Follow the same plan with a narrator, Arthur, D.W., and other main characters.

Spelling: Arthur's Spellathon

What the children will learn
To spell words associated with the book

Materials you will need
Paper, pencils

What to do
1. In addition to the words Arthur and his classmates spell in *Arthur's Teacher Trouble*, select words associated with the book, such as *Marc, Brown, author, Arthur, teacher, Ratburn, narrator, cover, drawing, illustration, page, front, back, beginning, ending, story*.
2. Construct a spelling test of the words from the mathematical, musical, and *Arthur's Teacher Trouble* lists.
3. After the spelling test, conduct a spelling bee using the words. Arrange them from the simplest to the most complex.

Something to think about
Some children are better spellers when they write the word rather than spelling it in front of the class in a spelling bee. Consider letting primary-age children have pencils and paper to practice and then spell aloud to the class.

Book Fair Day

By Lynn Plourde
Illustrated by Thor Wickstrom

Story Line

Mrs. Shepherd's class is the last one scheduled to go to the once-a-year book fair, and Dewey, a real book lover, is worried that all the good books will be taken. He tries several tricks to get in ahead of the rest of the school. Dewey tries sneaking in with his kindergarten book buddy, crawling through the library window, and searching for the lost hamster while looking at the book fair. When the time finally arrives, Dewey is such an expert on the books that his classmates are all asking his advice, and he does not have time to make his own selections. The librarian comes to the rescue by saving a copy of each of the books Dewey wants. The story ends with Dewey loading all his books in his wagon, which he calls Dewey's Book Mobile. Thor Wickstrom's cartoon illustrations are an excellent match for Dewey's antics and the activity-filled, primary-grade classrooms.

Read-Aloud Presentation

Recall with the children their experiences with a book fair. What books did they purchase? How did they go about selecting them? What do they plan to buy at the next book fair, and when is it? Read *Book Fair Day,* and at the end ask who in their classroom they would ask for advice about books.

STORY S-T-R-E-T-C-H-E-R

Art: Design a Book Cover for Our Book Fair

What the children will learn
To plan and draw an appropriate book cover

Materials you will need
Drawing paper, markers, crayons, colored pencils

What to do
1. Look at the cover of *Book Fair Day.*
2. Discuss how the children and the classroom in Wickstrom's illustrations are similar to and different from your classroom.
3. Notice the titles of the books that the children are reading and that are on display.
4. Ask the children to make a new cover for *Book Fair Day* with illustrations that would be true to what happens in their own classroom.
5. Display the book covers in the classroom reading area or the library.

Something to think about
Make other book cover illustrations that are based on the five other books about Mrs. Shepherd's class, *Pajama Day, School Picture Day, Teacher Appreciation Day, Field Trip Day,* and *Science Fair Day.*

STORY S-T-R-E-T-C-H-E-R

Art and Writing: Posters Announcing Book Fair Day

What the children will learn
To design attractive posters that provide all the pertinent information for an announcement

Materials you will need
Poster board, markers, tempera paint, camera, photo paper, printer

What to do
1. Discuss with the children the information they will need to provide to the readers of their posters, such as, who, what, when, where, how much money is needed, and any other rules.
2. Brainstorm some ideas that would call attention to the posters, such as photos of a variety of children reading different books.
3. Plan the layouts for as many posters as are needed to make the announcement at school.

Something to think about
Ask the person who is responsible for the school's website to come to class and discuss what is needed to place an announcement on the website. If possible, scan the children's posters and photos and add those to the site.

Physical Activity: Dewey's Book Clues Trail

What the children will learn
To listen and to follow clues

Materials you will need
Chalkboard, chalk, index cards, markers

What to do
1. Read *Book Fair Day* again and note all the places Dewey goes trying to get into the book fair early, which include the playground, the hallway, and the library.
2. Arrange ahead of time with the kindergarten teacher, physical activity director, custodian, and librarian to have these locations ready for the children's arrival.
3. Write a clue for each of these places, such as, "This is the place where Dewey reads to his book buddy. Go to that place and wait for your next clue." (kindergarten)
4. Give the kindergarten teacher this clue card. "This is the place Dewey is found trying to crawl through a window. Go to that place and wait for your next clue." (playground)
5. Give the physical activity teacher this clue card. "This is the place Dewey is found trying to track down the hamster. Go to that place and wait for your next clue." (hallway)
6. Give the custodian this clue card. "This is the place Dewey most wants to go all day long. Go to that place and wait for your next clue." (library).
7. Give the librarian this clue card. "This is the place Dewey goes after he helps all the children find their books. Go to that place." (their classroom).

Something to think about
Create a different trail by putting index cards with clues on them in certain books and hiding these books around the school. When the children locate one of these books, they find a clue inside hinting at the next book they need to find.

Reading: Book Buddies

What the children will learn
To practice their reading with younger children and to select books that will interest kindergarteners

Materials you will need
Collection of books appropriate for younger children

What to do
1. Partner with a kindergarten teacher and plan a weekly or twice weekly "Book Buddies" reading.
2. For the first Book Buddies reading, try to match the children as buddies, but plan that the book buddies may need to change after a few weeks when you can determine if the matches are appropriate.
3. Have the children recall their favorite kindergarten books and help the children find these books in the library. Also, check the book collection in the kindergarten classroom.
4. If possible schedule the Book Buddies at least twice weekly.

Something to think about
Working together with the kindergarten teacher, plan some STORY S-T-R-E-T-C-H-E-R-S for the books the children have selected for their Book Buddies. Let the older students become the helpers with the Book Buddies to complete the activities.

Reading: Dewey's Favorite Types of Literature

What the children will learn
To classify books by their genres or types

Materials you will need
Collection of variety of genres of books, strips of poster board, markers

What to do
1. Read *Book Fair Day* again. Notice the different books Dewey wants to buy at the book fair.
2. Biographies, fables, mysteries, fantasies, comics, and histories are some of the types Dewey dreams about. From the illustrations, notice his interest in detective books, dinosaur books, an atlas, and books about famous explorers.
3. With the librarian's help, set up a display of books. Let the children stack the books that go together, such as dinosaur books, detective stories, biographies, fantasy, and so on.

Something to think about
Further categorize books by whether they are fact (nonfiction) or fiction. For example, a dinosaur book may be fact, or if it is the story of an imaginary dinosaur, it could be fiction.

References

Allard, Harry. 1977. *Miss Nelson Is Missing!* Illustrated by James Marshall. New York: Houghton Mifflin Company.

Brown, Marc. 1989. *Arthur's Teacher Trouble*. New York: Hachette/Little, Brown.

Carlson, Nancy. 2006. *First Grade, Here I Come!* New York: Penguin.

Martin, Bill Jr., Michael Sampson, and Michael D. Chesworth. 2000. *Swish!* New York: Henry Holt.

Plourde, Lynn. 2006. *Book Fair Day*. Illustrated by Thor Wickstrom. New York: Penguin.

Additional References

Harper, Jessica. 2004. *Four Boys Named Jordan*. Illustrated by Tara Calahan King. New York: Putnam. *Four Jordans in one third-grade classroom cause chaos and confusion for teacher and students alike.*

Prelutsky, Jack. 2009. *What a Day It Was at School!* Illustrated by Doug Cushman. New York: Greenwillow. *School has never been so much fun! When your science homework eats your dog, you spend lunch dodging flying food, and your backpack weighs a thousand pounds, you know you've got a great answer to the question, "What did you do at school today?"*

Schulevitz, Uri. 2008. *How I Learned Geography*. New York: Farrar, Straus, and Giroux. *As he spends hours studying his father's world map, a young boy escapes the hunger and misery of refugee life. Based on the author's childhood in Kazakhstan, where he lived as a Polish refugee during World War II.*

Websites

1. Teacher Planet:
   www.teacherplanet.com/resource/back2school.php<http://www.teacherplanet.com/resource/back2school.php
   - Back-to-school resource page
   - Lesson plans and worksheets
   - First day activities
   - Printable clip art
2. Long Beach Kids: www.lb-kids.com
   - Featured authors printed interviews
   - Video archive of author interviews
   - Parents' Choice Awards

3. The Teacher's Corner.Net:
   http://www.theteacherscorner.net/seasonal/back-to-school
   - Sample lesson plans
   - Activities
   - Bulletin board ideas
4. Kids Reads: www.kidsreads.com
   - Author biographies
   - Classic reading lists
   - Trivia questions

Dogs and Cats

Madeline's Rescue

By Ludwig Bemelmans

Story Line

Madeline, a beloved character for primary-age children, is rescued by Genevieve the dog from the River Seine in Paris. When they return home to the boarding school, the dog becomes a companion to Madeline, the twelve little girls, and their teacher, Miss Clavel. When the trustees visit, they enforce the rule of "No dogs allowed," and Genevieve is banished to the streets. Though they search throughout the city, the girls and Miss Clavel cannot find Genevieve. Months later, Genevieve returns with a litter of puppies—one for each little girl, "enough hounds to go around." In classic Bemelmans writing style, the story is told in rhymed couplets. True to his drawing style, most of the illustrations are charcoal drawings with a yellow background, with some full-color pages included. This Caldecott Medal book is a classroom and library winner.

Read-Aloud Presentation

Ask the children their favorite Madeline books. If they do not know Madeline yet, refer them to the classroom library, where you have assembled a collection of Madeline books. Show the cover of the book and have the children guess what pet will be rescued and from where. Read *Madeline's Rescue* without pausing so that they can enjoy the entire story. (For older children, provide a biography of Ludwig Bemelmans from the Madeline website, www.madeline.com.)

STORY S-T-R-E-T-C-H-E-R

Art: Madeline's Paris Scenes

What the children will learn
To interpret some of the locations shown in Paris prints

Materials you will need
Prints or children's reference books on Paris

What to do
1. Display some Paris prints of the Eiffel Tower, Arc de Triomphe, River Seine, or Notre Dame Cathedral.
2. Compare the sites in the prints to Ludwig Bemelmans's illustrations.

Something to think about
If someone you know has been to Paris, ask that person to come to the class and show the children photographs of Paris. Compare the photos to the prints.

STORY S-T-R-E-T-C-H-E-R

Art: Charcoal Pictures

What the children will learn
To explore and to handle the medium of charcoal

Materials you will need
Scrap paper, yellow construction paper, charcoals, hair spray **(for adult use only)**

What to do
1. Show the children Bemelmans's illustrations in *Madeline's Rescue*. Notice the thick line drawings using charcoals with a yellow background.
2. Distribute scrap paper and let the children experiment with the charcoal, using the points, sides, and different sizes of charcoal.
3. When the children feel comfortable with the medium, let them draw on the yellow backgrounds a scene from the book or one of their own choosing.
4. When the children are out of the classroom, spray the finished charcoal drawings with hair spray to keep the drawings from smearing.

Something to think about

Experimentation is a valuable first step for children to explore a medium, whether charcoals and pastels, which smear easily, or bright temperas, oils, and watercolors. Each has distinctive properties that young artists need to explore.

Mathematics: Enough Hounds to Go Around, One-to-One Correspondence

What the children will learn
The mathematical concept of one-to-one correspondence

Materials you will need
Construction paper cutouts of small dogs (one for each child), markers, glue sticks

What to do
1. Reread the ending of *Madeline's Rescue,* and call attention to the part of the story when there are suddenly "enough hounds to go around," meaning Genevieve has enough puppies for each little girl to have one.
2. Show the illustrations and note that "each one has one" is called *one-to-one correspondence* in mathematical terms.
3. Give each child one of the cutouts of the small dogs.
4. Let the children write their names on the cutouts and paste them onto something they want to identify, such as a notebook.

Something to think about
After children have the concept of one-to-one correspondence, try counting by twos for the number of puppies Genevieve brought to Miss Clavel.

Reading: French Vocabulary Words

What the children will learn
To pronounce, read, and know the meaning of the French vocabulary words found in *Madeline's Rescue*

Materials you will need
Strips of paper or poster board, markers, thumbtacks or push pins

What to do
1. Reread *Madeline's Rescue*, pausing to note some of the French words in the text and illustrations.
2. Write the words on strips of paper or poster board, and display them on a bulletin board with a copy of the cover of *Madeline's Rescue.*
3. Among the French vocabulary words you could select are *Madeline, Genevieve, gendarmes, chamomile, Institut de France,* and *Blvd. St. Michel. Gendarmes* are police officers, *chamomile* is a kind of tea, *Institut de France* is the Institute of France, and *Blvd. St. Michel* is the Boulevard Saint Michael.

Something to think about
Consider adding the French words to your class word wall, so that children read the words on the wall and when they encounter them in the book. As they read *Madeline's Rescue* on their own, they will know the words.

Writing: The Next Madeline Adventure

What the children will learn
To use what they know about Madeline and about puppies to imagine another adventure

Materials you will need
Writing paper, pencils, chalkboard or whiteboard, chalk or markers

What to do
1. Brainstorm with groups of writers about what might happen when each of the little girls has her own puppy in Paris.
2. Ask individual children to write their own stories based on something the class has brainstormed or based on their own ideas.
3. Encourage the children to think of the first scene of the story and the last scene, then to think about what needs to happen in between.
4. Edit the stories with the children and select a variety for publishing to final form.

Something to think about
First graders may benefit from drawing a picture of what they think might happen, then writing some sentences about their stories. Second graders can draw beginning pictures on one side of the paper and ending pictures on the other as a way to get the writing process going. Third graders may be able to do a storyboard of all of the scenes of their stories.

Riptide

By Frances Ward Weller
Illustrated by Robert J. Blake

Story Line

Riptide is the true adventure of a dog who becomes the nineteenth lifeguard at a beach after saving a little girl from drowning. Rip belongs to Zach's family, who runs a fruit-and-vegetable stand near Nauset Beach. The dog spends most of his time romping and playing on the beach and diving and swimming in the ocean, even though dogs are not allowed. The lifeguards run him off the beach all summer until one hot, sultry day when there is a tremendous storm with huge riptides. A little girl gets pulled out to sea and is drowning. Rip swims out to her, and she catches his tail so he can pull her over to the lifeguard. Blake's oil paintings are truly works of art, with deep blue, turquoise, and azure seas, white-capped waves, sandy beaches with lapping surf, beautiful sunny days with billowing clouds, as well as stormy skies.

Read-Aloud Presentation

If the children have visited a beach, ask them about the rules at the beach. Find out if dogs were allowed on the beach. Discuss why animals might be prohibited. If your students do not know about beaches, talk with them about your own experiences. Show the children the cover of the book, and tell them that this is a true story. Read *Riptide* without pausing. At the end of the book, read the author's note about the newspaper clipping and interview information used to write the story. The book is such a popular one with children that they will want you to read it again. Don't hesitate to read it a second time or to show the beautiful paintings that illustrate the book, pausing for the children to recall what happens in each scene.

Classroom Library:
Pictures and Pet Stories

What the children will learn
To tell information about their pets in a way that will interest listeners

Materials you will need
Photographs of pets, CDs and CD recorder or tapes and tape recorder

What to do
1. Ask the children to bring pictures of their pets or of pets they would like to have.
2. In small groups, have the children show their pet pictures and tell a bit about their animals. Record the discussion.
3. Listen to the recordings and let each group brainstorm ideas for stories based on what the children said. For example, one child might tell why he wants a certain pet that he does not have. Someone else might talk about a time when her pet was heroic or was lost and found his way back.
4. Ask each child to make a recording.
5. Place the recordings and the photographs of the pets in the classroom library.

Something to think about
Have older children work with partners and interview each other like television reporters.

Classroom Library: Collection of Animal Adventure Books

What the children will learn
To find other animal adventure stories

Materials you will need
Librarian's reference books

What to do
1. Talk with the librarian ahead of time and tell him or her that some of your children will be coming to the library to find more true animal adventure stories.
2. With a small group of children who show particular interest in *Riptide* and other adventure stories, go through the steps of finding the books. Let the children browse through the books and decide whether or not to check them out for the classroom collection.

Something to think about

When children are allowed to select books on topics that interest them, they read more difficult stories.

STORY S-T-R-E-T-C-H-E-R

Mathematics: How Many Children in Our Class Have Pets?

What the children will learn

To prepare a graph and compare total numbers by categories

Materials you will need

Notepads, pencils, chart tablet or poster board, black marker and three other different colors of markers

What to do

1. With a black marker, draw a baseline across the bottom of the poster board or a sheet of chart tablet paper.
2. The first question is "How many children do we have in class?" Each child marks a horizontal straight line an inch or two long, starting at the baseline or the bottom of the chart tablet or poster board.
3. The second question is "How many students have one pet at home?" Using another color marker, each child who has one pet draws a line in a second column up from the baseline.
4. The third question is "How many students have more than one pet at home?" Use a third color and each child who has more than one pet makes a mark.
5. Call this information *data*. Discuss with the children what kinds of questions data can answer.
6. Discuss how to make the bar graph more readable. One idea is to label each bar with a shorter version of the question, such as "number of children," "one pet," "more than one pet."

Something to think about

Consider drawing a straight black line across each column when ten children have made their marks. This allows the children to count more easily.

STORY S-T-R-E-T-C-H-E-R

Special Event: Visit from a Veterinarian or Animal Control Officer

What the children will learn

About the safety laws and recommendations for their communities

Materials you will need

Poster board or chart tablet, marker

What to do

1. Invite a veterinarian or an animal control officer from your community to visit the classroom and discuss how to practice good safety around an animal.
2. Talk with the guest ahead of time and discuss some of the important points you want to emphasize.
3. Prepare a "K-W-L" chart. Under the *K* column, let the children list all the safety precautions for pets they already *know*. Under the *W* column, list their general questions, or what the children *want* to know.
4. After the guest shares information with the class, complete writing in the *L* column by answering the questions and writing other information the students *learned*.

Something to think about

Invite someone in your community who has a dog trained to work with a handicapped person to come to your classroom and talk about the special care and training the pet received and what the dog does.

STORY S-T-R-E-T-C-H-E-R

Writing: My Pet

What the children will learn

To use drawing as a prewriting device and to determine at least three main events

Materials you will need

art paper, colored pencils, markers, crayons

What to do

1. Talk with the children about the three main events in *Riptide*: the dog enjoying the beach, the lifeguards chasing him away, and the time he saved the little girl's life.
2. Fold a sheet of art paper into thirds. Tell the children that if you were illustrating this story, you would place each of the main events on a third of the paper.
3. Ask the children to fold their papers, then think of three main events that tell their pets' stories.
4. Have the children draw their main events.
5. Then ask the students to write about each main event.

Something to think about

The children who made recordings in the "Pictures and Pet Stories" STORY S-T-R-E-T-C-H-E-R may be interested in writing a story to illustrate.

Officer Buckle and Gloria

By Peggy Rathmann

Story Line

Officer Buckle is a regular visitor to schools to give programs on safety tips. Few people pay attention until a police dog named Gloria begins accompanying him. Then Officer Buckle and Gloria are in such demand that 313 schools ask them to give programs. They receive tons of fan mail with children remembering their safety tips, until Officer Buckle sees a film of their performance and realizes the children are watching Gloria, not him. He tries going to the schools alone, and he is a flop. And when Gloria tries going to the schools alone, she is a flop. There are even more accidents without Officer Buckle's reminders. Officer Buckle and Gloria reunite, and the children once again remember the safety tips. In this Caldecott Medal book, Rathmann has created winning personalities with Officer Buckle and Gloria.

Read-Aloud Presentation

Discuss what police dogs do, such as go with police officers to schools, search for people lost in earthquakes or tornadoes, sniff for drugs at airports. Read *Officer Buckle and Gloria*. Discuss how the police officer and the dog are a team and a good illustration of the safety tip, "Always stick with your buddy!"

STORY S-T-R-E-T-C-H-E-R

Art: School Safety Posters

What the children will learn
To interpret the meaning of safety tips in their own environments

Materials you will need
Poster board, drawing paper, markers, crayons, colored pens

What to do
1. Sign your classroom up for a safety poster contest, often given by police or fire departments.
2. Construct posters of favorite safety sayings that children think are important.
3. Make a list of the safety tips, and ask each child to make a different safety-tip poster.

Something to think about
Consider making a banner that can be draped near the front of the school announcing the safety poster contest.

STORY S-T-R-E-T-C-H-E-R

Safety: Tips from a Pet Owner

What the children will learn
The responsibilities of being a pet owner include ensuring the safety of the pet

Materials you will need
Chalkboard and chalk or whiteboard and markers, poster board, markers

What to do
1. Discuss what we as pet owners must do to keep our pets safe, such as place an owner's collar on the pet, never let the dog out without a leash, never leave a pet in a hot car, supervise people who want to pet your animal, keep the pet inside in extreme cold or extreme heat, and so on. For more tips on pet care, see the website of the Humane Society of the United States (www.humanesociety.org).
2. After listing all of the rules the children think are important, plan a visit from owners of a small puppy and a large dog.
3. Let the children ask questions of the pet owner or owners and recall the pet safety rules for petting.

Something to think about

Officer Buckle and Gloria is about a specially trained K-9 animal. Discuss the difference between family pets and highly trained animals that work with police departments. Both require safe handling rules.

STORY S-T-R-E-T-C-H-E-R

Social Studies: Community Helper—Dog Trainer

What the children will learn

To interact with someone who helps the community by being a dog trainer

Materials you will need

Leash, dog, dog treats, permission from parents

What to do

1. Invite a dog trainer to come to your classroom. Mention the age of your students and what they will need to know to interact effectively with a dog and what the trainer can expect.
2. Plan for the visit by reminding the children of the expectations that only a few children will be near the dog at one time, and that the children must follow the instructions of the trainer exactly.
3. Decide which children will pet the dog first and which will assist the trainer.

Something to think about

Some young children are afraid of dogs. Be sure to inform parents of the visit of the dog and trainer. Help children who are afraid so they can have a calm and easy visit with the animal, but do not force the interaction if children are uncomfortable.

STORY S-T-R-E-T-C-H-E-R

Social Studies: Community Helper—K-9 Police Officer and Dog

What the children will learn

To recognize the difference between a real K-9 police dog and the imaginary Gloria in the book

Materials you will need

Police or K-9 dog and officer, trainer, permission from parents

What to do

1. Meet with the officer and his police dog ahead of time to get a sense of the demeanor of the dog.
2. Discuss with the children how this dog is different from their pets at home and from Gloria in *Officer Buckle and Gloria*.
3. Arrange for small groups to interact with the police officer and with the police dog.

Something to think about

Welcome parents who are skilled pet owners to be a part of the classroom visits with pets and with working dogs.

STORY S-T-R-E-T-C-H-E-R

Writing: Thank-You Letters to the Officer and the Dog

What the children will learn

To express their appreciation using specifics from the visit

Materials you will need

Chalkboard, chalk, thank-you notes, notepaper, crayons or drawing paper, colored pencils

What to do

1. Help the children to recall the name of the officer who visited the class with his or her dog.
2. Write the names on the board.
3. Discuss some specifics of what the children enjoyed about the visit, including what the officer said and how the dog acted.
4. Write a group thank-you note from the whole class, modeling everything that should be included in the thank-you note.
5. Allow the children to write their own notes and draw small pictures on notepaper.

Something to think about

Some children may want to make star-shaped cards like the one Claire makes in *Officer Buckle and Gloria*.

Dewey: There's a Cat in the Library!

By Vicki Myron and Bret Witter
Illustrated by Steve James

Story Line

Inspired by the adult book *Dewey, the Library Cat*, the children's version is beautifully illustrated and captures the essence of the true story, but it is told from Dewey's perspective and with an imaginary mouse friend. The cat's full name is Dewey Readmore Books. Dewey finds a home in the library, but often feels frustrated by the children until he learns to be a helper and enjoy the interactions. Dewey learns from his friend Marty Mouse that libraries are places where people get help. The compelling story of a lonely kitten that becomes a much-loved library cat ends with Dewey helping a sad little girl become happy. Illustrated in glowing, warm pastels, James captures the feelings and endears Dewey to the reader.

Read-Aloud Presentation

Ask the children to look at the cover of the book and read the title, *Dewey: There's a Cat in the Library!* Have them guess how a cat got in the library. Ask the children to think about their own library and how a cat could get into it. Read the book and have the children recall how Dewey wants to be treated by the children. After reading the book, let the children tell about their pet cats and what the cats like to do that is silly. See www.kindnews.org for a discussion of kindness.

STORY S-T-R-E-T-C-H-E-R

Art: Dewey Prints from Cat Calendars

What the children will learn
To select and display favorite cat pictures

Materials you will need
Old calendars with pictures of cats and kittens, scissors, tape, construction paper

What to do
1. Collect old cat calendars from families and friends.
2. Have the children look through the calendars and select pictures of cats that look like Dewey.
3. Cut pictures from the calendars and glue the pictures onto construction paper frames.
4. Make a bulletin board display of Dewey cats.

Something to think about
Include in the display some photos of children with their cats.

STORY S-T-R-E-T-C-H-E-R

Game: Dewey's Hide-and-Seek

What the children will learn
To abide by the rules of the game

Materials you will need
None

What to do
1. Remind everyone that Dewey is a "hider." He hides from the librarians and from the patrons, but he enjoys being around the children.
2. Review the rules of hide-and-seek. Model one turn, with you counting while the children hide as if they were Dewey. Say, "Where's Dewey? Ready or not, here comes Vicki the Librarian." Let the last one found become the "finder" for the next turn, and use the child's name for that of the librarian, "Here comes Riley the Librarian."
3. When you find the children, have them move to the center of the room until everyone is found.

Something to think about
Ask the librarian if, after reading *Dewey: There's a Cat in the Library!* the children could have a game of hide-and-seek and she or he could be the "finder."

Mathematics: Favorite Cat Names

What the children will learn
To tabulate the answers to questions

Materials you will need
Chart tablet, markers, chalkboard, chalk

What to do
1. Discuss that "Dewey Readmore Books," is the name the townspeople in Spencer, Iowa, gave to the kitten that came to live in the library.
2. Survey the children to find out the names of their pet cats or cats they have known.
3. Designate two children as writers and two children as number recorders.
4. Each child says the name of his or her cat, the name of a cat or kitten they have known, or what they would name their cats if they had cat pets.
5. Group the names into categories. For instance, a group of people names, like Reggie and Dewey; a group named after their colors or markings, such as Smokey, Blacky and Patches; and a group made up of other names, such as Spanky, Princess, Autumn, or Bootsy.
6. Count the names and find out the types of names that are most common among the children's cats.

Something to think about
Ask the children to imagine that their school library has a library cat, and then ask the children what they would give the cat as its first name? "Readmore Books" would be the middle and last names.

Reading: The Dewey Story from Beginning to End

What the children will learn
To sequence the main scenes of a story

Materials you will need
Poster board, markers, scissors

What to do
1. Reread *Dewey: There's a Cat in the Library!* Pause after each scene and ask the children to describe the scene. For instance, the children would say that in scene one, Dewey is left in the book slot. In the last scene, Dewey is being held by a happy little girl.
2. Write the descriptions of the scenes on strips of poster board.
3. Shuffle the scenes and then let the children arrange them in order.

Something to think about
Consider having the children write a scene where each of them meets Dewey in the school or their community library.

Science and Social Studies: How to Interact with a Cat

What the children will learn
To critique the way the children in the story interact with Dewey

Materials you will need
Whiteboard and markers or chalkboard and chalk

What to do
1. Look back through the pages of the book, and notice the things that the children do to Dewey that bother him, such as petting him in the wrong direction, pulling his ears, chasing him, and carrying him upside down.
2. Let the children who are cat owners describe how to pet cats, how cats behave, and what cats like to do.

Something to think about
Ask a cat owner who has a docile cat to bring the cat to school, and let the children learn how to pet the cat.
Note: Before bringing a cat to class, make sure no one is allergic to cats.

For the Love of Autumn

By Patricia Polacco

Story Line

Polacco's text and illustrations tell the story of Danielle Parks as she goes from being a student teacher to moving to another state for her first teaching job. Autumn, a tiny kitty, moves with her. Miss Parks loves teaching and enjoys her class. Autumn loves the cottage with a garden by the sea, until she is scared by a storm and runs away. The schoolchildren help search for her, yet Autumn is lost until she returns one day with a new collar and a new name. The surprise ending is that Miss Parks finds more than her runaway cat; she finds the man who becomes her husband. *For the Love of Autumn* is a suspenseful story told with an expansive vocabulary and with lovely, expressive illustrations that are pencil drawings washed with watercolors.

Read-Aloud Presentation

Show the cover of *For the Love of Autumn*, and ask the children what they would like to know about the book, based on what they see on the cover. List their questions on a chalkboard or whiteboard. Read the story through from beginning to end so that the story flows without interruptions. After the story is over, let the children answer their own questions. If the answer is not found in the story, let the children suggest imaginary answers.

Art: Cat Photography

What the children will learn
To evaluate photographs

Materials you will need
Cat calendars, personal photos of cats from your collection or from those of the children's family members, scissors, bulletin board, tape or thumbtacks

What to do
1. Cut out the photographs of cats in cat calendars.
2. Make a bulletin board display of different breeds of cats.
3. Ask children who have cats to bring family photos of their cats and to add them to the bulletin boards.
4. Compare the differences in family photos and in professional photos: background, lighting, poses.

Something to think about
Invite a parent who is adept at photography or a pet photographer to your classroom, and ask him or her to illustrate how to get cats to pose and make suggestions to the children for taking pictures of their pet cats.

Science: K-W-L Chart on Cats

What the children will learn
To look for answers to their questions about cats

Materials you will need
Extra reference books, such as online encyclopedias, pet books, and additional references at the end of this unit, chart tablet or poster board, markers

What to do
1. Construct a K-W-L chart. *K* means what we *know* about cats. *W* means what we *want to know* about cats, and *L* stands for what we have *learned* about cats.
2. Divide the chart tablet, whiteboard or poster board into three columns, labeled *K, W,* and *L.*
3. Ask the children to say what they already know about cats, then what they want to know.
4. Based on the information in *For the Love of Autumn,* answer the question "What did we learn about cats?" For example, cats are afraid of loud noises such as

thunderstorms. Let the children generate other questions they have about cats.

5. Plan how the children might find answers. Whom would they ask, where would they search, and how will they remember what they have learned?

6. After their research, come back to the K-W-L chart and collectively answer the questions.

Something to think about
Use K-W-L charts for the study of dogs as well.

STORY S-T-R-E-T-C-H-E-R

Social Studies: Geography—Moving to Washington State

What the children will learn
To improve map-reading skills by finding their location and using a map of the United States to find the state of Washington

Materials you will need
Large map of the United States, pushpins, yarn, construction paper shape of a cat

What to do
1. Reread the part of *For the Love of Autumn* that describes Danielle Parks's move to the state of Washington from the coast of California.

2. Place a pushpin on the coast of Washington State on the U.S. map.

3. Use the construction paper cat to trace Danielle's and Autumn's route from the coast of California through Oregon to the coast of Washington.

4. Have the children locate some towns and cities along the way.

Something to think about
Write to some small towns on the coast of Washington and ask them to send brochures for a class display. Look at the maps the towns provided and locate the towns on a state map.

STORY S-T-R-E-T-C-H-E-R

Writing: Cats I Have Known

What the children will learn
To use adjectives to describe cats

Materials you will need
Book, whiteboard and markers *or* chalkboard and chalk

What to do
1. Select passages from *For the Love of Autumn* where the author, Patricia Polacco, describes the kitten Autumn.

2. List these descriptive passages on the board.

3. Ask the children to use color words, types of stripes, whiskers, shapes of ears, curls of tails, and other words to describe kittens and cats they know or have known.

Something to think about
Second and third graders may be ready for a study of adverbs that can be added to the story to describe the actions, such as *happily, surprisingly, sadly,* and *hurriedly.* See the website from the Cat Fancier's Association at http://kids.cfa.org and compare the words they use to describe cats.

STORY S-T-R-E-T-C-H-E-R

Writing: An Invitation to Visit

What the children will learn
To write in the form of an invitation

Materials you will need
Samples of some printed invitations, scrap notepaper, pens, pencils, or markers

What to do
1. Show the children the sample of a printed invitation, read it to them, and note what information is contained in the note. Often there are blanks for the person to fill in who, what, when, and where.

2. Also, read an invitation you have received that is written in sentence form.

3. Distribute blank notepaper and let the children write their own versions of an invitation to Mr. Norton to come to Miss Parks's house to meet each other and to see Autumn.

Something to think about
Consider composing a sample apology note, like the one Miss Parks might have written to Mr. Norton.

References

Bemelmans, Ludwig. 1953. *Madeline's Rescue*. New York: Penguin.

Myron, Vicki and Bret Witter. 2009. *Dewey: There's a Cat in the Library!* Illustrated by Steve James. New York: Little, Brown.

Polacco, Patricia. 2008. *For the Love of Autumn*. New York: Penguin.

Rathmann, Peggy. 1995. *Officer Buckle and Gloria*. New York: Penguin.

Weller, Frances Ward. 1999. *Riptide*. Illustrated by Robert J. Blake. New York: Penguin.

Additional References

Averill, Esther. 1983. *The Fire Cat*. New York: HarperCollins. *In this beginning reader, Pickles the neighborhood cat is rescued often by the firefighters, until he finds a home at the fire station helping rescue other cats stranded in trees and high places.*

Byars, Betsy, Betsy Duffey, and Laurie Myers. 2007. *Dog Diaries: Secret Writings of the WOOF Society*. New York: Henry Holt. *At the first annual meeting of WOOF—Words of Our Friends—assorted dogs preserve their heritage by sharing tales of canines through history, including Abu, who ruled all of Egypt except for one pesky cat.*

Himmelman, John. 2008. *Katie Loves the Kittens*. New York: Henry Holt. *When Sara Ann brings home three little kittens, Katie the dog's enthusiasm frightens the kittens away, until she learns that quiet patience is sometimes needed to begin a friendship.*

Websites

1. Humane Society of the United States: www.humanesociety.org/parents_educators
   - Games and academic programs
   - News and video
   - Stories
2. Humane Society of the United States, Kind News: www.kindnews.org
   - All animals
   - Games, stories, and humane heroes feature
3. The Cat Fanciers' Association: http://kids.cfa.org
   - Cats: Sections on breeds, careers, and parent/teacher
4. www.madeline.com
   - Biographical information about Ludwig Bemelmans
   - History of Madeline
   - Other stories by Bemelmans in "Friends of Madeline"

Chapter **7**

Frogs and Turtles

Growing Frogs

Frogs

Look Out for Turtles!

Box Turtle at
Long Pond

Turtle Summer: A
Journal for
My Daughter

Growing Frogs

By Vivian French
Illustrated by Alison Bartlett

Story Line

A mother helps a little girl understand the metamorphosis of a frog. From pond water, they scoop up "gray jelly stuff," which contains the frog eggs. They place the stuff in a fish tank and watch the changes as the eggs develop, first into tadpoles, and later into tiny frogs, and then into larger frogs that have to hop out of the water to breathe. When the frogs start hopping out of the water, the mother and child return the frogs to the pond. This book brilliantly combines a story with scientific information. The illustrations and the type treatment are appealing to the young reader.

Read–Aloud Presentation

Explore what children know about frogs and their development. They may know about tadpoles, but ask the children to think about what tadpoles were before they were tadpoles (eggs). Read the story, pausing for children to talk about their experiences with frogs and visiting ponds. Complete the story and ask the children what they learned from the story that they did not know ahead of time. See the Frogland! website at http://allaboutfrogs.org to follow up on some of the interesting facts found in the book.

STORY S-T-R-E-T-C-H-E-R

Art: Pond Scenes

What the children will learn
To interpret the scenes from the book into their own pond scenes

Materials you will need
Variety of art media, paints, brushes, and papers

What to do
1. Look at the pond scenes from *Growing Frogs* and scenes from the other books in this chapter about frogs, toads, and turtles.
2. Let the children choose their art media, the types of paints, and the papers.
3. Teach the students how to sketch an outline of the pond and the banks, adding reeds and grasses around the pond edges and on the banks.
4. Allow different amounts of time to complete the pond scenes, depending on the drying time for the different paints.
5. Create a display of the pond scenes to surround the books covers of the various feature books from this STORY S-T-R-E-T-C-H-E-R-S unit.

Something to think about
Let the children practice with crayon resist by drawing their frogs with crayons on the paper, then washing over them with watercolor paints.

STORY S-T-R-E-T-C-H-E-R

Reading: Comparisons of Real and Imaginary Frogs

What the children will learn
To compare the real frogs in *Growing Frogs* to imaginary frog characters in children's books and on television

Materials you will need
Paper, ruler, pencils, green markers

What to do
1. Fold sheets of paper in half vertically. With a ruler draw a large line down the middle along the fold.
2. Think of some imaginary frogs, such as Frog from the Frog and Toad series by Arnold Lobel, or Kermit the Frog from television, or Frog in Kenneth Grahamme's classic story, *The Wind in the Willows*.
3. Label the first column, "Imaginary."
4. Label the second column, "Real."
5. Have the children make comparisons, such as, "Imaginary frogs wear clothes." "Imaginary frogs tell stories." "Imaginary frogs are puppets." "Imaginary frogs row boats." "Imaginary frogs are princes in disguise." Compare them to real frogs that "do not wear clothes," "croak, not talk," "have real, slick skin not puppet felt,"

"leap and jump, but do not row boats," and "do not kiss princesses."

Something to think about
Compare the drawings in books about real frogs and to those about imaginary frogs.

STORY S-T-R-E-T-C-H-E-R

Reading: K-W-L Chart

What the children will learn
To remember what they know, to ask questions about what they want to know, and to recall new information

Materials you will need
Whiteboard or chart tablet and markers

What to do
1. Construct a K-W-L chart. Divide a whiteboard or a large sheet of chart paper into three columns and label the columns *K, W,* and *L,* respectively.
2. Ask the children to remember what they already know about frogs, and write the keywords from what they remember on the chart in the first column.
3. For the second column, have children state what they would like to know about frogs. Write the question in the *W* column.
4. Read *Growing Frogs,* and after the reading it, complete the *L* column by having the children recall what they learned from hearing or reading this book.

Something to think about
For young first graders, begin with a K-L chart. List what they know, and after listening to the book, list what they have learned. If older children ask questions not answered by the book, challenge the children by making their questions assignments for them to research from various sources in the library and online.

STORY S-T-R-E-T-C-H-E-R

Science: Notes, Scientific Observations

What the children will learn
To observe the growth of frogs and write accurate descriptions of what they see

Materials you will need
Frogs, fish tank, small notepads *or* notepaper and construction paper books, pencils

What to do
1. If frogs are not available through a nature center, order frog eggs from a biology-supply house.
2. Place frog eggs in a fish tank, following the instructions for pond water collection.
3. Observe the changes from specks in the jellylike material (the eggs) to tadpoles emerging to the refinement of the tadpoles growing their legs and losing their tails.
4. Have the children draw each stage of the frogs' development and record the day of the week when they saw the changes.

Something to think about
Contact a nature center and find out the best times of the year for the children to collect frog eggs, and invite a naturalist to your classroom to talk about working in pond environments.

STORY S-T-R-E-T-C-H-E-R

Special Project: Visiting a Pond

What the children will learn
To describe the natural habitat of frogs

Materials you will need
Access to a pond or a nature center, permission for the children to take a field trip, parent assistants, boots or shoes that can get muddy, old clothes, paper, pencils

What to do
1. Plan the trip with a naturalist or with an educator who knows the pond environment well.
2. Inform the parents or assistants of the types of learning you hope the children will gain from the visit.
3. Prepare the children by highlighting what they can expect to see, the safety requirements, and the groups to which they will be assigned.
4. Enjoy the visit to the pond.
5. After returning to the classroom, help the children to recall what they saw and to draw their observations.

Something to think about
For children who are less familiar with ponds, spend some time with them just getting comfortable in the environment. Have plenty of helpers—as many as two per child—to provide the best experience for primary-aged children.

Frogs

By Nic Bishop

Story Line

The forty-eight-page book is a stunning collection of twenty-four different frogs and toads found in parts of the world ranging from the Amazon to the desert, from backyards to swamps. General frog characteristics and metamorphosis are presented. Each frog is described with specific characteristics of different parts of its body, size, color, unique features, and habitat. The frogs have unusual names and unusual colors caught in crisp images, with some fold-out pages showing frogs in action. The frogs in the book—the Goliath, gliding frog, dart frog, mossy frog, spade foot frog, Australian water-holding frog, wood frogs and peepers, bullfrog, African bullfrog, strawberry dart poison frogs, red-eyed tree frog—are all described and photographed beautifully. The book contains a glossary and two pages of information about Nic Bishop as an explorer and photographer.

Read-Aloud Presentation

This nonfiction book is one to be enjoyed in a read-aloud session, but it also lends itself to being pored over by individual children to see the details in the vivid photographs. Begin at the back of the book, and read about Nic Bishop as an explorer and a photographer. Select a few of your favorite frog photos and read about them. Use the additional information in the book to talk with the children about a particular frog. Plan to spend extra time presenting this book, and let the children refer back to certain pages they enjoy.

STORY S-T-R-E-T-C-H-E-R

Art: Nature Photography

What the children will learn

To use simple cameras

Materials you will need

Simple digital camera or disposable cameras, printer, paper

What to do

1. Photograph the tadpoles and the frogs in the fish tank from earlier STORY S-T-R-E-T-C-H-E-R activity for the book *Growing Frogs* (see page 91).
2. Help the children learn to use the wide-angle and the close-up lenses of the camera.
3. Print the digital photographs on a printer. **Note:** If using disposable cameras, have the film developed.
4. Compare the photographs the children took with those in *Frogs*.

Something to think about

Invite an experienced photographer to class and ask him or her to bring in photographs from nature and to describe what he or she she had to do to capture the images.

STORY S-T-R-E-T-C-H-E-R

Mathematics: Comparisons of Features in Mathematical Terms

What the children will learn

To assemble the facts and write mathematical questions

Materials you will need

Chalkboard and chalk *or* whiteboard and markers, large index cards, markers, book

What to do

1. Read about the largest and smallest frogs, such as the Goliath frog that weighs as much as a human baby and the gold frog that can fit on the tip of your finger.
2. Compare how much a baby might weigh at birth, such as 7 pounds and 6 ounces, which would be the equivalent of a Goliath frog, with a gold frog that might be 3 ounces. The math question could be "How much more does the Goliath frog weigh than the gold frog?"

3. Write a series of math questions on the index cards, such as "How many insects does a frog eat in a summer?" (5,000) "How many insects would it eat in one half of the summer?" "Gliding frogs can leap from a tree and glide 50 feet. If the frog leaped five times, how many feet would it glide?" "Bullfrogs lay as many as 20,000 eggs. How many eggs would five bullfrogs lay?"
4. Intersperse the frog mathematics problems throughout the book, so the children can solve them as they are rereading the book.

Something to think about
Older children can write math problems based on the text that they read and can pose problems to each other.

STORY S-T-R-E-T-C-H-E-R

Physical Activity: Movements Like Frogs

What the children will learn
To imitate the movements of various frogs

Materials you will need
Chalkboard, chalk

What to do
1. Write some of the action words or movement words found in Bishop's *Frogs*, such as *jump, hop, glide, burrow, dig, swim, puff up, grasp, shooting tongue, freeze,* and *hiccup.*
2. Have the children imitate the movements.
3. For older primary children, say the name of a frog, and challenge them move like that frog would move.

Something to think about
If you have a full-length mirror in your classroom, let the children rehearse their movements so they are more exaggerated.

STORY S-T-R-E-T-C-H-E-R

Reading: Finding Out More About Interesting Frogs

What the children will learn
To use reference resources to find out even more about interesting frog species

Materials you will need
Children's reference books, websites for nature preserves and nature centers, chalkboard, chalk

What to do
1. Let the children decide which frogs described in the Bishop book they would like to learn more about.
2. Write the names of these frogs on the board. Group children who are interested in the same frogs.
3. Assign roles to each of the members: one is the Bishop reader; one is the reference book or website reader; another writes key words to help everyone remember the facts; and another is the illustrator.

Something to think about
Visit multiple websites on frogs and compare the information found on sites for young children with those for older students.

STORY S-T-R-E-T-C-H-E-R

Science: Matching Frogs and Toads to Their Habitats

What the children will learn
To match frogs and their locations or habitats

Materials you will need
Chart tablet, markers, index cards

What to do
1. Read the book again and select some of the most interesting frogs. Read for names and locations of their habitats. Some examples are Goliath frog—Africa, Strawberry dart frog—rain forest, Mossy frog—Amazon, Glass frogs—Central and South America, Tree frogs—South America, and Gliding frogs—rain forests.
2. Write the name of each frog on a separate index card, and on other cards write the locations.
3. Shuffle the cards and let the children try to make the matches. The children can check their matches by revisiting the text of the book.

Something to think about
Ask the children to match frogs to their descriptive characteristics, such as gliding frog—webbed feet, spadefoot frog—digs underground, and so on.

Look Out for Turtles!

By Melvin Berger
Illustrated by Megan Lloyd

Story Line

Turtles live longer than many other animals because they have remarkable survival skills. Both land and sea turtles can live almost anywhere and eat almost anything. *Look Out for Turtles!* provides amazing facts about the red-footed tortoise, desert tortoise, Marion's tortoise, diamondback terrapin, loggerhead turtle, wood turtle, eastern box turtle, common snapping turtle, green turtle, eastern mud turtle, leatherback turtle, Galapagos turtle, eastern painted turtle, Kemp's ridley turtle, and spotted turtle. The reader learns about turtle habitats and ways we can protect them. *Look Out for Turtles!* is a part of Roma Gans's Let's-Read-and-Find-Out Science book series. These books are written with an understanding of how young children think: texts brief enough for children to understand, yet complex enough to challenge them. Megan Lloyd's realistic watercolor illustrations are nature art for elementary-age children at its best.

Read-Aloud Presentation

Show the children an illustration in the book of a turtle found in your geographic location. Let the children share any personal experiences they have had with turtles, such as seeing them in their backyards, on the side of the road, or at the zoo. Read *Look Out for Turtles!* and ask the children what they think the title means. The children will probably think that the title means to watch out or a turtle might bite them. Read the book and guide the children towards understanding the title's message, that even though the turtle is a survivor, some species have become endangered. Note that the book also calls turtles *tortoises* and *terrapins*. Land-dwelling turtles are often called tortoises. Terrapin is usually used with the name *diamondback*.

Art: Patterns of Shells

What the children will learn

To recognize, describe, and produce patterns that look like turtle shells

Materials you will need

Light brown or green construction paper, scissors, pastel chalks, colored pencils, hair spray **(for adult use only)**

What to do

1. Help the children cut large shapes like turtle shells from light brown or light green construction paper.
2. Ask the children to look through the illustrations of the turtles and describe the patterns found on their shells. Explain and use the term *geometric patterns*.
3. Call the children's attention to the eastern painted turtle, eastern box turtle, and red-footed tortoise, or a turtle that lives in your geographic location.
4. Ask the children to make turtle-like patterns on the construction paper shapes using pastel chalks, colored pencils, or a combination of the two.
5. When the artists are out of the classroom, spray their patterns with hair spray to prevent smudging.

Something to think about

Explain to the children why they should never paint or carve the shell of a real turtle. See www.allturtles.com for turtle news from around the world and for videos of turtles.

Classroom Library: Turtles in Reality and in Fantasy

What the children will learn

To compare what is real and what is not, and to think about how fantasy is often based on reality

Materials you will need

Various turtle stories like Aesop's fable of "The Tortoise and the Hare," chart tablet, marker

What to do

1. Make a chart with two columns. Label one column "reality" and one column "fantasy based on reality."
2. Read to the children Janet Stevens's adaptation of Aesop's fable "The Tortoise and the Hare."

3. After reading the fable, discuss the story's basis in the observation that land turtles move very slowly.
4. Write the title of the fable in the column "fantasy based on reality."
5. Show the children *Look Out for Turtles!* and have them decide in which column to write the title of the book.

Something to think about
Find Native American stories that feature turtles, such as the retold story of *Fire Race: A Karuk Coyote Tale* by Jonathan London. Read an African story like *How Turtle Got Its Shell: An African Tale* by Sandra Robbins. Also consider reading *Tortoise Solves a Problem* by Avner Katz.

STORY S-T-R-E-T-C-H-E-R

Mathematics: How Many Turtle Eggs in a Clutch?

What the children will learn
To recognize, count, and prove quantity

Materials you will need
Cotton balls, container

What to do
1. Have the children who are interested find the description of the green turtle in *Look Out for Turtles!* Read that section again.
2. Discuss the female turtle's habit of laying 150 eggs.
3. Let the children take cotton balls from a bag or container and try to guess how many 150 is.
4. Depending upon how many cotton balls you have, let the children pile them up, then count to see if they have close to 150.
5. Ask the children to count out exactly 150 cotton balls and place them in the science display area with a sign that states, "Green turtles lay up to 150 eggs in a clutch."

Something to think about
Let the children investigate other comparisons of measurement made in the book, like the comparison between the speed of a human being and a tortoise on land.

STORY S-T-R-E-T-C-H-E-R

Science and Nature: Studying a Turtle

What the children will learn
To observe the habits of a turtle at close range

Materials you will need
A turtle, protected outdoor environment, water supply, notepads, pencils

What to do
1. Contact a zoo director or naturalist in your community.
2. Arrange for a turtle to live in a protected area of the school grounds.
3. Let teams of children study the turtle by observing its behavior over the course of a week.
4. Each week the teams can answer simple questions: "Where is the turtle?" "Has the turtle moved from one place to another since yesterday at this time?" "What is the turtle doing?" "What is the turtle eating?"
5. When the naturalist comes to take the turtle back to its natural environment, let the children tell the naturalist what they observed and ask any questions they have.

Something to think about
If it is not possible to have the turtle on the grounds, or you fear it would not be safe, contact a pet store and arrange for a turtle and a terrarium to visit for a week.

STORY S-T-R-E-T-C-H-E-R

Science Display: Amazing Facts, True or False

What the children will learn
To recall interesting facts and realize that some facts that sound amazing are true, while others are false

Materials you will need
Index cards or sticky notes, markers, two empty tissue boxes

What to do
1. Have a group of writers recall, check, and then print amazing facts from *Look Out for Turtles!*
2. Label one box "true" and the other "false."
3. Ask the writers to think up false and funny statements, such as, "Green sea turtles turn green because they eat green algae." After the statement, print, "Place this statement in the box marked 'true,'" or "Place this statement in the box marked 'false.'"
4. Let the writers think of funny statements such as, "Ninja turtles once lived and now appear on Saturday-morning cartoons."

Something to think about
Make a chart from page 31 of *Look Out for Turtles!* that states what children can do to help turtles survive.

Box Turtle at Long Pond

By William T. George
Illustrated by
Lindsay Barrett George

Story Line

The reader visits Long Pond by tagging along with a box turtle for a day. The turtle awakes, forages for food, encounters other animals that live along the banks, and drinks from Long Pond. The reader sees the turtle as it suns on a rock, finds shelter during a rainstorm, eats worms, and escapes from a raccoon by closing its shell. At the end of the day, the turtle searches for more food before hiding in the tall grasses, a camouflaged sleeping place. Lindsay Barrett George's beautiful yet realistic illustrations welcome the reader to the calm and excitement of a natural setting, helping us experience what it is like to live there.

Read-Aloud Presentation

Have the children recall *Look Out for Turtles!*. Discuss some of the fascinating facts they learned about turtles. Read again the pages on the eastern box turtle. Show the children the cover of *Box Turtle at Long Pond,* and help them identify the turtle pictured as an eastern box turtle. Read the book. Pause before the illustration of the raccoon to place your hand over the turtle. Ask the children what will happen to a box turtle if a young raccoon comes too close. After reading, go back through the book, page by page, and let the children describe the natural surroundings.

STORY S-T-R-E-T-C-H-E-R

Art: Misty Morning Painting

What the children will learn
To use a watercolor technique

Materials you will need
Watercolors, heavy paper, small brushes, masking tape, paper towels, tissues, water

What to do
1. Show the children the first of Lindsay Barrett George's illustrations of Long Pond, pointing out how the mist rises from the pond's surface.
2. Tape the watercolor paper to a flat surface.
3. Demonstrate how to wet the watercolor paper lightly by loading water into a brush and swishing it over the paper, then drying the paper with paper towels to leave a slightly damp surface.
4. On a scrap of watercolor paper, paint some watercolors. Show the children how to crumple tissue and paper towels and lightly touch these to the surface of the watercolor paper. The paint will be absorbed, leaving a whiter, lighter area with some color showing.
5. Let the children experiment with these techniques, then encourage them to paint their own misty morning landscapes. Allow the art to dry thoroughly.

Something to think about
Plan to leave the watercolors out for several days to encourage the children to experiment. Experimentation leads children to paint with more confidence and creativity.

STORY S-T-R-E-T-C-H-E-R

Cooking and Snack Time: Turtle's Grapes

What the children will learn
To decide their preferences in grapes

Materials you will need
White grapes, red grapes, black grapes, wild grapes (if possible), scissors, napkins, chalkboard, chalk

What to do
1. Have the snack helper wash the grapes and use the scissors to snip them into small bunches.
2. Print at the top of the chalkboard, "white," "red," and "black."
3. Ask each child to sample all three varieties of grapes and to mark his or her preference on the chalkboard by making a hash mark under the color.
4. Discuss the wild grapes that the box turtle eats, and look at the illustrations of the turtle at the grape vines.

Something to think about

Ask the produce manager in a supermarket which grapes are the most popular.

Science and Nature: Investigation Plots

What the children will learn

To sharpen their observation skills

Materials you will need

Yarn, notepads, pencils, paper bags

What to do

1. Before visiting a pond, talk with the children about how scientists gather information by observing and describing an area. If an area is too large to allow close observation of all the terrain, scientists observe smaller sections and generalize based upon these. Demonstrate for the children how to set up their investigation plots.
2. At the pond site, give each child a yard of yarn.
3. Have the child select a plot and mark it off by placing the yarn in a square on the ground.
4. Each child then observes everything within their marked-off area and takes field notes. Explain that field notes should contain a list or inventory of everything they see, sketches, and notes of what happens.
5. Have each child collect three specimens or objects to represent his or her plot, such as a blade of grass, a twig, a pebble, or loam.

Something to think about

Create a science display for the science center in the classroom using specimens collected during the visit to the pond.

Special Event: Visit to a Pond

What the children will learn

To explore a natural environment leaving little evidence that they have been there

Materials you will need

Field trip permission forms, transportation, volunteers, biodegradable garbage bags, old clothes

What to do

1. Arrange for a visit to a pond. Inquire at nature centers if you live in an urban area.

2. Get parents to sign the field trip permission forms and instruct them to have their children dress in old clothes.
3. Prepare the volunteers for their responsibilities by telling them what you hope the children will learn from the visit.
4. Talk with the children about the investigations planned and the behavior expected of them.
5. Take paper or biodegradable garbage bags and pick up any litter found at the site.

Note: Follow all appropriate safety precautions.

6. Consult ahead of time with the naturalist or the pond owner about any areas that are off-limits.
7. Mark out a trail or path so as not to disturb the grasses or other plants.
8. Plan for relaxation time to allow the children simply to enjoy being in a natural environment.

Something to think about

See www.gma.org/turtles for activities related to turtles.

Writing: Science Learning Log

What the children will learn

To synthesize information from reading, observing, and sharing data

Materials you will need

Field notes from observations, writing folders, pencils, colored pens, crayons, markers

What to do

1. Assemble small groups of children around the science display, and discuss the different ways they learned about life at a pond and what they learned.
2. Invite the children to look at the specimens in the science display to remind them of what they observed. For instance, one child might see the leaf she placed in the display and remember how the grubs dug further into the earth after the leaves that covered them were lifted.
3. Ask the children to write in their science learning logs what they learned from visiting the pond. Encourage the students to use their field notes and specimen samples and to talk with their friends.
4. Encourage the children to add illustrations.

Something to think about

Continue writing in learning logs to help children synthesize the information they acquire in each unit.

Turtle Summer: A Journal for My Daughter

By Mary Alice Monroe Photographs by Barbara J. Bergwerf, Illustrations by Lisa Downey

Turtle Summer
A Journal for My Daughter

Mary Alice Monroe
Barbara J. Bergwerf

Story Line

Turtle Summer: A Journal for My Daughter is a collection of photographs and a narrative that tells about a mother and daughter who volunteer to patrol the beaches for signs of loggerhead turtles nesting. The beautiful photographs capture the action of the book, as well as common shorebirds, shells, and actual turtle eggs. The illustrations serve as beautiful backgrounds and emphasize key points. The text offers factual information about turtles, including suggestions on how to protect them. Also, photos of turtle rescues, special shells, and the mother-daughter team may move the listeners to want to volunteer for the turtle patrol. The book is excellent for sharing with a class, but individual children can also learn a lot by looking at its photographs and illustrations.

Read-Aloud Presentation

Talk with the children about their study of turtles. In *Look Out for Turtles!* and *Box Turtle at Long Pond*, the turtles live on land and in the pond. In the book *Turtle Summer*, a mother and daughter are protecting turtles that live in the sea but that lay their eggs on the beach. Talk with the children about this author and her daughter volunteering to do work at the beach as they patrol for signs of loggerhead turtles. Ask the children to listen for interesting facts about protecting the turtles. After reading the book, place it in a science display on turtles for children to see on their own.

STORY S-T-R-E-T-C-H-E-R

Art: Designing Our Volunteer Badges

What the children will learn

To associate badges as ways to identify special causes and to know a person's interests

Materials you will need

Badge maker (if available), pencils, markers, laminator, pins

What to do

1. Look at the "Turtle Rescue" badge and the "Aquarium Member" badge in the book.
2. Ask the children to design badges they would wear that have something to do with turtles or another animal they want to protect.

Something to think about

Make the children's designs into real badges if you have a badge maker at your school or library. If not, let the children draw their designs, laminate them, and wear them for the time that you are studying turtles.

STORY S-T-R-E-T-C-H-E-R

Art: Sandy Beach Scenes

What the children will learn

To paint beach scenes using textured paint for the sandy beach

Materials you will need

Construction paper, glue, sand, tempera paints, saltshakers

What to do

1. Let the children draw beach scenes and paint them with tempera paints.
2. Demonstrate how to make a sandy texture by painting a sandy color for the beach, then sprinkling the sandy part with sand from a saltshaker.
3. Allow the art to dry flat so that the sand does not shake off.

Something to think about

After the children finish their sand paintings and leave the area, spray the paintings with hair spray to make the sand stay in place. Allow to dry overnight.

Mathematics: "Guesstimates" of 80–150

What the children will learn
To practice making estimates by guessing and counting to confirm

Materials you will need
Clear plastic pail or large glass jar, 150 golf balls or ping-pong balls, gift box or bag, small notepad

What to do
1. Read the part of the book that describes the nest of the loggerhead turtle as containing 80–150 eggs that are about the size of ping-pong balls.
2. Pour ping-pong or golf balls into a container, and let the children tell you when to stop. When they say, "Stop," let a child count the balls by counting aloud and placing the balls in a bag or box. Do this several times for the children to get a sense of the quantity.
3. Continue counting to 80 and stopping, and then to 150 and stopping.
4. Have each child write his or her name on a sheet of notepaper. Pour some golf balls in the pail or jar. Ask each child to guess how many golf balls are in the pail or jar and then write their individual guesses on their papers.
5. Count the number of eggs (balls) in the pail or jar. The child who comes closest to guessing the correct number gets to be the person who pours the next set of "eggs" the children will count.

Something to think about
The next day, place the ping-pong or golf balls with the supplies for the children to use independently.

Science: Sorting Shells

What the children will learn
To recognize and sort by similarities and differences

Materials you will need
Large collection of shells, shoeboxes or gift boxes, index cards, marker, tape or glue

What to do
1. Show the children the pictures of the shells found in *Turtle Summer*, and write the names of the shells on index cards: moon snail, mussel, ark, clam, lettered olive shell, tulip shells, knobbed whelk, oyster, jackknife clam, slipper, large cockle, southern sand dollar, sea star (also known as starfish), urchin, and angel wing shell.
2. Place the index cards on shoeboxes. Also tape or glue a sample shell on the box.
3. Let the children sort the shells into the appropriate boxes.

Something to think about
First graders will need fewer choices of shells. Vary the amount and the complexity of the sorting tasks by the ages and abilities of the students.

Writing: K-W-L Answers to Turtle Mysteries

What the children will learn
To use information in books to answer questions

Materials you will need
Chart tablet, markers

What to do
1. Have the children complete a K-W-L chart: what we *know,* what we *want* to know, and what we have *learned.* Have the children say what they know about turtles. Have five or six key facts in mind. If needed, refer back to *Box Turtle at Long Pond* or *Look Out for Turtles!*
2. Generate a list of five or more questions the children would like to know about turtles. Often their questions are about the size and weight, whether turtles bite, and where to see turtles.
3. Read *Turtle Summer* and answer their questions.
4. After reading the book, refer back to the children's questions and answer them for the "what we learned" completion of the chart. However, continue the "what we learned" chart with more than the answers to their initial questions.

Something to think about
Generating questions ahead of time gives purpose to children's listening and to their reading. Completing the K-W-L chart is a helpful classroom tool; it also can be used individually with older children.

References

Berger, Melvin. 1992. *Look Out For Turtles!* Illustrated by Megan Lloyd. New York: HarperCollins.

Bishop, Nic. 2008. *Frogs.* New York: Scholastic.

French, Vivian. 2003. *Growing Frogs.* Illustrated by Alison Bartlett. Somerville, MA: Candlewick.

George, William T. 1989. *Box Turtle at Long Pond.* Illustrated by Lindsay Barrett George. New York: HarperCollins.

Monroe, Mary Alice. 2007. *Turtle Summer: A Journal for My Daughter.* Photographs by Barbara Bergwerf. Illustrated by Lisa Downey. Mt. Pleasant, SC: Sylvan Dell.

Additional References

Chrustowski, Rick. 2003. *Hop Frog.* New York: Henry Holt. *Describes the life cycle of a leopard frog from tadpole to adulthood.*

Fleming, Denise. 1998. *In the Small, Small Pond.* New York: Henry Holt. *Illustrations and rhyming text describe the activities of animals living in and near a small pond as spring progresses to autumn.*

Katz, Avner. 1993. *Tortoise Solves a Problem.* New York: HarperCollins. *A classic Aesop's fable with a famous artist's illustrations.*

London, Jonathan. 1993. *Fire Race: A Karuk Coyote Tale.* Illustrated by Sylvia Long. San Francisco: Chronicle. *A folktale of how fire was brought to earth by different animals including Turtle.*

Parker, Nancy Winslow and Joan Richards Wright. 1990. *Frogs, Toads, Lizards, and Salamanders.* Illustrated by Nancy Winslow Parker. New York: Greenwillow. *Describes the physical characteristics, habits, and natural environment of a variety of frogs, toads, lizards, and salamanders.*

Robbins, Sandra. 2001. *How the Turtle Got Its Shell: An African Tale.* Illustrated by Iku Oseki. New York: See-Mores Workshop. *An African folktale with scenes appropriate for children's dramatics.*

Stevens, Janet. 1985. *The Tortoise and the Hare.* New York: Holiday House. *A classic Aesop's fable in an easy-to-read format.*

Websites

1. Frogland! AllAboutFrogs.org: www.allaboutfrogs.org
   - Everything frog: games, facts, news, art, etc.
   - Teachers' corner
   - Book reviews
2. All About Turtles: www.gma.org/turtles
   - Turtle defense
   - Exploring a pond
   - Turtle Species
3. All Turtles: www.allturtles.com
   - Videos and clip art
   - Turtle news from around the world
   - Ask a vet

Endangered Animals

Polar Bears

By Mark Newman

Story Line

Renowned wildlife photographer Mark Newman presents exquisite photographs of a mother bear and her cubs on land and in the water. The book presents basic science concepts for primary-age children. The main ideas appear in bold print as the opening statement on each two page spread of photographs. For instance, "Polar bears are big," is followed by descriptions of their size, but the next pages show tiny polar bear cubs, following the sentence, "Polar bears are tiny." Interesting facts are interwoven into the book as it describes the playfulness of the cub on the ice and in the ocean. Extra information is provided at the end of the book, "More Facts About Polar Bears," with lists of conservation organizations concerned about polar bears and their artic environment. The "Author's Note" provides insights into Mark Newman's work and his feelings about animals and photographing them. Newman's photographs have appeared in *Newsweek, National Geographic,* and *Life.*

Read–Aloud Presentation

Show the children the cover of the book and ask them where polar bears live. Some will know they live in the Arctic, near the North Pole. Call attention to the photos on the beginning pages before the text begins. Discuss who a photojournalist is and read some selected parts of the "Author's Note," which you can describe as a message to the reader. Show the endpaper pages with the baby polar bear in many playful positions. Point out the polar bear scientist dressed in a lab coat and glasses talking with children bundled up in warm coats and boots. Read the book through without pausing so that the flow of the story is continued. At the end of the reading, talk about the Arctic ice that is melting, and read some of the things that the children can do to help.

STORY S-T-R-E-T-C-H-E-R

Art: White on White and Pastels

What the children will learn

To illustrate Arctic ice and to use colored pencils effectively

Materials you will need

White construction paper, colored pencils

What to do

1. Look at Mark Newman's photographs and notice the white polar bear has some shading of brown that shows her fur. Notice the white ice with shades of blue shadows on one side. Notice that the ripples in the light blue water have darker blue lines that show movement.
2. Ask the children to use shading as they draw a mother polar bear and her cub and to show the habitat of the Arctic Ice.
3. Display the pictures in the classroom library or science center, along with the book for children to explore on their own.

Something to think about

Help the children learn how to use colored pencils to create the shading effect on the fur by holding the pencil on the side and slanting toward the paper. Practice making different kinds of strokes for lightness, darkness, and shading.

STORY S-T-R-E-T-C-H-E-R

Mathematics: Sizes, Heights, Weights, Distances, Numbers

What the children will learn

To note how numbers are used to describe polar bears, their cubs and the population

Materials you will need

Chalkboard and chalk, whiteboard and markers, or computer projector and screen

What to do

1. Reread the book and pause for each description that uses a number, such as "giant male weighs 1,700 pounds." Every page has some numerical amount noted.
2. After each numerical statement, write on the board or screen the number, such as "6," and a sentence in the

children's own words. For example, "The polar bear can swim at about six miles per hour," or "20,000 to 25,000 polar bears live in the Arctic."

Something to think about
Try some relative measurements, such as the height to the ceiling compared to the height of a male polar bear or the width of a dinner plate to help children understand the relative size of a grown bear's paw.

STORY S-T-R-E-T-C-H-E-R

Science: What Can We Do to Help the Polar Bears?

What the children will learn
To begin to understand that using less energy and recycling help save energy and thus help the polar bear

Materials you will need
Chart tablet, markers

What to do
1. Find the sentence, "Polar bears are endangered." Discuss the concept of climate change and melting ice.
2. Discuss how families can conserve energy so it is less necessary to get oil from the polar bears' territory.
3. Have the children compose some rules that will help the earth: Walk whenever possible. Recycle cans, bottles, and paper. Buy twisty light bulbs (compact fluorescent light bulbs). Use a fan or open a window instead of using the air conditioner. Put a sweater on instead of turning up the heat.

Something to think about
Help children recall what they learned in the thematic unit, "Recycle, Reuse, Repurpose." Connect the two units, "Endangered Animals" and "Recycle, Reuse, Repurpose."

STORY S-T-R-E-T-C-H-E-R

Social Studies: Where Is the Arctic?

What the children will learn
To locate the Arctic and the North Pole on a globe or map

Materials you will need
Globes or maps

What to do
1. Help the children use the globe or map to find the Arctic. The North Pole is there, but many globes and maps do not indicate it. Discuss the North Pole and the South Pole and the temperatures at each.
2. Introduce the concept of the equator, where the hottest temperatures are around the middle of the earth, and the North and South Poles, the Arctic and Antarctica, where the coldest temperatures are.
3. Discuss that polar bears only live in the Arctic, near the North Pole.

Something to think about
It is important when children encounter a problem that they think about what they can do so that we improve the environment. It is difficult for first and second graders to get these complex cause and effect relationships.

STORY S-T-R-E-T-C-H-E-R

Special Event: Polar Bears Also Live in Zoos

What the children will learn
To state observations and compare the book to the live animals

Materials you will need
Permission from parents, transportation, chaperones

What to do
1. Make all of the necessary arrangements required by your school or center for a field trip.
2. Go over the rules for the trip with the chaperones as well as the students.
3. Have the zoologist or zoo educator meet your bus and come on the bus to give instructions about the visit. See the Polar Bears exhibit first, if possible, so that the children will be fresh for the experience.
4. Ask to see any other endangered animals that may live at the zoo, including mammals, birds, even insects.

Something to think about
The excitement of new places and new sights takes children's energy. Be sure to plan lunch and snacks at the same time as your school schedule and to include frequent water and toileting breaks.

Sam the Sea Cow

By Francine Jacobs
Illustrated by Laura Kelly

Story Line

This four-chapter adventure tells the story of Sam the sea cow. The book is based on the true story of a sea cow (or manatee) that becomes stuck in a sewer pipe and is named Sam by the media. The story tells of Sam's life from the minutes after he is born up until he is ready to mate. Sam's adventures include an encounter with the blades of a motorboat, a rescue from the sewer pipe, a stay in a marine park, and his return to Crystal River in Florida. Additional factual information is provided about sea cows, as well as an address for the Save the Manatee Club. Laura Kelly's illustrations of plants, animals, insects, and manatees are well-matched to the text. The full-color pages make this small book easily shared with a large group of children.

Read–Aloud Presentation

Read the explanation at the back of the book of why Francine Jacobs was inspired to write this story. Show the front cover of the book and explain to the children that the sea cow is also called the manatee. Pause between each of the four chapters to let the children predict what will happen to Sam. After reading the entire book, ask the children to think about why these animals have become endangered. Announce the STORY S-T-R-E-T-C-H-E-R-S planned for *Sam the Sea Cow*. See the video on manatees at Defenders of Wildlife—Kids' Planet website, as well as the fact sheet: www.defenders.org/wildlife_and_habitat/wildlife/manatee.php.

STORY S-T-R-E-T-C-H-E-R

Art: Mural of *Sam the Sea Cow*

What the children will learn
To plan and create a cooperative art project

Materials you will need
Butcher paper, art materials, bulletin board, construction paper, stapler

What to do
1. With a group of eight children, plan a bulletin board for the hallway that will tell the story of *Sam the Sea Cow*.
2. Read the story again and plan a major scene for each of the four chapters. Let pairs of children work together, with each pair responsible for one chapter.
3. Each pair of artists makes a small sketch of what they want to do on a larger scale.
4. Divide the mural into five sections by drawing lines across the butcher paper. In the first section, print the title and author of the book.
5. Let each pair of artists create their section of the mural.
6. After the artists finish sketching and painting each section of the mural, staple the mural to the hallway bulletin board.

Something to think about
If younger children are working together, cut the sections of the butcher paper apart, then staple them back together after the children complete their work.

STORY S-T-R-E-T-C-H-E-R

Mathematics: Numbers Tell a Story

What the children will learn
To use numbers to represent the various parts of the story

Materials you will need
Large index cards, colored markers, hole punch, yarn

What to do
1. Distribute twelve index cards and markers to a small group of children.
2. Read *Sam the Sea Cow*. Each time the story mentions a number, have the children write that number on an index card.
3. After the story, have the children retell the story using the index cards as prompts.

4. Link the cards together by punching two holes in the top and in the bottom of each index card about an inch in from either side of the cards.
5. Thread yarn through the holes and tie the cards together so that they are aligned vertically.
6. Because they only need ten cards for the numbers, ask the children to draw a picture of Sam as a baby on the top card and as an adult on the bottom card.

Something to think about
With older students, continue adding numbers from the factual information provided at the end of the story.

STORY S-T-R-E-T-C-H-E-R

Science and Nature: Sam's Water Hyacinths

What the children will learn
To observe the growth patterns of water plants

Materials you will need
Aquarium or child's plastic swimming pool, water hyacinths, plant food

What to do
1. Visit a nursery and find specimens of water hyacinths.
2. Explain to the nursery owner or worker what you are trying to help the children understand.
3. Set up a water habitat for the hyacinths using an aquarium or a child's plastic swimming pool.
4. Maintain the plants and feed them as directed.
5. Observe the growth patterns and measure the changes every two to three days.
6. Ask the children to note in their science learning logs what they are learning.

Something to think about
If possible, visit a water garden or botanical garden that has water hyacinths and other plants that live in rivers, swamps, and marshy areas.

STORY S-T-R-E-T-C-H-E-R

Writing: Writing the News Report about Sam the Sea Cow

What the children will learn
To write a report using who, what, where, when, how

Materials you will need
Chalkboard and chalk or chart tablet paper and markers

What to do
1. With a small group of children in the writing area, pretend to be newspaper reporters who have heard about a manatee stuck in a sewer pipe. They must write an article with all the facts.
2. On the chalkboard or chart paper, print, "who," "what," "when," "where," "why," and "how."
3. Invite the children to write a newspaper article based on the story in the book about the manatee's becoming stuck, getting rescued, and being released.
4. As an alternative, let the children write their reports as if they were radio or television newscasters.

Something to think about
Consider having the children answer a list of questions using library reference books or Internet searches.

STORY S-T-R-E-T-C-H-E-R

Writing: Communicating with the Save the Manatee Club

What the children will learn
To write for information about what the club does to help the manatee

Materials you will need
Map of Florida, paper, pencil, envelope, postage

What to do
1. Show the children the address in the back of *Sam the Sea Cow* for the Save the Manatee Club.
2. Ask the children what they would want to know if they contacted the club, such as how much membership will cost, what the club does to protect the manatee, how much money the club raised last year, and what the children can do to help if they don't live near the manatees.
3. Compose one class letter asking these questions.
4. After the club receives your letter, they may send a brochure and catalog. Read this information with the students and think of additional questions the class would like to ask.
5. Call 1-800-432-JOIN and ask if someone would be willing to speak to the class by phone.
6. Place the call using a speakerphone, letting the children ask their questions.
7. Send a thank-you letter to the person with whom the class spoke. If funds are available, join the club.

Something to think about
If you live near an aquarium or natural preserve that cares for manatees, take the children to visit a manatee.

Whales

By Seymour Simon

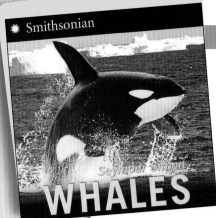

Story Line

Photographs of whales accompany text full of lively descriptions of the characteristics, habits, and natural habitats of different whales. Beginning with the humpback, Simon clears up common misconceptions about whales. He explains how they breathe and their identity as mammals and describes how scientists use the markings on flukes and tails to recognize individual whales. Additional information covers baby whales, nurturing of young, anatomy, and different kinds of whales. Simon writes about the sperm, narwhal, and orca, as well as the baleen whales like the right, gray, minke, blue, and humpback. The book concludes with information about the International Whaling Commission. Simon's photographs are magnificent and majestic as well as informative.

Read–Aloud Presentation

Ask the children to imagine that they are on a ship, when suddenly a huge humpback whale careens alongside, arching its entire body up above the water, falling back into a giant belly flop before sinking down below the waves. Show the children the cover photograph of *Whales*. Read the entire book, pausing for the children to look closely at every picture. Ask each child to identify one whale he or she would like to learn more about. Have the children write the names of these whales in their science learning logs.

Art: Photographic Display

What the children will learn

To mount a photographic display

Materials you will need

Tempera paints, brushes, butcher paper or colored bulletin board paper, scissors, pictures of whales from nature magazines and brochures, construction paper, glue, stapler

What to do

1. Have the children paint the ocean on white butcher paper or staple colored bulletin board paper to a bulletin board.
2. Cut pictures of whales from nature magazines and brochures.
3. Have the children cut black construction paper one-quarter to one-half inch larger than each of the whale pictures.
4. Mount the magazine pictures by gluing them onto the black construction paper.
5. Staple or glue the mounted pictures onto the ocean background.

Something to think about

Make a small label for each print, or number them and provide an identification key on a smaller poster. See also photographs of whales in the species section on whales and dolphins at the website for the World Wildlife Fund (www.worldwildlife.org/species).

Classroom Library: Finding Out More from Whale Books

What the children will learn

To locate additional information

Materials you will need

Reference books or other children's books on whales

What to do

1. Collect as many different books on whales as you can find. Try to include realistic fiction, fantastic, and factual books.

2. Leave the books on display in the classroom library for the children to browse through or to use when searching for information about the whale they select to study in more detail.

3. After the children have had a few days to read the books, have them stage a "read more" book report session. Several children can report on different books each day.

Something to think about

As an extension of this STORY S-T-R-E-T-C-H-E-R, compare the information found in realistic fiction, in fantastic books, and in factual books. Use Simon's *Whales* as the example of a factual book. You could use Joanne Ryder's *Winter Whale* as an example of a fantastic book and Judy Allen's *Whale* as an example of realistic fiction.

STORY S-T-R-E-T-C-H-E-R

Science and Nature: Amazing Facts Riddles

What the children will learn

To write riddles using facts

Materials you will need

Chalkboard and chalk or chart tablet paper and markers, large index cards

What to do

1. List all the different whales mentioned in Simon's *Whales*.

2. Form writing partnerships by assigning two children to work together to write about one kind of whale.

3. Have the writing partners read again about their particular whale, either in Simon's book or another from the class library.

4. Ask the partners to write a riddle card and an answer card about their whale. For example, on the riddle card, the partners could write, "Which kind of whale performs in marine parks?" On the answer card, they could write, "Orcas or killer whales perform in marine parks."

5. Mix up the cards and leave them in the science display area for the children to read and answer.

Something to think about

Let the writers make a riddle book, which can be bound and kept in the class library. The children can illustrate the book and provide the answers to their riddles at the back of the book.

STORY S-T-R-E-T-C-H-E-R

Social Studies: World of Whales

What the children will learn

To locate on a world map the places where the whales Simon describes have been seen

Materials you will need

World map, sticky notes, markers

What to do

1. As the children complete their writing in the writing center and their investigations in the library area, ask them to place sticky notes on the ocean locations where various whales have been spotted.

2. Print the name of the whale on the sticky note.

Something to think about

You can do this STORY S-T-R-E-T-C-H-E-R with first graders by reading *Whales* again, pausing to locate each place mentioned.

STORY S-T-R-E-T-C-H-E-R

Writing: Revisiting the Text for More Information

What the children will learn

That a book filled with information will need to be read more than once

Materials you will need

Writing paper, stapler, pencils, notebooks or file folders

What to do

1. Construct science learning logs by stapling writing paper in file folders or using notebooks. Ask a small group of children at the writing center which whales they selected at the end of the read-aloud presentation.

2. One child might say the orca or killer whale. Read just that section of *Whales*, then ask the child to write in the log what she or he wants to be sure to remember.

3. If the children are proficient readers, allow them to continue on their own, reading from *Whales* and writing what they want to recall. If they are less proficient, read the information to them or help them record it.

Something to think about

Ask every child to collect at least five specific facts about the whale they have chosen to study.

Giant Pandas in a Shrinking Forest: A Cause and Effect Investigation

By Kathy Allen

Story Line

The author uses photos of real pandas to answer frequently asked questions about the giant panda, such as where do giant pandas live? what do they eat? why is the giant panda in danger? what can be done to help the giant panda? The short chapters provide facts and explore the lives of giant pandas in the wild and in zoos and reserves. Also included are an excellent glossary of simple terms, which are in bold print throughout the book, and a table of some of the world's endangered animals. The author keeps the children's interest with well-selected facts and a pleasing narrative flow, while the photos are captivating.

Read-Aloud Presentation

Ask the children to name some of the animals they think are in danger. Someone will probably mention the panda. Before reading the book, tell the children you want to make a list of all the surprising facts they hear in the book. Read *Giant Pandas in a Shrinking Forest* and then have the children recall some significant facts. For children to explore the book on their own, place it in the science center or the library area with other books on endangered animals. See also the Giant Panda section of the website Kids' Planet (www.kidsplanet.org). Have children make a sound they think the Giant Panda would make and then play the audio from the website to surprise them.

Art: Black-and-White Pandas

What the children will learn
To use different media to create black-and-white prints

Materials you will need
White construction paper, black construction paper, glue sticks, scissors

What to do
1. Look at the photos of the pandas in *Giant Pandas in a Shrinking Forest*. Help the children to notice which parts of the panda are black and which parts are white.
2. The children can choose whether to make their background white or black, but let them draw their panda with a pencil and cut out the parts that are white and glue them onto a black background (or the parts that are black and glue them onto a white background).
3. After making their pandas, the children can sketch in the remaining parts of their pandas so that the picture feels complete.

Something to think about
For second and third graders, use swatches of black and white fabric and do the project. If available, furry fabric helps to add to the appeal of the art pandas.

Mathematics: How Many Giant Pandas Are Alive Today?

What the children will learn
To interpret simple graphs

Materials you will need
Graph paper, pen or marker

What to do
1. Read on page 4 that there are "only about 1,600 giant pandas in the wild." And, read on page 18 that "scientists are hoping to increase the wild panda population to 5,000 by 2025."
2. Have the children think about the difference between 5,000 and 1,600. Do a simple subtraction problem.

3. Demonstrate to children how to make and to read a graph showing the two points, 1,600 now and 5,000 by 2025.

Something to think about
Consider making graphs of all other comparisons, such as their age now and how old they will be in 2025.

STORY S-T-R-E-T-C-H-E-R

Reading: Panda Word Wall

What the children will learn
To read the words highlighted in the text and in the glossary

Materials you will need
Chalkboard, chalk, markers, scissors, poster board, optional—magnetic strips and magnets

What to do
1. Look through the book with the children and, when you encounter a term in bold, have a child write the word on the chalkboard.
2. From the eleven words highlighted in the book, select some that you want to emphasize, such as *endangered, habitat, extinction, captive and species.*
3. Make poster board strips of these words and let the children tell about the word in relationship to the facts or meaning in the book.
4. Display the poster board strips on a word wall for *Giant Panda*s *in the Shrinking Forest*

Something to think about
Create a word wall for the entire endangered animals unit. The compilation helps the children to recall the books from which they learned these words.

STORY S-T-R-E-T-C-H-E-R

Science: Favorite Facts About Pandas

What the children will learn
To add specificity to interesting information from the book

Materials you will need
Words from the word wall

What to do
1. Let the students choose a word from the word wall they made in the previous STORY S-T-R-E-T-C-H-E-R. Ask the children to talk about the word as a piece of information about the giant panda.

2. Refer back to the book and add specifics to the information. Help the children to understand that scientists use facts but they have to be precise.

Something to think about
Check other reference books on the giant panda to find more interesting facts to which the children can add specificity.

STORY S-T-R-E-T-C-H-E-R

Social Studies—Geography: Locating China

What the children will learn
To use a globe or map to locate a country

Materials you will need
Globe, map

What to do
1. Collect globes and maps from around the school.
2. From the map in the book, create a larger map of China by hand or using a photocopier, and point out the six reserves where the giant pandas live.
3. Help the students locate China on a globe and on a map.

Something to think about
If you have students whose parents have Chinese ancestry, ask them to show the children the places where their family lived in China and locate those on a map.

Will We Miss Them? Endangered Species

By Alexandra Wright
Illustrated by Marshall Peck III

Story Line

As a sixth grader in Countryside Elementary in Newton, Massachusetts, Alexandra Wright wrote *Will We Miss Them? Endangered Species*. She describes where endangered animals live, why they are vanishing, interesting facts, and special needs they have. The book includes information about the bald eagle, elephant, blue whale, panda, Galapagos tortoise, mountain lion, whooping crane, grizzly bear, manatee, muriqui, rhinoceros, mountain gorilla, and crocodile. The book also includes a world map showing habitats and a few encouraging words about protection of wildlife. Marshall Peck III's brightly colored illustrations in acrylic show animals in a variety of natural poses and native surroundings.

Read-Aloud Presentation

Engage the children in a discussion of the implications of the title, *Will We Miss Them? Endangered Species*. Lead the discussion into consideration of endangered species. Read *Will We Miss Them? Endangered Species*. Point out on the map the endangered animal species nearest your home. After reading the book, announce that it was written by the author when she was in the sixth grade. Turn to the back dust jacket cover, and read about Alexandra Wright and the illustrator, Marshall Peck III. For older primary children, see the World Wildlife website (www.worldwildlife.org/species) for podcasts from journalists around the globe.

STORY S-T-R-E-T-C-H-E-R

Art: Animal Cutouts

What the children will learn
To make a drawing using the most effective medium

Materials you will need
Assortment of art supplies, hair spray **(for adult use only)**, construction paper, poster board, scissors, stapler, hole punch, yarn or string

What to do
1. With the children who come to the art area, look at Marshall Peck III's illustrations. Ask the children which art medium they would choose to portray the different animals. For example, watercolor for a whale, because it swims under water, or colored pen for the whooping crane.
2. Let the children sketch or paint any animal using any medium or mix of media that they choose.
3. Ask the children to cut out the animals they have drawn or painted.
4. Glue or staple a small poster board tab at the top of each animal. Punch a hole in the poster board and thread yarn through it to make a loop.
5. Use the animal cutouts in the "Sorting by Habitat Bulletin Board" STORY S-T-R-E-T-C-H-E-R.

Something to think about
When the children are out of the classroom, finish charcoal and pastel chalk drawings by lightly spraying with hair spray to keep them from smudging.

STORY S-T-R-E-T-C-H-E-R

Classroom Library: Riddle Writers Write Animal Riddles

What the children will learn
To confirm their knowledge about animals

Materials you will need
Large index cards, markers

What to do
1. With a small group of children, write out riddles based on the information in *Will We Miss Them? Endangered Species*.

2. Create riddle cards and answer cards. Write a question on a riddle card. On an answer card, restate the question as an answer. For example, the riddle card might read, "What animal can spot small animals moving in a field a mile away?" The answer card could reply, "When bald eagles fly in search of their dinner, they can spot small animals moving in a field a mile away."

3. Leave the riddle cards in the classroom library with the endangered-animal books.

4. Ask the riddle writers to making riddle cards for all the endangered animals they have studied.

Something to think about

For younger children, make riddle puzzles by cutting the index cards into two puzzle shapes that fit together.

Science and Nature: Sorting by Habitat Bulletin Board

What the children will learn

To determine the habitats of endangered species

Materials you will need

Bulletin board, butcher paper, scissors, colored chalks, crayons, markers, animal cutouts from the art STORY S-T-R-E-T-C-H-E-R, push pins, small step stool

What to do

1. Staple butcher paper onto two bulletin boards.
2. On one bulletin board, use long, sweeping lines with colored chalk to create the six habitats: sky, flatland, mountains, cave, rocky seashore, and ocean.
3. On the second bulletin board, use long, sweeping lines with colored chalk to represent four habitats: rain forest, jungle, water hole, marshland.
4. Let the children color in the habitats with crayons and markers.
5. Place push pins into the habitats and the animal cutouts near the bulletin boards, so the children can place the animal cutouts in the habitats where they belong.
6. Encourage different choices: the bald eagle could be placed in the sky or in the trees near the mountains.

Something to think about

You do not have to be an artist to make these bulletin boards. Even faint lines will be sufficient to remind the children of the habitats that they are supposed to represent. The step stool allows the children to reach high enough to place the eagles in the sky and the muriqui near the top of the rain-forest canopy.

Science and Nature: Visiting a Zoo

What the children will learn

The role that zoos play in protecting species

Materials you will need

Transportation, field trip permission forms, volunteers

What to do

1. Arrange a class visit to the zoo by talking with the education director of the zoo ahead of time. Ask the education director to come to your class to talk before the visit, if possible, and also to greet the children on the day of the class visit.
2. Obtain maps of the zoo before the visit, and show the children the path the class plans to take through the zoo.
3. On the maps, mark the locations of endangered animals the children have studied.
4. Ask a parent volunteer who is a good photographer to take pictures of the endangered animals, or purchase slides at the gift shop. Ask another parent to take candid photographs of the children.

Something to think about

Prepare parent volunteers to supervise and interact educationally with the students. With first graders, plan to have one volunteer for every two children. With second and third graders, plan one volunteer per four children.

Writing: Writing Thank-You Letters to the Zoo

What the children will learn

To write a thank-you note and to express their feelings

Materials you will need

Construction paper, colored pencils, markers, large mailing envelope

What to do

1. Ask each child to fold a piece of construction paper in half, vertically or horizontally, to make a thank-you note.
2. On the outside, write and decorate the words, *Thank You*.
3. On the inside, ask the children to write their appreciation to the zoo for protecting animals from

extinction, for building a habitat, or for researching the best care of endangered species.

4. Somewhere on the note, ask the children to sketch one of their favorite animals.
5. Mail the thank-you notes in the large envelope to the education director of the zoo.

Something to think about

Older children can cut shapes in the construction paper and place their drawing of the animal inside the note, where it can be seen through the cutout.References

References

Allen, Kathy. 2011. *Giant Pandas in a Shrinking Forest*. Mankato, MN: Capstone Press.

Jacobs, Francine. 1979. *Sam the Sea Cow*. Illustrated by Laura Kelly. New York: Walker.

Newman, Mark. 2011. *Polar Bears*. New York: Henry Holt.

Simon, Seymour. 1989. *Whales*. Illustrated by Seymour Simon. New York: HarperCollins.

Wright, Alexandra. 1992. *Will We Miss Them? Endangered Species*. Illustrated by Marshall H. Peck III. Waterton, MA: Charlesbridge.

Additional References

Allen, Judy. 1992. *Whale*. Illustrated by Tudor Humphries. New York: Candlewick. *Realistic fictional story about the life of a whale in an ocean that has an oil slick.*

Caper, William. 2008. *Florida Panthers: Struggle for Survival*. New York: Bearport. *Children relive the inspiring and heroic efforts of people who stepped in to save Florida panthers when all seemed lost. Through this true tale of wildlife survival, children discover the bold and creative ideas that Americans and their government have used to protect and care for the country's endangered wildlife.*

Guiberson, Brenda. 2000. *Into the Sea*. Illustrated by Alix Berenzy. New York: Henry Holt. *Follows the life of a sea turtle from its hatching on a beach through its years in the sea and its return to land where it lays its eggs.*

Ryder, Joanne. 1991. *Winter Whale*. Illustrated by Michael Rothman. New York: Morrow. *A fantasy book of a child transformed into a humpback whale.*

Thomson, Sarah L. 2009. *Where Do Polar Bears Live?* Illustrated by Jason Chin. New York: HarperCollins. *This book not only offers interesting facts about polar bears, but also helps children begin to understand the changing environment.*

Websites

1. Endangered Species: www.endangeredspecie.com
   - Books on endangered species
   - Teachers' page
   - Kids' corner featuring games and reports written by students
2. World Wildlife Fund, Species, Protecting the Future of Nature: www.worldwildlife.org/species
   - Audio and video reports on species
   - Map finder of species' indigenous homes
   - Podcasts from journalists around the globe
3. Defenders of Wildlife: Kids' Planet: www.kidsplanet.org
   - Games and puzzles
   - Stories
   - Lessons for elementary students

Oceans

The Magic School Bus on the Ocean Floor

By Joanna Cole
Illustrated by Bruce Degen

Story Line

When Ms. Frizzle announces a class trip to the ocean, the children think she means a day at the beach, but Ms. Frizzle drives the Magic School Bus right into the sea. The class explores the intertidal zone (where the tide meets the shore), the continental shelf (where the land slants down and is covered by the ocean), the deep ocean floor (where little light reaches), and the coral reef before returning to shore. The Magic School Bus changes into a submarine, a submersible, a glass-bottomed boat, and a giant surfboard. When the children return, Ms. Frizzle's classroom has also transformed, becoming a giant science display that explains everything the children have learned. Readers will recognize Bruce Degen's trademark illustrations. The Cole-and-Degen combination is magical, and the mix of fact, humor, and fantasy makes this an excellent book with which to launch a study of the oceans. See an interview with author Joanna Cole at www.readingrockets.org/ books/interviews/cole in which she discusses the process of writing about Ms. Frizzle.

Read-Aloud Presentation

Recall with the children other *Magic School Bus* adventures, such as *The Magic School Bus at the Waterworks*, *The Magic School Bus Inside the Earth*, *The Magic School Bus Inside the Human Body*, and *The Magic School Bus Lost in the Solar System*. Ask the children what they like so much about the *Magic School Bus* books. Read *The Magic School Bus on the Ocean Floor* without pausing to read the children's written reports or the classroom charts on the sidebars. After reading, first let the children comment on the story, then ask everyone to write in their learning logs at least one amazing fact they learned.

Art: Factual Ocean Murals

What the children will learn
To present information in an aesthetically pleasing manner

Materials you will need
Butcher paper, stapler, masking tape, colored pencils, chalks, markers

What to do
1. With the children, decide on the subjects for a number of different ocean murals. Examples might include an ocean food chain, continental shelf, coral reef, or a favorite fish.
2. Talk with the students about making the information on the murals both accurate and aesthetically pleasing.
3. Cut table-length strips of butcher paper. Let the paper hang off the edge and tape it down to the.
4. Let teams of children work on each mural.
5. When the murals are complete, trim the edges and hang them around the room for the children to study.

Something to think about
For a related STORY S-T-R-E-T-C-H-E-R, create a Ms. Frizzle print using liquid embroidery paint or fabric paint to create an ocean scene on old T-shirts.

Art: Fish Mobiles and Balloons

What the children will learn
To improvise a three-dimensional representation

Materials you will need
Construction paper, tissue paper, newspaper, coat hangers, fishing line, tempera paints, brushes, balloons, markers, glue, tape, stapler, gift wrap ribbon

What to do
1. Look at the artistic representations of fish that Ms. Frizzle's students create.
2. Have the children brainstorm ways to portray fish.
3. Demonstrate how to make a fish mobile by cutting fish shapes from construction paper and gluing them around the edges, leaving a small opening through which crumpled newspaper can be stuffed.

4. Let the children also experiment with decorating the balloons to create jellyfish and octopi.
5. Create fish mobiles by stapling fishing line onto the construction paper fish and tying the line to a hanger.

Something to think about
Plan a huge Magic School Bus display by covering a bulletin board with yellow construction paper and inviting the children to decorate it.

Classroom Library: "I Have Always Wondered"

What the children will learn
To find answers to their questions

Materials you will need
Reference books on the ocean, chart tablet, marker

What to do
1. Begin by thinking aloud. For example, say, "I have always wondered why the sea is salty."
2. Ask the children to think of questions they have always wondered about and write them on chart tablet paper.
3. Find answers in the margins of each page of the book, where the reports and charts made by Ms. Frizzle's class are printed. Search for other answers in books read as a part of this unit and in reference books.
4. Begin another chart of "Amazing Facts," such as "Whale sharks are not whales."
5. Include a third set of questions, but instead of labeling them "Ms. Frizzle's questions," insert your name.

Something to think about
Ms. Frizzle's classroom offers an excellent example of the many ways children can investigate a topic. If you live near an ocean, plan a trip there, or visit a website about oceans. See photos from the Smithsonian National Zoological Park at www.nationalzoo.si.edu/Animals/OceanLiving/ForKids/default.cfm or the National Oceanic and Atmospheric Administration at http://oceanservice.noaa.gov/education.

Mathematics: Sorting Seashells and Coral

What the children will learn
To name and categorize seashells and coral

Materials you will need
Small baskets or boxes, many seashells and coral, index cards, markers

What to do
1. Help the children identify a number of seashells by comparing them to the drawings in *The Magic School Bus on the Ocean Floor*.
2. Ask the children to categorize the seashells by attributes such as size, shape, or color.

Something to think about
Older children may be able to categorize the seashells by whether the animals live in the intertidal zone, on the continental shelf, or on a coral reef.

Science Display: Salting the Water

What the children will learn
To create a three-dimensional display of different geological formations

Materials you will need
Empty aquarium, plastic pan or dish about twelve inches by twelve inches, two pounds of salt, spoons, pebbles, sand

What to do
1. To illustrate how salty most of the ocean is, fill a twelve-by-twelve-inch pan or dish with water. Let the children pour in two pounds of salt and taste the water.
2. Pour the salt water into the aquarium.
3. Let groups of children take turns creating geological formations in the aquarium by adding sand and pebbles. Encourage the groups to make their representations demonstrate that what looks like an island above the water is really a mountaintop. They can create the intertidal zone, the continental shelf, and the mountains and valleys of the deep ocean.

Something to think about
If resources are available, invite a pet store owner to help the children establish and monitor a salt water aquarium.

My Visit to the Aquarium

By Aliki

Story Line

With big brother and little sister, a boy visits an aquarium and observes a variety of fish and animals in their many environments. They include brightly colored fish in a tropical coral reef, seahorses and jellyfish in coastal waters, penguins in Antarctic waters, eels and schools of sardines in a giant kelp garden, sharks in cold open seas, and starfish and crabs in tidal pools. Near the rain forest, they notice piranhas, while in freshwater they see perch, catfish, turtles, and alligators. In coastal waters, they see bluefish and bass with salmon migrating to freshwater. In the beach environment, the children notice birds and shells, while in a bay environment there are seals and otters. This is a great book to introduce children to aquariums, with detailed watercolor illustrations and labels that help children see the creatures mentioned in the text.

Read-Aloud Presentation

Select five of the more unusually named fish and animals, such as leopard shark, parrot fish, wolf eel, longnose gar, and beluga whale. Have the children listen when those fish and animals are mentioned and to raise one finger when they hear the first one, two fingers for the second one, three fingers for the third, four fingers for the fourth, and five fingers for the fifth. At the end of the reading, ask several children which pictures they would like to see again. Place the book in the library corner of the room or in the science display on oceans, and let the children read the book on their own. See the live cameras in exhibits at the website for the National Zoo (www.nationalzoo.si.edu).

Art: Watercolor Environments

What the children will learn

To use watercolors to paint a variety of water environments

Materials you will need

Watercolors, variety of sizes of brushes, scrap paper, watercolor paper, tape

What to do

1. Ask the children to decide which environment they want to paint in their watercolor picture: the coral reef, coastal waters, Arctic waters, kelp gardens, open sea, or tidal pools.
2. After they identify their environments, show pictures for Aliki's *My Visit to the Aquarium,* and help children notice the predominant colors used in the backgrounds and those used for the details of the fish.
3. Allow children time to experiment with the watercolors on scraps of paper before taping down watercolor art paper onto tables or desktops.
4. Consider having one group of painters paint at the end of each day until there are at least the five scenes that represent ocean environments.

Something to think about

Create a display of a large class mural depicting an ocean theme. *My Visit to the Aquarium* also contains environments that are freshwater rivers and streams, which can be an extension of the study of oceans.

Movement: Mimicking Movements of the Fish

What the children will learn

To demonstrate the types of movement suggested by the words in the text

Materials you will need

Chart tablet, markers

What to do

1. Read the words or phrases from the book that suggest movement and write them on the chart tablet, such as *hiding, poking around, puffed up, waddling, swimming*

close together in circles, chasing, swarming, slid behind rocks, darted up, floating, and *zoomed past.*

2. Read the words or phrases together.
3. Let different children show what these movements might look like.
4. Have the children create their own space by measuring arms' lengths away from each other, then read out the movement phrases in random order from the chart and have the students move in the ways the words suggest.

Something to think about
Write the names of fish on the chart, and let the children demonstrate how these ocean and coastal creatures move.

STORY S-T-R-E-T-C-H-E-R

Mathematics: Aliki's Fish

What the children will learn
To count, compare, and record their results

Materials you will need
Multiple copies of the book, if possible, chalkboard and chalk or whiteboard and markers

What to do
1. Count all of the fish on the cover of Aliki's *My Visit to the Aquarium.*
2. Write the number on the board.
3. Designate groups of three children, with one as the counter, one as the checker, and one as the recorder.
4. Assign each group a different page and have them count, check, and record on the board the number of fish on their pages.
5. At the end of the exercise, answer the question, "How many fish did Aliki paint in her book?"

Something to think about
Do the exercise on a different day using shells, birds, or other animals instead of fish.

STORY S-T-R-E-T-C-H-E-R

Science: Naming the Environments

What the children will learn
To associate the type of ocean environment with the fish, animals, or birds found there

Materials you will need
Multiple copies of the book, chalkboard and chalk or whiteboard and markers

What to do
1. Select a few passages from the book that describe the different ocean environments that the children saw in their visit to the aquarium.
2. Notice the different fish and animals that were there.
3. Place the names of some of the fish on the board, and let the children select the appropriate environment. For example, sharks in cold open water, penguins in the Antarctic, seals in the harbor, parrot fish in the coral reef, eels in the kelp garden, and so on.

Something to think about
Let the children devise their own matching game. Have them draw a fish or animal on an index card, write the name of the environment on other cards, and then match the cards.

STORY S-T-R-E-T-C-H-E-R

Science: Visiting an Ocean Aquarium

What the children will learn
To observe the ocean environments and inhabitants in the aquarium

Materials you will need
Permission from parents or guardians, transportation, staff and parent assistants

What to do
1. After securing the permission and making plans to adequately staff the visit, talk with the curator or director of the aquarium to explain the interests and ages of your students.
2. Visit the aquarium in advance to decide how much time you will spend at each exhibit or display. Do not rush.
3. Plan for an aquarium worker to describe what he or she does at the aquarium and discuss how he or she learned to do that job.
4. After the trip to the aquarium, invite the children to reflect on it by drawing pictures or writing observations in their science notebooks.

Something to think about
It is important to discuss the dangers to marine life. Use the last page of the Aliki book to talk about environmental hazards to ocean life.

Alphabet of Ocean Animals

By Laura Gates Galvin
Illustrated by Steven James
Petruccio, Joanie Popeo,
Walter Stuart, Stephen Marchesi,
Katie Lee, Jon Weiman,
Bob Dacey, Debra Bandelin,
and Daniel Stegos

Alphabet of OCEAN ANIMALS

By Laura Gates Galvin | Illustrated by Steven James Petruccio, Joanie Popeo, Walter Stuart, Stephen Marchesi, Katie Lee, Jon Weiman, Bob Dacey, Debra Bandelin, and Daniel Stegos

Story Line

This information-rich resource book includes a recording, a glossary, and a poster of the alphabet letters and their corresponding ocean animals. Magnificently illustrated by the many artists listed above, there is a consistency of form and style. Key descriptive information is written in rhyming couplets. Each letter of the alphabet represents an animal or ocean habitat such as reef, ice floe, or kelp. Approved by the Smithsonian Institution's National Museum of Natural History, the interesting facts provide an excellent introduction to a unit on oceans.

Read–Aloud Presentation

Remove the poster from the back of the book and have the children recite the alphabet and try to identify as many of the pictures of the ocean animals that they can, such as *D* for dolphin and *S* for shark. As you read the book, let the children practice saying some of the words they may not know, such as *anemone, manatee, urchin,* and *xiphias gladius.* After reading the book, return to the poster and let the children try again to identify all the pictures.

STORY S-T-R-E-T-C-H-E-R

Art: Underwater Watercolors

What the children will learn
To use the medium of watercolors

Materials you will need
Watercolor paints, different sizes of brushes, scraps of construction paper and watercolor paper, masking tape, small containers, paper towels, water

What to do
1. Demonstrate for the children the different qualities of the watercolors when they are concentrated and when they are diluted by adding more water to the brush.
2. Help children in their experimenting with watercolors by letting them paint on scraps of paper to discover how much water and now much paint they want to load onto their brushes.
3. After the students' experimentation, tape sheets of watercolor paper onto tables or flat desktops.
4. Encourage children to paint underwater scenes like the ones seen in *Alphabet of Ocean Animals.*
5. Create a display of the watercolor paintings surrounding the poster from the book.

Something to think about
Watercolors take some time to dry. Consider painting at the end of the day so that the watercolor backgrounds can dry overnight. Then, let the children add their featured fish or ocean animal the next morning. Usually the watercolor backgrounds have more moisture or water in them and are done with larger brushes, while the featured fish will probably be painted with smaller brushes for more detail.

STORY S-T-R-E-T-C-H-E-R

Language Arts: Listening to the CD of *Alphabet of Ocean Animals*

What the children will learn
To follow along with the CD and the text

Materials you will need
CD player, optional—listening station

What to do
1. Assign some children the CD listening experience so that they can hear and practice following along.

2. Ask them to listen for certain purposes. For example, answer the questions, "Which fish is called a clownfish?" "Which fish has a powerful sting and swims near the beach?" Create a list of questions that move from the front of the book to the back.

Something to think about

Create a list of more comparative questions, such as "Which was the largest fish you heard about on the CD?" "Which was the smallest fish?" "Which was the hardest to pronounce?" "Which was the easiest to pronounce?" "Which was an ocean animal that you would like to see up close?" "Which is an ocean animal you would only like to see from a distance?"

Reading: Glossary

What the children will learn

To read the information found in the glossary and identify key words

Materials you will need

Numerous reprints of the glossary or one large one, highlighters

What to do

1. Choose some of the children's favorite ocean animals, such as dolphin, great white shark, humpback whale, and octopus.
2. Read aloud these selections from the glossary, and pick out the key words, such as *dolphin*—mammal, warm-blooded; *great white shark*—hunting, 4,800 pounds, eats anything; *humpback whale*—whale watches, dark gray or black, 60 feet long; *octopus*—cloud of ink, escape.
3. Complete the key word study for the remaining ocean animals listed in the glossary.

Something to think about

Construct a board matching game of the ocean animals and the key words associated with them, such as *octopus*—cloud of ink. The game can be made with poster board and magnetic tape.

Science: Further Research on Ocean Animals

What the children will learn

To use resource materials that help them learn more scientific facts

Materials you will need

Computer with internet access, library books

What to do

1. Search websites of local or regional aquariums, museums near oceans, and encyclopedia sites.
2. Check out additional reference materials from the school or community libraries.
3. Have the children use both the websites and the reference books to find out more about the ocean animals they selected.
4. Ask the students to write notes of the additional facts they learned about the ocean animal they researched.

Something to think about

Consider making a large display of the interesting facts the children located. Revisit the *Alphabet of Ocean Animals* glossary and help the children decide which information they would add to what is already available to them.

Writing: My Real or Imaginary Visit to the Ocean

What the children will learn

To incorporate information they have learned into their writing

Materials you will need

Chart tablet or whiteboard, markers, writing paper, pencils

What to do

1. Ask the children who have taken trips to the ocean talk about their experiences.
2. Discuss how this is a trip others may take someday, so they can imagine what their trip would be like.
3. Brainstorm some key words that the children will use in their writing, such as *beach*, weather words, names of shells and fish, and other ocean-related words.
4. Ask the children to write about a real trip or an imaginary trip to the ocean, but ask them to include at least three ocean animals in their story, with specific information they learned during their studies of oceans.

Something to think about

Have the children draw at least three pictures, one for the beginning of their story, one for the middle, and one for the ending. Then, they can write their stories in a sequence.

The Fantastic Undersea Life of Jacques Cousteau

By Dan Yaccarino

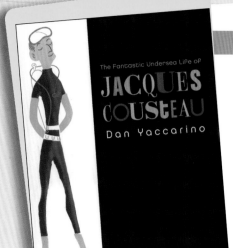

Story Line

Using gouache and an airbrush on watercolor paper, Yaccarino has written and illustrated a biography that is of interest to children who enjoy adventure and to their teachers and parents who would like to introduce children to great explorers. As an inventor, Jacques Cousteau devised diving equipment and waterproof cameras. He made documentaries and television shows and wrote books. In this book, his early life and the driving force behind his life's work are explored. In small bubbles, famous quotes of Cousteau's add to the text without taking away from the story. Yaccarino shares with primary-grade children Cousteau's love for the beauty and mystery of the undersea world.

Read-Aloud Presentation

Show the children the cover of the book, and ask if anyone can guess what Jacques Cousteau's job was. From the flippers and the air tank, some will guess a diver. Write the words, *diver, inventor, explorer,* and *oceanographer* on the board. Ask the children to listen for examples of each of these in the book. Read the book aloud, and after the reading let the children give examples associated with each word.

Art: Airbrushing Ocean Scenes

What the children will learn
To control liquid paints with airbrushes

Materials you will need
Watercolor paper, scraps of paper, watercolor paints, lunch trays, tape, brushes, airbrushes (or straws)

What to do
1. Demonstrate how to make watercolor pictures.
2. Tape the watercolor paper to a lunch tray so it is easy to turn.
3. Show the children the illustrations in *The Fantastic Undersea Life of Jacques Cousteau*. Notice the different colors of the undersea illustrations.
4. Let the children paint the backgrounds appropriate for an underwater scene, and allow the art to dry overnight.
5. Demonstrate how to use an airbrush filled with a small amount of paint. Allow the children to experiment on scraps of paper.
6. If airbrushes are not available, use drinking straws and let the children place paint on their papers and blow through the straw to create an effect of spraying water.

Something to think about
If the art teacher does not have an airbrush, contact a cosmetologist or theater actors, who often have airbrushes that they use with makeup.

STORY S-T-R-E-T-C-H-E-R

Reading: Famous Cousteau Sayings

What the children will learn
To read and interpret the meanings of Cousteau's sayings

Materials you will need
Round pizza pan, different colors of paper, scissors, markers, tape

What to do
1. Using the pizza pan as a pattern, cut colored paper into circles.
2. Have a small group of children find all the Cousteau sayings Yaccarino has scattered throughout the undersea illustrations and write them on separate sheets of paper.

3. Display the Cousteau sayings in the classroom. Every day, discuss one or two of the sayings with the children. Arrange the sayings in the same order as those in the book, starting with "The sea, once it casts its spell, holds one in its net of wonder forever," which describes Cousteau's early fascination with the sea. The last saying is, "If we were logical, the future would be bleak indeed. But we are more than logical. We are human beings, and we have faith, and we have hope, and we can work." The last quote reflects Cousteau's concern about pollution.

Something to think about
Do not be concerned if primary-age children do not get the full meaning of these famous sayings. Often they understand at one level, but they may lack the expressive capabilities or the logic to express their views of these abstract but worthy concepts.

STORY S-T-R-E-T-C-H-E-R

Science: Goggles, Snorkels, and Diving Equipment

What the children will Learn
To identify different types of diving equipment

Materials you will need
Goggles, snorkels, diving air tank, mouth piece, children's plastic pool, plastic toys

What to do
1. Invite a diver or a diving-equipment store owner to the class.
2. Ask the diver to explain the equipment.
3. Let children try on the goggles, snorkels, and diving equipment.
4. Float different plastic toys in the swimming pool and let the children look through the devices at the toys.

Something to think about
Emphasize the importance of safety even in small pools, as young children can drown in a small amount of water.

STORY S-T-R-E-T-C-H-E-R

Social Studies: Mapping Jacques Cousteau's Adventures

What the children will learn
To locate some of the oceans and seas that Cousteau explored

Materials you will need
Large world map or large globe, sticky notes, scissors, push pins

What to do
1. Read again the parts of the book mentioning the Mediterranean Sea and Antarctic Ocean. Locate these on a map or globe.
2. Find the names of other seas and oceans on the map.
3. Read reference books to see if Cousteau explored those bodies of water.
4. Cut small *Calypso* boat shapes from sticky notes, and ask the children to place the boat shapes on the map or globe for each sea or ocean that Cousteau explored.

Something to think about
With first graders, simply reading this book and finding the seas on a map is sufficient. As they read other Cousteau reference materials, help second and third graders to find other locations. Since Cousteau wrote fifty books, two encyclopedias, and made films and television shows, we know he explored almost every sea and ocean on earth.

STORY S-T-R-E-T-C-H-E-R

Writing: *Diving Saucer, Sea Flea, Calypso*

What the children will learn
To imagine the adventure of being inside the devices and on the ship

Materials you will need
Writing paper, pencils, drawing paper, choice of markers, colored pencils, crayons

What to do
1. Reread the section of the book in which Yaccarino describes the *Diving Saucer*, the *Sea Flea*, and the *Calypso*.
2. Ask the children to imagine what each of these was like and to draw sketches of them.
3. Brainstorm what it must have looked like inside the *Diving Saucer* and what a conversation between two people might have been like in the *Diving Saucer*.
4. Have the children write about an adventure on any of the three ships.

Something to think about
The children's adventure stories could lend themselves well to dramatization.

Ibis: A True Whale Story

By John Himmelman

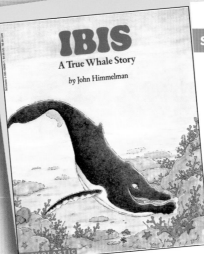

Story Line

Ibis is a story based on real events that happened to a humpback whale calf that lived near a fishing village. Ibis and Blizzard, two whales, like looking at little fish, particularly the starfish. Friendly whale-watching boats cause the whales to lose their fear of all boats and ships. Unfortunately, one boat brings a fishing net, and Ibis is entangled. With the net wrapped around her mouth, she cannot eat and does not respond to her friend Blizzard's approaches. Blizzard, knowing something is wrong, pushes Ibis's body to the surface where whale watchers find a way to rescue her. Ibis responds to the humans wiggling their fingers in the water because it reminds her of starfish. John Himmelman's watercolor-and-ink drawings accurately capture the mood of the book.

Read-Aloud Presentation

Show the cover of *Ibis: A True Whale Story* and read the book. Also read the afterword, where John Himmelman tells about the origin of the story. Based on Himmelman's account in the afterword, discuss what in the story is fact and what is fiction. It is fact that Ibis the whale was entangled in the nets and that the whale watchers rescued her. We do not know if she really thought about starfish or wished for Blizzard to play with her. The story is based in truth but has some parts we cannot prove. This is one of the books that the children will want you to read again because it evokes such sympathetic feelings and a sense of triumph when Ibis is rescued.

STORY S-T-R-E-T-C-H-E-R

Art: Underwater/ Overwater Scenes

What the children will learn
To show different views

Materials you will need
Pencils, paper, watercolors, margarine tubs with water, and brushes, or colored pencils

What to do
1. Look again at John Himmelman's illustrations in *Ibis: A True Whale Story.* Have the children notice the way they can see part of Ibis above the water and part below the water.
2. Encourage the children to experiment with drawing whales and the hulls of boats above and below the water line.
3. When the children have finished their underwater/overwater scenes, display the art in the library area with the book jacket from *Ibis: A True Whale Story.*

Something to think about
For younger children, let them fold their papers horizontally. On the top half, ask them to draw what appears above the water, using the fold as the water line. On the bottom half, the children can draw the parts of their pictures that would be under water.

STORY S-T-R-E-T-C-H-E-R

Classroom Library: Story Retelling

What the children will learn
To retell the story in their own words

Materials you will need
Paper bag, scraps of paper, pencil, optional—CDs and CD recorder or tapes and tape recorder

What to do
1. With a group of five children, look through the illustrations of *Ibis: A True Whale Story,* and let the children recall what was happening in each scene.
2. Ask the children to retell the story.
3. Print the numbers *1, 2, 3, 4,* and *5* on scraps of paper. Place the numbers in a paper bag and have the children draw out a number. That is the order in which the children will take turns telling the story.

4. Let the children sit in that order around you. Pass the book from person to person, or select one child to hold the book.

5. If the children are interested, let them retell the story and record it.

Something to think about
Books with powerful themes and a sense of suspense are excellent choices for story retelling.

STORY S-T-R-E-T-C-H-E-R

Music and Movement: Writing a Song for Ibis

What the children will learn
To write a song that tells a story

Materials you will need
Chart tablet, marker, optional—recording of whale sounds

What to do
1. If you can get a recording of whale songs, play it for the children. Discuss how different sounds communicate different needs.

2. Ask the children to write a song telling the story of Ibis. Write it to a familiar tune such as "Row, Row, Row Your Boat." Sing:

> Row, row, row your boat
> Out to see the whales.
> Merrily, merrily, merrily,
> There a big whale blows.
> (See page 236 in the Appendix for more verses.)

3. Print the words on chart tablet paper.

4. Record the song on the flip side of the tape with the recording of *Ibis: A True Whale Story* from the Story Retelling activity.

Something to think about
If your school has a music teacher, ask the teacher to play the tune on the piano, write in the appropriate musical notes near the words of the song on the chart paper, and teach the song to other classes.

STORY S-T-R-E-T-C-H-E-R

Science and Nature: Like Ibis, Different from Ibis

What the children will learn
To compare other whales to Ibis the humpback

Materials you will need
Reference books on whales, charts or pictures of whales if possible, chart tablet or poster board, marker

What to do
1. The story of Ibis will undoubtedly generate more interest in whales. Send a small group of children, "reference checkers," to the school library, and have them tell the librarian about the Ibis book and the class's interest in whales.

2. Let the librarian collect an array of reference books, charts, and pictures, and have the reference checkers decide which books would be most helpful to the class.

3. Place the books on display along with *Ibis: A True Whale Story* in the science and nature center.

4. After the children have had some time to learn more about whales, discuss what they learned, including the similarities and differences. Help the children see how scientists studying a species begin to classify the different subspecies.

5. Draw a line down the center of the chart. On one side print, "Like Ibis," on the other side write, "Different from Ibis."

6. Ask the children to compare other whales to Ibis according to what they have read and seen in the reference books on whales. Write their comparisons on the chart.

Something to think about
Let the children continue their studies by looking at dolphins and sharks. Younger children can compare dolphins, sharks, and whales, rather than trying to discern similarities and differences among whales.

STORY S-T-R-E-T-C-H-E-R

Writing: Inquiring About Rescues

What the children will learn
To compose group letters asking questions

Materials you will need
Chalkboard and chalk or chart tablet and marker

What to do
1. Reread the afterword from *Ibis: A True Whale Story*, in which the author tells about the work of the Center for Coastal Studies in Provincetown, Massachusetts.

2. Have the children think of questions they would like to ask the people who work there. For example, "Have they ever rescued any other whales?" "Did Ibis go back to that sea?"

3. After the children have thought of questions, form small groups and work with each group on composing a letter to the director of the center.
4. If interested, request any additional materials about the work of their center.
5. Mail the letters to Provincetown Center for Coastal Studies, 115 Bradford Street, Provincetown, MA 02657.

Something to think about

If you live near a coastal area, find out about any sea life rescue efforts in your area, and contact them instead of the Provincetown Center.

References

Aliki. 1993. *My Visit to the Aquarium*. New York: HarperCollins.

Cole, Joanna. 1992. *The Magic School Bus on the Ocean Floor*. Illustrated by Bruce Degen. New York: Scholastic.

Galvin, Laura. 2007. *Alphabet of Ocean Animals (Smithsonian Institute Series)*. Illustrated by Steve James Petruccio, Joanie Popeo, Walter Stuart, Stephen Marchesi, Katie Lee, Jon Weiman, Bob Dacey, Debra Bandelin, and Daniel Stegos. Norwalk, CT: Soundprints.

Himmelman, John. 1990. *Ibis: A True Whale Story*. New York: Scholastic.

Yaccarino, Dan. 2009. *The Fantastic Undersea Life of Jacques Cousteau*. New York: Random House.

Additional References

Koch, Michelle. 1993. *World Water Watch*. New York: Greenwillow. *Briefly describes some of the dangers caused mainly by humans for such animals as otters, sea turtles, seals, penguins, polar bears, and whales.*

Kranking, Kathleen W. 2003. *The Ocean Is*. Photographs by Norbert Wu. New York: Henry Holt. *The reader is invited on an underwater tour of the ocean to view the varied plant and animal life there.*

Lauber, Patricia. 1990. *An Octopus Is Amazing*. Illustrated by Holly Keller. New York: HarperCollins. *An introduction to one of the curiosities of the sea: the multitentacled, highly intelligent octopus.*

Websites

1. National Oceanic and Atmospheric Administration: http://oceanservice.noaa.gov/education
   - Ocean-themed mystery games
   - Lesson plan library
   - Links to ocean-themed activities
2. Smithsonian National Zoological Park: www.nationalzoo.si.edu/Animals/OceanLiving/ForKids/default.cfm
   - Ocean animal fact sheets
   - Jigsaw puzzles and other games
3. Reading Rockets: www.readingrockets.org/books/interviews
   - Video interviews of children's book authors
   - Lists of books by theme
   - ABCs of Teaching Reading

Birds

Unbeatable Beaks

By Stephen R. Swinburne,
Illustrated by Joan Paley

Story Line

The beautifully and boldly illustrated book is a superb way to introduce children to a variety of birds and help them to appreciate the ways birds use their beaks. Swinburne has written a rhyming poem with couplets on each page, and Paley has illustrated the pages brightly using a collage approach. Each bird is identified in large print. The book is excellent for sharing with a group of children. It includes a matching game with answer key at the back and a glossary with a brief description of each bird, its beak, food, and geographic area.

Read-Aloud Presentation

Show the children the cover of the book and have them describe what is happening—the mother bird is holding out a bug to give to three hungry baby birds in a nest. Encourage the children to make the association that birds have to use their beaks like we use our hands: How do flickers build their nests? How do robins dig for worms? How do woodpeckers get bugs from under the bark of trees? How do hummingbirds sip nectar from a flower? How do toucans crack nuts? Read the book and show the pictures for each page.

STORY S-T-R-E-T-C-H-E-R

Art: Colorful Collages of Birds

What the children will learn
To create pictures using torn and cut pieces of paper to add texture and contrast

Materials you will need
Scraps of brightly colored construction paper, black and white paper, scissors, glue, pencils

What to do
1. Look again at the pictures created by illustrator, Joan Paley, for *Unbeatable Beaks*. Notice the brightly colored birds and bold backgrounds.
2. Ask each child to draw an outline of a large bird on brightly colored construction paper. Their drawing should cover most of the page.
3. Demonstrate for the children how to cut and tear paper and use it to fill their bird shapes.
4. After the children glue the paper pieces in place, leave the art lying flat until the glue is dry.

Something to think about
Children often learn to draw birds by simply making large *V*s in the sky; therefore, you may have to refer to the cover of the book for children to get the size perspective for their collages.

STORY S-T-R-E-T-C-H-E-R

Reading: Finding Out More from a Glossary

What the children will learn
To use a glossary

Materials you will need
Copies of the glossary, chalkboard, chalk

What to do
1. Have the children name several of their favorite birds from the book. Write the names of the birds the children mention and emphasize the first letter of each bird name.
2. Distribute a copy of the glossary to each child, or point out their favorite birds on the list. Lead them to notice that the glossary is an alphabetized list with some additional information, but the list includes more of the birds' names than children are used to using, such as *Brown pelican* instead of just *pelican*.
3. Read or let the children read aloud some of the descriptions of their favorite birds.

Something to think about
For younger primary-grade children, demonstrate the use of the glossary by asking questions, such as, "I want to

find out more about flamingoes. Where do I find out more about them?" Lead the children to the listing for *Greater Flamingo* in the glossary.

STORY S-T-R-E-T-C-H-E-R

Reading: Unusual Birds Research

What the children will learn
To use reference resources

Materials you will need
Computer with internet access or library books about birds

What to do
1. Select a bird from *Unbeatable Beaks* that lives in a habitat near you, or one the students may have seen at a zoo. Show the picture of the bird, and then read about it in the book and from the glossary.
2. Ask the children how they could find out more about the bird if they wanted even more information.
3. Conduct an Internet search, and read from one of the sources that is appropriate for children. If you have a computer with a projector, show the children the steps.
4. Compare the information found on the Internet with information in a library or classroom book on birds.

Something to think about
Using the computer versus using books is a debate in elementary education. We prefer to use both so children become proficient in the use of a variety of sources.

STORY S-T-R-E-T-C-H-E-R

Science: Amazing Facts About Birds

What the children will learn
To learn a new amazing fact to share with the class

Materials you will need
Collection of bird books for the science center or the classroom library, large index cards, hole punch, pencils, markers, yarn or string or twist ties

What to do
1. Punch a hole in the middle of one of the short sides of each index card.
2. Let each child select a bird with an unusual beak, and write the name of that bird on his or her index card.
3. Read about the bird in the glossary of *Unbeatable Beaks* and from one other book.

4. Have each child find out an "amazing fact" about the bird and write the fact on the index card.
5. Distribute a second index card and marker to each child and allow the children to draw their birds.
6. Using yarn, string, or a twist tie, connect the two cards so that when they are opened the bird drawing and the amazing fact are facing each other.

Something to think about
Display the index cards in the classroom library or in the science center. Encourage the children to read each other's "Amazing Facts about Birds" cards and to consider their cards as another reference source.

STORY S-T-R-E-T-C-H-E-R

Writing: Write to the National Audubon Society

What the children will learn
To compose a group letter or e-mail requesting materials

Materials you will need
Chalkboard and chalk or computer with projector, markers, paper

What to do
1. Talk about the fact that the National Audubon Society was founded in honor of John James Audubon, a naturalist who drew birds. The National Audubon Society has materials for teachers and children.
2. Suggest that as a class you compose a letter or e-mail to the National Audubon Society to find out special projects children can be involved in to protect birds.
3. With the children's ideas in mind, begin composing a letter on the computer or on the chalkboard. Let the children make suggestions while you are composing.
4. Edit the finished letter or e-mail, crossing out and adding words or phrases as well as adding information about the class.
5. Print the finished letter or e-mail and send it to the National Audubon Society, 225 Varick St., New York, NY 10014.

Something to think about
Contact the wildlife authorities for your state and ask for materials written for primary grades.

White Owl, Barn Owl

By Nicola Davies
Illustrated by
Michael Foreman

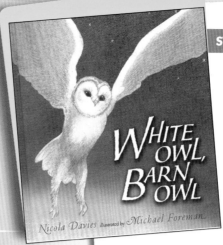

Story Line

A little girl tells the story of helping her Grandpa build a special box and then accompanying him on his search for a barn owl to inhabit it. Their adventure includes looking for signs of owls, waiting patiently after sunset, and making owl sounds. Factual information appears both in the little girl's observations and in additional, smaller print. The detailed watercolor and pastel illustrations set a soothing tone. A CD accompanies the 2009 edition.

Read-Aloud Presentation

Show the children the beginning page of *White Owl, Barn Owl* with the child and her Grandpa. Have the children make guesses about the structure the two are carrying. Then, show the children the cover of the book and read the title. Let them predict what might happen in the story. Expect some winces when Grandpa tells the little girl that the barn owl pellets are tiny bones and fur from mice the owl has eaten. Change your voice to one of anticipation as Grandpa and the little girl wait for an owl to appear. Whisper when the child describes the owl fluttering down to a branch and a tiny feather drifting down, and for their discovery of the baby owls. Place the book in the science center for the children to explore on their own. See the Audubon website (web4.audubon.org/educate/kids) for information and for a live camera view of a barn owl.

Art: Feather Painting

What the children will learn
To draw a bird using feathering strokes

Materials you will need
Prints of owls or those from the book, drawing paper and scraps, pencils, colored pencils, crayons

What to do
1. Let the children look at the prints of owls and then draw an owl or any other bird that interests them.
2. Help the children notice the feathers and the ways that Michael Foreman, the illustrator, used soft strokes to show the delicate feathers.
3. Have the children experiment with the feathering technique, as well as with some darker shading.
4. After some practice, ask the children to draw another owl or one of their favorite scenes from the book.

Something to think about
Often teachers move on to the next art project without allowing children ample time to practice new techniques. Encourage children by giving specific compliments for the feathering techniques, but also allow them to draw pictures of birds at more than one session.

Classroom Library: Read More About Owls

What the children will learn
To compare information found in two sources

Materials you will need
Copy of *White Owl, Barn Owl* and an owl reference book, such as *Owls* by Adrienne Mason, chart tablet and marker or chalk and chalkboard

What to do
1. Recall some of the interesting facts about owls from *White Owl, Barn Owl*. Write the facts on a chart for easy reference for the class.
2. Read *Owls* by Adrienne Mason or another reference book about owls. Show children the table of contents. Enlarge it for a larger group. Compare the table of contents in *Owls* to the index in *White Owl, Barn Owl*.

3. Add to your chart of new information at least one fact learned from this new source.
4. Place the two books in the classroom library for children to explore on their own.

Something to think about
Young children may be able to find only one or two facts and may become overwhelmed by the amount of information. Help the children by asking them to find one fact about size, or nests, or another type of owl, such as the elf owl. Some second graders and third graders should be able to decide what they want to know and look for it in the two texts.

STORY S-T-R-E-T-C-H-E-R

Reading: Facts with a Story

What the children will learn
To read accompanying print for facts

Materials you will need
Chart tablet and markers or computer with projector screen

What to do
1. Read some of the print that is in a smaller and different print type from the illustrations on facing pages.
2. Add these facts to a chart.
3. Read the story again, and ask the children to listen for information that is provided in the story as well as in the fact notes.
4. Place a check mark by each fact from your chart when it is heard in the story.

Something to think about
Children will become better listeners when they have a tool for thinking about a story, such as the fact chart. However, it is best to read the original story straight through for the first hearing.

STORY S-T-R-E-T-C-H-E-R

Reading: Using an Index

What the children will learn
To use an index to find information from a book

Materials you will need
Enlargements of last page of the book

What to do
1. Look at the index in *White Owl, Barn Owl*. Discuss how an index can be helpful for finding specific information in a book. Help the children to notice that the index is in alphabetical order.
2. Let the children search for information they want to find, such as baby owls. Help the children understand that baby owls are called chicks. Look up the information, and read it again to them.

Something to think about
Pose a problem for the children. Have them decide some of the most interesting parts of the book that they would like to share with their parents or a friend. Use the key words in their descriptions and create your own class index for *White Owl, Barn Owl*.

STORY S-T-R-E-T-C-H-E-R

Science: Using Binoculars to Identify Birds

What the children will learn
To use an observation tool that bird watchers use

Materials you will need
Several sets of inexpensive, lightweight binoculars

What to do
1. Collect binoculars from friends and families of students, specifying lightweight and inexpensive ones with a magnification power of about four and a wide range of vision.
2. Let the children focus on fixed objects, such as buildings, trees, birdbaths, and bird feeders.
3. Help children to follow a moving object with their eyes and then with binoculars, as when a bird flies from the feeder.

Something to think about
Younger children will enjoy looking at each other and objects in the classroom, discovering the magnification power of the binoculars. Older primary-grade students can use the binoculars with fixed objects and can begin to track birds flying from feeders to low branches.

About Birds: A Guide for Children

By Cathryn Sill
Illustrated by John Sill

Story Line

Sill and Sill provide facts about common birds that are familiar to children, such as the Canadian goose or the American robin. Characteristics of birds are presented in simple sentences that primary children can learn to read, but the details of physical markings in the accurate watercolors make it a good selection for reading to a group as well. Nine birds are featured, and the pictures in the book illustrate their habitats.

Read-Aloud Presentation

Show the cover and let the children determine what bird is on the cover—a robin. Ask the children to name some other birds that are often found in their backyards. Have the children listen to see if the birds they named are in the book. At the end of the reading, have the children recall the names of the nine birds in the book. If needed, thumb through the book, showing the illustrations and letting the children identify the birds.

STORY S-T-R-E-T-C-H-E-R

Art: Watercolors over Pencil Drawings

What the children will learn
To practice painting with watercolors

Materials you will need
Watercolor paints, water in plastic bowls, pallets or mixing trays, scraps of construction paper, watercolor paper, brushes, paper towels

What to do
1. Let children experiment with mixing colors of watercolor paints. Use scraps of construction paper for practice.
2. Look at John Sill's illustrations of birds in *About Birds: A Guide for Children*. Help the children to notice the watercolors are sometimes lighter and sometimes darker. Help them experiment with making lighter and darker colors by changing the amount of water they have on their brushes. Using paper towels to dry the brushes, help the children to see that a dry brush loaded with color makes a darker color, and a wet brush makes lighter colors.
3. Let the children draw birds with a pencil on sheets of watercolor paper and then paint their birds.

Something to think about
For young children who lack much experience with watercolors, the experimentation is the most important phase, not their finished products. Another way to help the children succeed is to use the watercolor paper and entirely cover the paper with watercolors, letting it dry overnight. The next day, the children can draw an imaginary bird over the watercolors.

STORY S-T-R-E-T-C-H-E-R

Art: Bird Bookmarks

What the children will learn
To draw in miniature

Materials you will need
Strips of white construction paper, rulers, scissors, colored pencils or fine-tipped markers, laminating machine and laminating film

What to do
1. Have the children cut strips of white construction paper about the size of bookmarks.

2. Show children the miniature picture keys that Sill used in the afterword of *About Birds: A Guide for Children*. Tell the children that you would like each child to select his or her favorite bird, draw a picture of the bird for his or her bookmark, and color it with colored pencils or fine-tipped markers.

3. Laminate the bookmarks and let the children cut them out from the film.

Something to think about
Let children take their bookmarks home to their parents as a gift, or keep them for their own use.

STORY S-T-R-E-T-C-H-E-R

Mathematics: Measuring Ingredients for Bird Cakes*

What the children will learn
To measure using whole and half cups and to follow directions

Materials you will need
Pinecones, stapler, string, birdseed, peanut butter, solid vegetable shortening, mixing bowl, knife or spatula, wooden spoon, measuring cups

What to do
1. Cut lengths of string, and staple the strings onto pinecones.
2. Pour a cup of birdseed into a mixing bowl.
3. Stir in a half cup of chunky peanut butter.
4. Add a half cup of solid vegetable shortening. Use a wooden spoon or spatula (or hands) to mix (or mush) the vegetable shortening with the peanut butter and the bird seeds.
5. Spread the mixture onto pinecones.
6. Hang the pinecones onto low-hanging tree branches as bird feeders.

Something to think about
*Do not do this STORY S-T-R-E-T-C-H-E-R if you have a child in your classroom who is allergic to peanut butter.

STORY S-T-R-E-T-C-H-E-R

Mathematics: What Size Are the Birds?

What the children will learn
To read and to make measurements

Materials you will need
Rulers, pencils, sticky notes

What to do
1. Look at the afterword of *About Birds: A Guide for Children* and help the students notice that the descriptions include the sizes of the birds.
2. Suggest that the children read about the nine birds and then add the measurements to the chart tablet in the STORY S-T-R-E-T-C-H-E-R for Science.
3. Let the children practice measuring those lengths on their rulers. They can draw a line on the chart tablet, using their rulers as the straight edge, to show the lengths of the birds.

Something to think about
For older children, let them find something in the classroom that is of equal measurement to the size of the bird. For example, the height of the robin might be about the same size as a chalkboard eraser, and the Canadian goose might be about the same size as a dodge ball.

STORY S-T-R-E-T-C-H-E-R

Science: Bird Habitats

What the children will learn
To associate certain birds with the habitats

Materials you will need
Chart tablet, markers

What to do
1. Write the names of the birds featured in the book on the chart tablet.
2. Look back through the book and compare the cover of the book, with the robin on a leafy green tree branch and a bird's nest with one blue robin's egg in it, to the page with the roadrunner and a desert scene.
3. Paging through the book, have the children describe the backgrounds or the habitats and write a descriptive phrase about each bird's habitat on the chart tablet.

Something to think about
Leave the chart tablet on display in the science center or the classroom library along with the book for the children to review.

Sparrows

*By Hans Post and
Kees Heij
Illustrated by Irene Goede*

![Sparrows book cover]

Hans Post & Kees Heij   Illustrations by Irene Goede

Sparrows

Story Line

In this book, Post, a teacher who worked as head of education at the Rotterdam Zoo, and Heij, a biologist specializing in sparrows, follow the life cycle of this familiar bird: from an egg in the nest to hatchling to fledgling to adulthood. The book includes information on sparrows' parenting, food, habitats, and how they survive each season. The book also has many other birds found in backyards, public spaces, and the edges of the forest. The story comes full circle when the sparrow lays her own eggs and her little ones hatch. Additional information is included about sparrows in North America. Goede's illustrations are beautifully drawn and realistically painted with watercolors. Children will find much to which they can relate in both the text and the illustrations, which are shown from multiple perspectives.

Read-Aloud Presentation

Have the children recall the birds they see around their homes. Invariably, someone will mention sparrows. At that time, show the front cover of the book and have the children notice the title and describe the bird. Then, look inside at the front book flap and notice the tiny bird coming from the egg. Turn to the back of the book and look at the full-grown sparrow. Tell them this is the story of how the tiny sparrow chick grows into a mother sparrow. The National Zoo website (www.nationalzoo.si.edu/animals/birds/forkids/default.cmf) has pictures of birds in zoos and migrating birds as well as information about rare sparrows.

Art: Unusual Places for Sparrows to Live

What the children will learn
To depict the many different places where sparrows build nests

Materials you will need
Drawing and painting paper, choice of colored pencils, markers, chalks, tempera paints, brushes

What to do
1. Show the children the pictures of sparrows' nests in strange places—on the neon sign and on top of a statue. Also, discuss the places they are commonly found, such as under the eaves of houses and corners of porches.
2. Ask the children where they would like to find a sparrow's nest around their homes or around their school.
3. Have the children draw a picture and write a caption about their sparrow's nest location.

Something to think about
Place the artwork near or in a display of bird-watching guides, Audubon prints, and other materials used in the unit on birds and their habitats.

Mathematics: Mathematical Comparisons of Birds We Have Studied

What the children will learn
To compare birds and make mathematical problems from their comparisons

Materials you will need
Feature books from the "Birds" unit, whiteboard, markers

What to do
1. Have the children recall all of the birds you have studied—the owls, sparrows, and the variety of birds that live in our own backyards.
2. Select several birds to focus on, and compare the birds in mathematical terms to the sparrow. For example, the sparrow weighs about as much as seven sugar cubes. How much does seven sugar cubes weigh? How much does a barn owl weigh?

3. Arrange the birds from smallest to largest in weight.
4. Continue the comparisons, based on the number of feathers, the flying range, and other characteristics.

Something to think about
Older children may be able to make sentences from the mathematical comparisons and solve problems. For example, "How many sparrows would it take to weigh as much as a hawk?"

STORY S-T-R-E-T-C-H-E-R

Reading: Roger Tory Peterson's House Sparrows

What the children will learn
About a famous naturalist, Roger Tory Peterson

Materials you will need
Peterson's field guides to birds, information from Wikipedia

What to do
1. Show the children copies of Peterson's field guides to birds.
2. Read a selection from Wikipedia about Roger Tory Peterson.
3. Read selections in a field guide about house sparrows, and compare to the information found in the Post and Heij book, *Sparrows*.

Something to think about
From the mathematics STORY S-T-R-E-T-C-H-E-R, look at the list of the other birds mentioned in *Sparrows*. Divide the class into teams, and let each team research the other birds found in the winter scene: crow, fieldfair, greenfinch, wood pigeon, blackbird, starling, dunnock, magpie, Blue titmouse, and chickadee.

STORY S-T-R-E-T-C-H-E-R

Science: Sparrow Facts

What the children will learn
To recall some facts about sparrows that may be surprising to others

Materials you will need
Construction paper or poster board, sticky notes, marker, pencil, scissors

What to do
1. Draw freehand the shape of a giant sparrow and cut it out as a display piece.
2. Have each child write a fact about sparrows and post them on the sparrow cutout.
3. Make questions from the children's facts and use these questions to help the children recall what they have learned. For example, if the child writes, "It does not run. It hops," you may write, "What hops but does not run?" Or, leave out a key word for the children to answer. "It has more than _____ feathers." (3,500) "The sparrow's heart beats _____ times a minute." (800)

Something to think about
After studying several birds from the unit, create different displays of the cutouts of birds, and use the sticky note exercise. Then, mix up the sticky notes and have the children try to arrange them into the appropriate bird shape, for the hawk, the sparrow, and the owl.

STORY S-T-R-E-T-C-H-E-R

Science: Stages of a Sparrow's Life

What the children will learn
To describe the stages of a sparrow's life

Materials you will need
Drawing paper or art paper, colored pencils or markers

What to do
1. Recall the stage of the life of the sparrow as described by Post and Heij: egg, chick, fledgling, adult or mother sparrow.
2. Let each child fold a large sheet of drawing or art paper in halves, then in quarters.
3. Help the children label each part of the papers with the stage of the sparrow's life: egg, chick, fledgling, adult.
4. Discuss how Peterson and other bird naturalists, who are called ornithologists, drew pictures of their observations.
5. Have the children draw the four stages of the life of the sparrow.

Something to think about
When a naturalist visits your class, have him or her bring along some field notes with drawings. If these are not available, check out field guides at your local library.

Arrowhawk

By Lola M. Schaefer
Illustrated by
Gabi Swiatkowska

Arrowhawk

Lola M. Schaefer ~ ILLUSTRATED BY *Gabi Swiatkowska*

Story Line

Schaefer, the author, is also a teacher, and the book is derived from the story she and her students followed of a hawk (which they named Arrowhawk), that was injured by a poacher's arrow. Told from the hawk's perspective, the language is action packed and sympathetic without being emotion laden. After the arrow, the hawk is caught in a snare. It appears that Arrowhawk will perish, but Arrowhawk is rescued and treated. The story of his rehabilitation and eventual release end the author's story, but an appendix provides the facts as well as more information about red-tailed hawks and other birds of prey, called *raptors*, as well as some discussion of conservation efforts. Swiatkowska's illustrations are beautifully naturalistic, and the realism of the landscapes complete the story.

Read-Aloud Presentation

Take the cover off the book and spread it out so that the children can see the whole body and wings of Arrowhawk. Describe the bird as a bird of prey or raptor, and explain that this means that the birds hunt small animals from the sky. Show the faint red on the tail feathers that denotes that Arrowhawk is a red-tailed hawk. Have the children notice the talons. Let them guess why the title of the book is *Arrowhawk*. Read the book from beginning to end without stopping. After reading the book, discuss the importance of conservation and rescue efforts. See the website http://www.abirdsworld.com/html/kidsnest.html for more information about hawks and other birds.

Art: Bird Prints

What the children will learn
To appreciate nature prints

Materials you will need
Book of Audubon bird prints

What to do
1. Revisit *Arrowhawk* by thumbing through the illustrations and noticing the various poses of the hawk landing, flying low, soaring, perching, attempting to fly, resting, and flying away.
2. Show the children the Audubon prints of birds, and include a red-tailed hawk, if available.
3. Notice the differences between the Audubon birds and the poses that show movement in the *Arrowhawk* illustrations.

Something to think about
If you have a naturalist painter in your community, invite him or her to visit the class and show some paintings. Discuss how the painter achieves the sense of movement in her or his paintings.

Field Trip: Aviary

What the children will learn
To observe the different birds in the aviary

Materials you will need
Field trip permission forms, transportation, chart tablet, markers, poster board, hole punchers, yarn, binoculars, cameras

What to do
1. Determine the nearest zoo or conservation aviary. Visit the aviary and talk with the directors or assistants about the ages of your students and their interests.
2. Prepare the students for the visit by telling them what you saw and by brainstorming some questions they would like to ask. "How many birds are in the aviary?" "Where did they come from?" "Are there any hawks, especially red-tailed hawks?" "Which birds are the oldest and youngest birds?"
3. Prepare the volunteers by going over the school rules, transportation rules, and aviary rules. Assign particular students to each volunteer.

4. Ask volunteers to bring cameras and binoculars, if possible.
5. Make name tags with the names of the children, their school, and any other required information.

Something to think about
If it is not possible to make a field trip to an aviary, see if someone from the zoo or the conservation aviary would visit the school and bring a hawk.

Reading: More Information About Hawks

What the children will learn
To use research tools and seek specific information about hawks in your area

Materials you will need
Computer with Internet access, printer, chart tablet, markers

What to do
1. Talk about Arrowhawk. Mention that he was a red-tailed hawk, a bird of prey (*raptor*).
2. Brainstorm questions the children would like to have answered, such as, "How many types of hawks are there?" "What are the names of the hawks that live where we live?" "Do people who live here see hawks often?"
3. Demonstrate how to find out information about hawks by going to the World Bird Database (avibase.bsc-eoc.org/avibase.jsp) or the National Geographic website (animals.nationalgeographic.com/animals/birds.html).
4. Answer specific questions about hawks from your region, but also have children recall additional information they learned from their searches. Write these facts on the *Arrowhawk* chart tablet.

Something to think about
As you and your students collect information about hawks, have them add other interesting facts to the chart tablet. Review it each day.

Science: Birds of Prey

What the children will learn
To classify and compare birds of prey

Materials you will need
Bird prints or bird-watching guides, index cards, markers

What to do
1. Read about several birds of prey, such as hawks, owls, eagles, falcons, and ospreys.
2. Notice the similarities in the information that is presented about each bird, such as region, size, color and markings, food source, behavior, males and females, nests, and eggs.
3. Divide the children into groups and assign each group a different bird of prey to research.
4. Have the children record their information onto large index cards.
5. Reassemble so that each group has one child from the hawk group, one child from the eagle group, one child from the owl group, one from the falcon group, and one from the osprey group.
6. The groups can compare their information about the various birds of prey. They can then determine the smallest, the largest, the ones in your region, the ones not in your region, habitats, food, endangered or not, and other similarities and differences among the birds of prey.

Something to think about
Of course, younger children might use fewer birds and only make comparisons between the hawk and one other bird of prey. Choose a comparison involving a bird that lives in your region.

Writing: Stories from the Aviary to the Wild

What the children will learn
To use knowledge of rescue of birds to write a real or an imaginary story

Materials you will need
Writing paper, pencils

What to do
1. Look through the pages of *Arrowhawk* with the children, and have them describe what they see or tell the story in their own words.
2. Recall other birds found in the aviary they visited or other birds they heard about being rescued when the naturalist visited the school.
3. Let the children describe a bird, tell what happened to cause the bird to need to be rescued, how it was rescued, how it was rehabilitated, and what it was like for the bird when set free.

Something to think about

Allow the children several days to work on their drafts, edit them, and then produce their stories in booklet form or have someone type the stories into a computer and produce a disk for each child.

References

Davies, Nicola. 2007. *White Owl, Barn Owl*. Illustrated by Michael Foreman. Somerville, MA: Candlewick.

Post, Hans and Kees Heij. 2008. *Sparrow*. Illustrated by Irene Goede. Honesdale, PA: Boyds Mills Press.

Schaefer, Lola. 2004. *Arrowhawk*. Illustrated by Gabi Swiatkowska. New York: Henry Holt.

Sill, Cathryn. 1997. *About Birds: A Guide for Children*. Illustrated by John Sill. Atlanta, GA: Peachtree Publishers.

Swinburne, Stephen. 1999. *Unbeatable Beaks*. Illustrated by Joan Paley. New York: Henry Holt.

Additional References

Guiberson, Brenda Z. 1992. *Spoonbill Swamp*. Illustrated by Megan Lloyd. New York: Henry Holt. *Guiberson's excellent account of nature's everyday drama is beautifully illustrated in watercolors, enhancing the readers' appreciation for the pink spoonbill and the aggressive alligator that narrowly misses capturing her.*

Herkert, Barbara H. 2001. *Birds in Your Backyard*. Nevada City, CA: Dawn Publications. *Find out about common backyard North American birds, building birdhouses, attracting birds, state and province birds, and maps of habitats.*

Mason, Adrienne. 2004. *Owls*. Illustrated by Nancy Gray Ogle. Toronto: Kids Can Press. *Learn about typical owls and barn owls through detailed illustrations and common questions children ask.*

Websites

1. BirdLife International Avibase—The World Bird Database: http://avibase.bsc-eoc.org/avibase.jsp
   - Comprehensive database
   - Interactive map of regional birds
2. National Geographic: http://animals.nationalgeographic.com/animals/birds.html
   - Brilliant pictures and videos
   - Links to bird-themed games and maps
   - Latest bird news headlines
3. Smithsonian National Zoological Park: www.nationalzoo.si.edu/Animals/Birds/ForKids/default.cfm
   - Fact sheets
   - Games
   - Bird exhibits
   - Virtual trip
4. Audubon: http://web4.audubon.org/educate/kids
   - Live camera of barn owl
5. Wild Bird Information: http://www.abirdsworld.com/html/kidsnest.html
   - Printable pages
   - Bird-watching tips
   - Schoolroom activities

Trees and Rain Forests

The Gift of the Tree

By Alvin Tresselt
Illustrated by
Henri Sorensen

Story Line

Alvin Tresselt helps the young reader see the life of an old tree that has lived in the forest for over one hundred years. The insects, birds, and animals it has sheltered and fed are testimony to its boundless worth. The text is not poetry, but the language is poetic, as in the phrase, "rich rain of acorns." The gift of the tree is the life it brings, even as it dies during a hurricane, whose winds slash through the forest. We see the way the tree and the forest creatures depend upon each other. In the end, a tiny acorn sprouts to carry on the life of the proud tree. Originally published in 1972 and reissued in 1992, the book is timely and timeless. Sorensen's illustrations are as splendid as Tresselt's words. Each tells the story of the natural cycle in a realistic yet respectful approach to the subject.

Read-Aloud Presentation

Open the book and flatten out the dust cover to let the children see that on the back is a beautiful painting of the forest. Invite them to note the season of the year. In addition to the deer and the birds on the cover, ask the children what other animals they might see if they visited this forest. Keep a chart tablet nearby, and as you read the book, ask one child to list the animals, birds, and insects. At the end of the book, let the children share their observations. See the How Stuff Works website for the "True Poetree" activity.

STORY S-T-R-E-T-C-H-E-R

Art: Leaf Rubbings

What the children will learn
To create rubbings

Materials you will need
Variety of leaves, newsprint, crayon, charcoal, pastel chalk

What to do
1. During a nature walk, collect a variety of fallen leaves.
2. Bring the leaves back to the classroom so the children can arrange the leaves in interesting patterns.
3. Place newsprint over the leaves.
4. With a piece of charcoal, pastel chalk, or crayon on its side show the children how to rub it on the newsprint over the leaves.
5. Display the leaf rubbings around the room.

Something to think about
Arrange some leaves with identification labels for the science center.

STORY S-T-R-E-T-C-H-E-R

Art: Twig Pictures

What the children will learn
To incorporate an object they find into a picture

Materials you will need
Fallen twigs, construction paper or poster board, glue

What to do
1. Ask the children to place a twig randomly on a piece of paper or poster board. Glue the twig in place.
2. After the glue dries, ask the children to make pictures that incorporate the twig. For example, if the twig is placed across the top of a page, it could look like a tree branch in front of a window.
3. Encourage the children to think of many imaginative alternatives.

Something to think about
Develop this activity by having the children use three, and then five, twigs in a design. See additional educational resources for connecting children with nature at the Arbor Day website, www.arborday.org.

Mathematics: Hugging a Tree

What the children will learn
To use parts of their own bodies to measure trees

Materials you will need
None needed

What to do
1. Ask the children to find trees that they can measure with different parts of their bodies.
2. Let the children brainstorm a few examples: a tree as big around as a hug, a tree as short as a hand, a tree as tall as an arm is long.
3. Have the volunteers write down at least one inventive measurement per child during a walking field trip.

Something to think about
Upon returning from the field trip, discuss the usefulness of using parts of the body to measure other things.

Science and Nature: Loam, a Natural Compost

What the children will learn
To use loam (naturally decomposing materials made by falling leaves) as planting material

Materials you will need
Acorns, loam, trowels, milk cartons (clean and dry), one per child, scissors

What to do
1. Cleanly cut the tops off the milk cartons and set them out to dry.
2. Have the children fill a milk carton with loam collected during a walking field trip.
3. Have the children plant acorns that they collected on the trip in the milk cartons.
4. Place in a sunny spot, water, and observe the changes over time.

Something to think about
Compare the growth of acorns in various soils—loam, potting soil, fertilized soil, overwatered soil, and underwatered soil.

Science and Nature: A Walk in the Forest

What the children will learn
To enjoy the beauty of trees and recognize various stages of growth and decay

Materials you will need
Parent volunteers, paper grocery bags, leaves, twigs, pebbles, other interesting objects found along the way, large milk cartons (clean and dry), loam

What to do
1. Schedule a field trip or walking excursion into a wooded area.
2. If possible, arrange for groups of children to walk on different nature trails to allow them to enjoy the pleasure of discovery without interruptions from the entire class.
3. Spend at least five minutes sitting in a quiet spot and simply listening to the sounds of nature.
4. Do the mathematics STORY S-T-R-E-T-C-H-E-R during the walking field trip.
5. Bring back leaves and twigs for art and science displays.
6. Fill milk cartons with loam collected from under a tree.
7. Look for sprouting acorns in the loam.
8. Bring the sprouting acorns back to the classroom for the science display center.

Something to think about
If you have a wooded area near your school, consider taking four or five children at a time with you for a special walk, rather than making it a class trip.

The Lorax

By Dr. Seuss

Story Line

A child goes to the wise Once-ler in search of answers to the question of what happened to the Truffula Trees. The tale is told in Seuss rhyme with many double messages. The answer is clear, however: The Truffula Trees disappear because the Once-ler's company is greedy and does not allow the trees to grow and replace themselves. They are warned by a character named the Lorax, but no one listens when he says that cutting down the trees will cause problems for the environment and for all the creatures that live in the Truffula Tree forest. The Once-ler company thinks it is more important to make *thneeds,* meaning "something that all people need." Soon there are lots of thneeds, but no trees. The last hope is one Truffula seed and a good citizen who might make it grow. This environmental tale, told by Dr. Seuss in his venerable style, is surely relevant today.

Read-Aloud Presentation

Show the children the cover of *The Lorax,* and tell them that the little creature with the beard gives advice that everyone should heed. Ask the children to listen for the Lorax's advice. Read *The Lorax,* pausing after the first thneed has been knitted. Ask the children to predict what they think will happen next. When the Lorax appears in the story, ask if the children think anyone will listen. Continue reading, pausing after the last Truffula Tree has been cut down, and then ask the children what they think will happen. At the end of the story, ask what the Lorax means when he says, "I speak for the trees." What do the trees want him to say?

Art: An Imaginative Place Where Truffula Trees Grow

What the children will learn
To use their imaginations to create a new kind of tree

Materials you will need
Cotton balls, yarn, Popsicle sticks, pipe cleaners, felt, tissue paper, fabric, glue, stapler, construction paper

What to do
1. Look again at the illustrations in *The Lorax,* and discuss how Dr. Seuss used his imagination to create a new tree, the Truffula Tree.
2. Ask the children to use their imaginations to create new trees.
3. Let the children invent the new trees using materials found around the classroom.

Something to think about
Invent new names for the trees. Print tiny signs for each tree and its inventor.

Cooking and Snack Time: Truffula Fruits

What the children will learn
To distinguish among the flavors of different grapes

Materials you will need
Scissors, napkins, green grapes, black grapes, red grapes

What to do
1. Call the grapes "Truffula Fruits." Let the cooking and snack helpers wash them.
2. With scissors, snip small bunches from the larger bunches.
3. Ask the children to decide which flavor of Truffula Fruit they like best. Ask them which is sweetest, which is tartest.

Something to think about
Bring kiwi, nectarines, or another fruit the children rarely see and call it Truffula Fruit.

Science and Nature: Planting a Truffula Tree

What the children will learn
To plant and take care of seedlings

Materials you will need
Seedlings, trowel, topsoil, compost or rich soil, flower pots or plastic containers, rulers

What to do
1. Secure enough seedlings from the county extension office or an environmental project to give one to every child.
2. Prepare a bed for the seedlings by mixing topsoil with compost or rich soil, turning it into the bed with the hand trowel.
3. Plant the seedlings in the prepared soil.
4. Measure the growth of the seedlings on the first of each month.
5. After the seedlings have grown for several months, transplant them into flower pots or plastic containers.
6. Give one to each child for a family tree-planting ceremony.

Something to think about
If some children do not have places to plant trees, ask for space on the school grounds or in a park where the children can plant their trees.

Writing: The Return of the Lorax

What the children will learn
To think constructively and write a message of hope

Materials you will need
Chalkboard, chalk, writing paper, pencils

What to do
1. Extend the story of the Lorax by asking the children to write about what happens after the child plants the Truffula Tree seed.
2. Invite the children to imagine the new world once the forest returns.
3. Let the children pretend that the Lorax, who lives far away, hears news of the Truffula Trees beginning to grow.

4. Encourage the children to write a scene in which the Lorax comes back and is greeted by the Once-ler, who has longed for his return.

Something to think about
Make a mural of "The Return of the Lorax."

Writing: Speaking for Trees

What the children will learn
To compose a passionate speech about caring for the environment

Materials you will need
Chalkboard, chalk, pencil, paper

What to do
1. Reread the passage in the story where the Lorax proclaims that he speaks for the trees.
2. Brainstorm with the children a list of things you think the Lorax might have said when he talked with the Once-ler, who would not listen to his speech.
3. Let the children write their speeches.
4. Encourage the children to give their speeches.

Something to think about
On another occasion, let the Lorax speak for the animals that were driven from the Truffula forest, or for the birds or the fish. Or write about what the Lorax would say if he came to our town.

The Great Kapok Tree: A Tale of the Amazon Rain Forest

By Lynne Cherry

THE GREAT KAPOK TREE
A TALE OF THE AMAZON RAIN FOREST
by Lynne Cherry

Story Line

Children will enjoy the adventure and the suspense of this Gulliver-like story, an environmental message wrapped in a magical tale. A woodchopper falls asleep, and in his dream, the creatures of the rain forest whisper to him not to chop down their trees. The boa constrictor, the bee, a troupe of monkeys, a toucan, a tree frog, a jaguar, a tree porcupine, an anteater, and a three-toed sloth whisper to the woodman. In the end, a child from the Yanomamo tribe implores the man to spare their tree. Cherry's full-page illustrations make the rain forest plants and animals come to life. They provide such a rich visual experience that the children will want to look at the pictures again and again. The endpapers are a map of the tropical rain forests of the world, bordered with small drawings of the insects and animals that inhabit them.

Read-Aloud Presentation

Read the author's note at the beginning of the book that describes the Amazon rain forest. Then open the book to the endpapers and show the children where the tropical rain forests are on the world map. They are highlighted in green. Read the story without pausing. Hand the book to a child who has not shown as much interest in reading as others have. Ask him or her to take the book to the classroom library and invite a friend to go along to look at the pictures more closely and see some of the animals, which are camouflaged in the pictures. See additional information on rain forests at the Rain Forest Alliance website, www.rainforest-alliance.org.

Art: Green-on-Green Collages

What the children will learn
To create collages

Materials you will need
Different shades of green construction paper, pencils, colored pencils, markers, crayons, chalks, glue sticks, scissors

What to do
1. Have the children look at Lynne Cherry's beautiful illustrations in *The Great Kapok Tree*. Call attention to the shades of green and the way Cherry drew the veins in leaves. Have the children notice how the insects and animals sit on top of a mass of greenery.
2. Let the children use the many shades of green construction paper, and draw many different types of leaf patterns, adding some darker veins or highlight the edges with white.
3. Cut out enough leaves to cover an entire sheet of paper.
4. Glue the leaves in place, and add any combination of flowers, insects, and animals to the pictures, but use the greenery as background.

Something to think about
Avoid providing patterns for the leaves. Have the children notice how the leaves are turned, twisted, and shaped so that there is no exact pattern.

STORY S-T-R-E-T-C-H-E-R

Classroom Library: Whispers to *Senhor*

What the children will learn
To use their voices expressively

Materials you will need
Chalkboard, chalk, CDs and CD player or tapes and tape recorder, tape player, stapler, listening station, headphones

What to do
1. Make a list of all the insects and animals that whisper in the woodchopper's ear.
2. Let the children volunteer to read the different parts. Write the volunteers' names beside the rain forest creatures' names on the chalkboard.
3. Practice reading the whispers.

4. Assign another child to be responsible for recording the page-turning signal on cue: clicking a stapler.
5. Record the book. You should read the narrative and the children should read what the insects, animals, and child whisper in the ear of *Senhor,* the woodchopper.

Something to think about
Practice the dialogue with reluctant children in private so that they can be confident readers for the recording session.

STORY S-T-R-E-T-C-H-E-R

Science and Nature: What Is a Kapok Tree?

What the children will learn
Some facts about the kapok tree

Materials you will need
Chalkboard, chalk, reference books on plants

What to do
1. Read the author's note at the beginning of *The Great Kapok Tree.* Have the children restate any facts that were stated or implied about the tree. List these facts.
2. Read *The Great Kapok Tree* and add more to the list.
3. Look up the kapok tree in reference books, and read the information aloud to the children. Let the students tell you other information to add to the list.
4. At the end of the information-gathering session, let the children restate in their own words what they want to be sure to remember about the tree.

Something to think about
Find out if there is a botanical garden near you that has a kapok tree. A plant specialist may be willing to provide additional information. Better still, plan a visit to the garden.

STORY S-T-R-E-T-C-H-E-R

Science and Nature: Animals of the Rain Forest

What the children will learn
To identify rain forest animals

Materials you will need
Chart tablet or poster board, marker, learning log notebooks or index cards, pencils, optional—reference books

What to do
1. Reread *The Great Kapok Tree.*
2. Have a child list on a chart the different animals mentioned in the story.

3. Compare the large illustrations of those animals to the smaller ones on the borders of the rain forest map.
4. Look closely at the smaller animal illustrations, and list other animals not mentioned in the story, such as the coati, the moustached tamarin, and the kinkajou.
5. Look at reference books and find out more about these animals. Leave the reference materials on display for several days for the children to browse through.
6. Have each child write a few sentences in his or her science and nature learning logs or on index cards about an animal he or she learned more about.

Something to think about
On other days, concentrate on insects of the rain forest or plants of the rain forest.

STORY S-T-R-E-T-C-H-E-R

Writing: Writing to Environmental Groups

What the children will learn
To compose a letter requesting information

Materials you will need
Sample letters, writing paper, pencils, chart tablet and marker or computer and projection screen, envelopes, stamps

What to do
1. Read the acknowledgments section on the back of the title page of *The Great Kapok Tree,* where the author expresses her appreciation to the World Wildlife Fund.
2. Tell the children that the World Wildlife Fund provides materials to students about their projects, but to receive them, they must write a letter requesting information.
3. Read the children part of a friendly letter you have received, and part of a business letter. Help them to hear the difference in language and expression.
4. Let each small group compose a letter. Be sure to state in the letter that the class has read *The Great Kapok Tree.*
5. Either print the letters on chart tablet paper or write them on a computer with a projection screen.
6. Reread the letters and help the children edit them.
7. Have volunteers print or write the finished letters from each small group. Mail the letters to World Wildlife Fund, PO Box 97180, Washington, DC 20090-7180.

Something to think about
Consult with the librarian for the names and addresses of other environmental groups who will provide information to primary-age children.

Welcome to the Green House

By Jane Yolen
Illustrated by Laura Regan

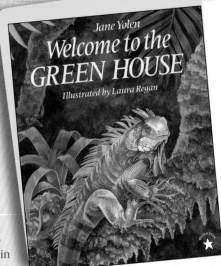

Story Line

Jane Yolen communicates the beauty, mystery, and wonder of the rain forest in wonderful rhyme. Her eloquent and accurate descriptions introduce the reader to the inhabitants of this fragile ecosystem. She helps the reader appreciate the color, climate, weather, and sounds of the rain forest. The last two pages offer a refrain that young children will enjoy chanting together. This is Laura Regan's first children's book. Her illustrations in gouache capture the splendid rain forest colors and the mysteries of camouflage.

Read-Aloud Presentation

Construct a K-W-L chart with the children, listing all the things they already know about the rainforest and the things they want to know. Read *Welcome to the Green House*, and add to the chart by listing what the children learned from the reading. After constructing the chart, read the last two pages of *Welcome to the Green House* again, and encourage the children to repeat the lines after you. Print these lines on chart paper for the classroom library and for the children to read on their own. Introduce the other rain forest books you have collected for the children to look at during free reading time. At another read-aloud session, present Helen Cowcher's *Rain Forest* and compare the animals included in that book to those in *Welcome to the Green House*.

Art: Rain Forests Are Every Shade of Green

What the children will learn
To shade and tint greens

Materials you will need
Display table, collection of green art supplies (many different shades of green construction paper, green crayons, green pencils, green chalk, etc.), tempera paints (green, black, and white), brushes, newsprint, easels

What to do
1. With the children who are working at the art center, collect all the art supplies in the classroom that are any shade or tint of green.
2. Look through all of Laura Regan's illustrations in *Welcome to the Green House*.
3. Have the children choose different art supplies and create as many different shades and tints of green as they can to represent the greens of the rain forest.
4. Demonstrate how to shade green with black tempera paint and to tint it with white.
5. Display the rainforest greens on a bulletin board.

Something to think about
Ask the children to think about which animal or bird could hide near this color and be camouflaged.

Music and Movement: Rainforest Creatures on the Move

What the children will learn
To move like the rainforest animals

Materials you will need
Chart tablet paper, marker

What to do
1. Read *Welcome to the Green House* again and list all the animals and birds, which include

Slow, green-coated sloth	Golden lion tamarin
Quick-fingered capuchin	Keel-billed toucan
Blue hummingbird	Wild pig
Golden toad	Chorusing frog
Waking lizard	Boat-billed heron
Howler monkey troop	Fluttering bat
Prowling ocelot	Kinkajou

2. Let the children move like they think these birds and animals would move. If they cannot decide, refer back to the text.

Something to think about

Plan another session for the children to interpret the movement of flowers and plants during different times of the day and different weather conditions.

Music and Movement: Connected to . . .

What the children will learn

To chant the names of rain forest animals

Materials you will need

List of rain forest animals from the music and movement STORY S-T-R-E-T-C-H-E-R, tagboard, scissors, marker

What to do

1. Discuss the rain forest ecology as an environment where all the species support each other, like a chain.
2. If the children do not know the song, "The head bone's connected to the neck bone. The neck bone's connected to the chest bone," then teach it to them.
   Note: The lyrics and a recording of the song can be found at http://kids.niehs.nih.gov/lyrics/bones.htm.
3. Ask the children to sing the song using the names and descriptions of rain forest animals. For example,
   > The slow-moving sloth's connected to the quick-fingered capuchin.
   > The quick-fingered capuchin's connected to the blue hummingbird.
   > The blue hummingbird's connected to the golden toad.

   Continue chanting down the list.
4. Cut strips of tagboard and have each child print the name of a rain forest animal on his or her strip.
5. Ask sixteen children to stand up, holding the names of the animals, but rearranged in random order. So the song might begin, "The blue hummingbird's connected to the fluttering bat."
6. Sing through the new arrangement of animals.

Something to think about

On the next day, add to the chain by inserting the names of rain forest plants and insects.

Science and Nature: Camouflage

What the children will learn

To recognize how camouflage aids in survival

Materials you will need

Field trip permission (if no wooded area is available nearby), parent volunteers

What to do

1. Walk to a wooded area.
2. Disperse the children in twos or threes and have them sit very quietly.
3. Ask the children to watch a small patch of soil or leaves.
4. Look closely to see whatever is living there—beetles, grubs, snails, ants.
5. Model for the children how to disturb the area gently by lifting leaves, moving a stick, looking on the underside of a leaf. Note how much life there is in the area, and how it is camouflaged.
6. Back in the classroom, discuss how insects and small animals use camouflage to help them survive.

Something to think about

Let the children try to find all the animals camouflaged in each scene in *Welcome to the Green House*.

Writing: Chain of Animals

What the children will learn

To write and sing a song about the rain forest creatures

Materials you will need

List of animals from the music and movement STORY S-T-R-E-T-C-H-E-R, chart paper, marker

What to do

1. Read over the list of animals compiled from *Welcome to the Green House*.
2. Adapt the children's chant, "Over in the Meadow," to create a chant about the rain forest. For example, the first verse might be:
   > Over in the rain forest, in their green, green home,
   > Lived an old mother sloth and her little sloth one.
   > "Move!" said the mother. "I move," said the one.
   > So they slowly move for a peek at the sun.

The entire song appears on page 238 of the Appendix.

Something to think about

Print all the songs and chants on a chart tablet. Call this the class *Big Book of Music*.

Planting the Trees of Kenya: The Story of Wangari Maathai

By Claire A. Nivola

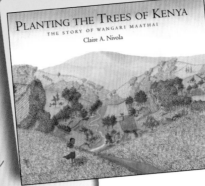

Story Line

Claire Nivola tells the compelling story of a strong Kenyan woman named Wangari Maathai, who won the Nobel Peace Prize in 2004 for her work as the founder of the Green Belt Movement in Kenya. When Wangari was a girl, the land was green and people could fish and grow their own food. But over the years, more and more trees were cut down, the land became dry and barren, and it became very hard for the people of Kenya to live. Wangari Maathai taught the women and children to grow seedlings and to plant trees. She convinced soldiers to plant trees. She taught prisoners to plant trees. In time, thirty million trees had been planted, and the people realized they could change their lives for the better. This true story is powerfully told in words and beautiful watercolors.

Read-Aloud Presentation

Show the cover of *Planting the Trees of Kenya: The Story of Wangari Maathai*. Explain that Wangari Maathai is a woman's name that may not sound familiar to them because she is Kenyan. Practice saying the name together: wan-'gar-ee muhth-'eye. Discuss the Nobel Peace Prize, and that it is not just about war and peace, but about things that help people live peaceful lives. In countries where people can grow their own food, they can take care of themselves and live peaceful lives. Read the story of Wangari Maathai and planting the trees. See the How Stuff Works website for a section on "Growing Tropical Trees."

STORY S-T-R-E-T-C-H-E-R

Art: Leaf Rubbings

What the children will learn
To use objects from nature to create art

Materials you will need
Leaves, bark, drawing paper or typing paper, tape, crayons

What to do
1. Take a nature walk and notice the trees around the school.
2. Collect leaves from the trees.
3. Demonstrate how to tape the leaves in an interesting arrangement to a sheet of paper.
4. Place another sheet on top, press down, and rub the sides of a crayon across the leaves to create a rubbing.
5. Arrange the leaf rubbings around the classroom for display.

Something to think about
Make bark rubbings by letting the children take typing paper out to the trees, and have one child hold the paper in place while another rubs the crayon to create the bark pattern. Display these around the classrooms with the names of the trees the bark prints represent.

STORY S-T-R-E-T-C-H-E-R

Mathematics: Two-for-One Equations

What the children will learn
To determine the answers each time a one is replaced by two

Materials you will need
Whiteboard, markers

What to do
1. Read the section of the book where Wangari Maathai tells the people to plant two trees for each one they cut down.
2. Have the children count how many students are in their class. Tell the children to imagine if each of them cut down one tree, then ask how many trees the class would need to plant in order to plant two for one. For example twenty-five children each planting two trees would need fifty seedlings.
3. Try the equation in various combinations: all the boys, all the girls, everyone wearing sneakers, everyone wearing boots, and so on.

Something to think about

Link this mathematics equation to the special projects of planting trees on the school grounds or in the community.

STORY S-T-R-E-T-C-H-E-R

Science: Demonstrating the Effects of Erosion

What the children will learn

To understand the effects of water and wind on soil erosion

Materials you will need

Large potted plant, water source, hose or watering can, large bucket or plastic container, fan, plastic garbage bag, optional—water table, sand

What to do

1. Reread the parts of the book where the author wrote about the erosion that occurred when the trees were all cut down and there were not enough roots to hold the soil.
2. Demonstrate this by removing a large plant from its container.
3. Help the children to see the root system and the soil that is held in place by the roots.
4. Break some of the roots off, and have a child pour water over the root ball. Note what is occurring. The roots will no longer hold the soil and it is washing away.
5. Leave the plant lying out on plastic all day and blow a fan on the roots. The next day have the children notice what the wind has done to the soil. It will be dried up and can be blown away.

Something to think about

Place sand in a sand-and-water table or child's plastic pool and let children moisten it to create hills and valleys. Let them play with the sand and water to create streams of water and notice the erosion.

STORY S-T-R-E-T-C-H-E-R

Special Project: Planting Trees Two for One

What the children will learn

To care for seedlings

Materials you will need

At least two seedlings for each child, watering cans, trowels

What to do

1. Contact the local arborist or county extension agent and find a source for seedlings of trees appropriate or indigenous to your area.
2. Secure permission to plant seedlings on the school grounds, and ask gardeners to help prepare the soil.
3. With the help of a professional, demonstrate to the children how to plant the seedlings and provide other instructions, such as how and when to water the seedlings. Plan for enough seedlings for each child to plant one tree at school and one tree at home.

Something to think about

If some children do not have space to plant a tree at home, they can grow their seedlings in large tin cans salvaged from the school cafeteria, which is an appropriate reuse of cans that would be discarded.

STORY S-T-R-E-T-C-H-E-R

Writing: Information on Arbor Day

What the children will learn

To seek information on a website and write a thank-you note for the information

Materials you will need

Computer with access to children's websites for various conservationist groups, such as the National Arbor Day Foundation, the Sierra Club, or the state or national forest in your area; whiteboard and markers

What to do

1. Find appropriate websites from the organizations (see the references).
2. Select a website your students will enjoy, and with a small group of children decide which information to download and read to the rest of the class.
3. Print the materials to place in the science area for the unit on trees.
4. After sharing the information with the class, with small groups of children compose e-mails or letters to the organization thanking them for having information for children.
5. Let various groups compose their messages and share the messages, conducting a group edit to see the differences in each small group's wording while still stating the same message.

Something to think about

Take your e-mail messages and turn them into letters or vice versa.

Trees and Rain Forests

References

Cherry, Lynne. 1990. *The Great Kapok Tree: A Tale of the Amazon Rain Forest*. New York: Houghton Mifflin Harcourt.

Nivola, Claire A. 2008. *Planting the Trees of Kenya: The Story of Wangari Maathai*. New York: Farrar, Straus, and Giroux.

Seuss, Dr. 1971. *The Lorax*. New York: Random House.

Tresselt, Alvin. 1972. *The Gift of the Tree*. Illustrated by Henry Sorensen. New York: HarperCollins.

Yolen, Jane. 1993. *Welcome to the Green House*. Illustrated by Laura Regan. New York: Penguin Group (USA).

Additional References

Bunting, Eve. 1996. *Someday a Tree*. Illustrated by Ronald Himler. New York: Sandpiper. *A young girl, her parents, and their neighbors try to save an old oak tree that has been poisoned by pollution.*

Fleming, Denise. 2000. *Where Once There Was a Wood*. Illustrated by David Powers. New York: Henry Holt. *Examines the many forms of wildlife that can be displaced if their environment is destroyed by development, and discusses how communities and schools can provide spaces for displaced wildlife to live.*

Zak, Monica. 1993. *Save My Rain Forest*. Illustrated by Bengt-Arne Runnerstrom. Volcano, CA: Volcano Press. *Eight-year-old Omar Castillo fulfills his dream of visiting the endangered rain forest of southern Mexico and wins an audience with the president of Mexico to express his concern.*

Websites

1. Arbor Day Foundation Youth Education: www.arborday.org/kids
   - Tree-themed games and activities
   - Contests
   - Educational resources
2. Rainforest Alliance Learning Site: www.rainforest-alliance.org/kids
   - Rain forest curriculum and resources
   - Pages for kids and teachers
   - Slideshows and pdf files organized by grade level
3. How Stuff Works Tree Activities for Kids: www.home.howstuffworks.com/tree-activities-for-kids.htm
   - Tree activities for kids
   - Links to craft pages

Chapter 12

Recycle, Reuse, Repurpose

Recycle! A Handbook for Kids

Stuff! Reduce, Reuse, Recycle

What Can You Do with an Old Red Shoe?

We Are Extremely Very Good Recyclers

Dinosaurs Go Green! A Guide to Protecting Our Planet

Recycle! A Handbook for Kids

By Gail Gibbons

Story Line

The story begins with a garbage truck and the question about what happens to all of the garbage. The story follows different types of garbage—paper, glass, aluminum cans, plastics—and what happens to them. The text also includes what children and families can do to recycle these materials. This much-needed information helps children understand their world and the community services provided for recycling. Gail Gibbons's full-page illustrations are saturated colors in her classic block style and are excellent for viewing individually or for sharing with an entire class.

Read-Aloud Presentation

Have children think about the garbage pick-up at their homes. How many times in a week is it picked up, and how many containers does their family have? Look at the picture of the garbage truck, and have the children discuss where the garbage truck goes to dispose of the waste from their homes. Read *Recycle! A Handbook for Kids*. Announce some of the STORY S-T-R-E-T-C-H-E-R-S associated with the book. See www.epa.gov/kids for additional ideas for kids helping the environment.

STORY S-T-R-E-T-C-H-E-R

Art: Posters for Recycling Campaign

What the children will learn
To use three-dimensional objects on a poster

Materials you will need
Chart tablet or whiteboard, whiteboard marker, heavy poster board, scissors, twist ties, colored markers

What to do
1. Have the children discuss things they use at home or in the classroom that can be recycled.
2. Ask the children to make posters that show other children in the school what can be recycled.
3. Discuss that they could draw pictures of these objects, but attaching some samples of the various objects could also be used.
4. Demonstrate how to connect twist ties and place them around an aluminum can or a glass juice bottle and how to attach these objects to the poster board.
5. Have the children add words to encourage the students in their school to recycle these objects.

Something to think about
Display the posters near the sources of these disposables, such as cafeterias and vending machines, but give directions to where the containers for recycling are located.

STORY S-T-R-E-T-C-H-E-R

Language Arts: Interviewing a Recycling Director

What the children will learn
To ask key questions for a good interview

Materials you will need
Chart tablet or whiteboard, markers

What to do
1. Invite the director of a recycling program to visit.
2. Write the questions the students would like to ask the director on chart tablet paper or a whiteboard.
3. Be sure that one of the questions is what can kids do to help with recycling.
4. Before the director arrives, review the questions from the chart tablet or whiteboard and ask for volunteers to pose these key questions.
5. After the key questions have been asked, let the children ask any other questions they have.

Something to think about
Visit with the director of the recycling program ahead of time and inform her or him of the ages of your students. Work with the director to help him or her focus the audiovisuals or any other part of his or her presentation to the level of the children.

Mathematics: Comparisons of Before and After Recycling at Our School

What the children will learn
To make comparisons based on their actions

Materials you will need
Large containers for recycling paper, glass, and aluminum cans; garbage cans; old shower curtain or a large piece of plastic; tape; marker

What to do
1. Ask the custodians not to pick up your classroom's trash for a day. Call the children's attention to the amount of trash the class generated. Look at the sizes of the containers and notice the gallons printed on them.
2. Spread the trash out onto a shower curtain or large strip of plastic, such as a painter's cloth.
3. Examine the trash to see what could be recycled, such as paper, glass, and aluminum cans.
4. Separate the trash and place it into recycle bins, leaving only the nonrecyclables in the garbage can.
5. Mark the height the trash reaches with a piece of tape on the outside of the garbage can and write a date on it.
6. After your study of recycling, do the exercise again. Compare the amounts of garbage left and the amounts of recyclable materials.

Something to think about
Help children become aware of how to use scraps and backs of paper for practice writing or drawing. Show them other ways you have changed, such as using double-sided printing.

Science: Associating Scientific Names

What the children will learn
To associate scientific names for ordinary materials

Materials you will need
Large index cards, markers

What to do
1. Review the book to find the scientific names Gibbons uses in the illustrations. They include *silica* for glass, *polystyrene* for Styrofoam, and *chlorofluorocarbons* for gases that cause harm to the ozone layer.
2. Write the words on index cards, and print a corresponding word or phrase on another index card. For example, *silica* on one card and *glass* on another.
3. Have the children match the more common term with the scientific terms.

Something to think about
Children often enjoy learning long names, such as *chlorofluorocarbons*.

Social Studies: Our Town's Recycling

What the children will learn
About recycling that they and their family can do

Materials you will need
Field trip permission forms, transportation, volunteers, chart tablet, marker

What to do
1. Visit your city's or town's landfill or recycling station. Talk with the director about what you are trying to teach the children.
2. Secure an appropriate number of volunteers for your class. Write assignments for the volunteers on the chart tablet and make plans for the trip.
3. Review the purposes of the special field trip and what you learned from visiting with the director.
4. With the students, plan for the visit, assigning them to specific volunteers, reviewing safety precautions, and explaining what you want them to observe.
5. After the field trip, review what the children observed, what surprised them, what they want to do differently to be better recyclers.

Something to think about
The recycling process varies by city or town. If you have a college or large high school nearby, they often have recycling programs.

Stuff! Reduce, Reuse, Recycle

By Steven Kroll
Illustrated by Steve Cox

Story Line

Pinch is a packrat who collects stuff and does not use it. When the children in the town have a tag sale, much like a community yard sale, everyone donates things to sell except Pinch. Eventually, when he sees others passing by his house with so many toys to sell, he decides to contribute. When everyone pools their money, they have enough to buy one tree, but when all the packrats in town bring in their stuff, they have enough for a dozen trees. The moral of reduce, reuse, and recycle also includes making a greener earth. Cox's illustrations are humorous and capture the tale in bright colors.

Read-Aloud Presentation

Ask the children if any of them have ever had a yard sale. Discuss the reasons that people have yard sales—to get rid of stuff they no longer need. Mention the term *packrat*, meaning "someone who collects things but does not get rid of things." Read the book and talk about the value of yard sales to reduce, reuse, and recycle. Announce the STORY S-T-R-E-T-C-H-E-R-S for this book.

STORY S-T-R-E-T-C-H-E-R

Art: Ads for a School Garage Sale

What the children will learn
To design and make attention-getting posters

Materials you will need
Sample posters, poster board, markers, scraps of paper, index cards, double-sided tape

What to do
1. Look at some posters announcing events, and discuss what about the posters draws attention.
2. Talk about attention-getters. Look through *Stuff! Reduce, Reuse, Recycle* and see which illustrations capture the children's attention (begin with the cover and beginning and ending scenes).
3. Ask the children to work with an art partner to determine what would make a good poster.
4. Let the children sketch out some ideas on scraps of paper. Tell them to leave a space about the size of a five-by-seven-inch index card for the information about the sale. Have the children position the index card on the poster board with double-stick tape.
5. Make the posters and then display them in various locations around the school.

Something to think about
Each of the STORY S-T-R-E-T-C-H-E-R-S for *Stuff! Reduce, Reuse, Recycle* is connected to having a tag sale. These sales are called different things in different parts of the country—*yard sale, garage sale, community bazaar*.

STORY S-T-R-E-T-C-H-E-R

Mathematics: How Much Does It Cost?

What the children will learn
To price items for a tag sale to earn money for a class tree

Materials you will need
Price tags or stickers, sale items

What to do
1. Ask the children if they have anything they would like to donate to a class tag sale so the class can buy, for example, a tree to plant for the school.
2. Place the cost of the tree, such as twenty dollars, on a poster or on the board. As children bring in items and tag them, subtract the amount from the cost of the tree.
3. Encourage participation. Begin bringing in items to contribute and suggest some prices.
4. Let the children make the price tags for your contributions after a discussion about what others would be willing to pay.
5. As the children bring in items, add them to the tag sale table, and let the children make the price tags for the items. Continue adding items and subtracting their costs from the price of a tree.

Something to think about

Helping children to reach a goal by their own efforts is important learning at any age.

Mathematics: Classification by Type

What the children will learn

To sort, group, and classify items

Materials you will need

Display space, baskets or plastic tubs, strips of poster board, markers, tape

What to do

1. After a few days of collecting items, begin to classify them by sorting, grouping, then naming the group. For example, toys, winter clothes, and things for babies.
2. Some of the groups can be sorted by subcategories, such as toys: dolls, blocks, trucks, cars.
3. Let the children sort by colors, function, or price.
4. Make signs out of poster board, and let the children place them on their groupings. When the children discover there can be more than one category in a grouping, let them make additional signs. Take the signs off at the end of the day, and let children resort and rename the next day.
5. Let the last sorting be done by how you want the tag sale to be organized, perhaps by types of items and then by prices. For example, toys are grouped together, then there may be a one-dollar table, a fifty-cents table, and a twenty-five-cents table.

Something to think about

Because the children may want to buy things at the tag sale as well, decide on some rules ahead of time.

Social Studies: School Tag Sale

What the children will learn

To take responsibility for contributing to a group effort and for individual tasks

Materials you will need

Chart tablet, markers, index cards or large sticky notes

What to do

1. Brainstorm the tasks for organizing a class or school tag sale. (Get permission from school administration first.)

2. Write a family newsletter describing the activity and how families can be involved. Also, explain how the tag sale fits into the larger unit of study, "Recycle, Reuse, Repurpose."
3. Working with the class, list all the things that need to be done to prepare for the tag sale, such as collecting the items, pricing them, making posters to advertise, setting up, selling, counting up the money earned, and so on.
4. Enlist assistance from family volunteers; have a child assistant for each parent. Encourage the parents to think aloud about what they are doing, so that the child learns the thinking behind the work.
5. As the work is going on, have the chart tablet of tasks available to check off.
6. Have the tag sale with children involved from start to finish, from set-up to clean-up, counting the money, and purchasing the tree.

Something to think about

Having a school tag sale or school yard sale is an excellent social studies activity as it requires organizing tasks with groups of people involved to accomplish a common goal.

Writing: W, W, W, W, H, + Information

What the children will learn

To write appropriate information to announce a tag sale

Materials you will need

Index cards, double-sided tape, scraps of paper, pencils, markers

What to do

1. Discuss the need to announce your tag sale to the school or to the community.
2. Begin by placing an index card on a poster board (see the art STORY S-T-R-E-T-C-H-E-R).
3. Discuss the importance of who, what, when, where, how, and any additional information. For example, who—Ms. Smith's class; what—Tag Sale; when—Friday, February 8, after lunch; where—school cafeteria; how—see a preview sale on Thursday, buy on Friday; + information—money to plant a tree.
4. Tell the children they can write the information as an invitation or as a promotion for a new tree for the school yard.

Something to think about

If there is a closed-circuit television system in the school, let the children write their own commercial to broadcast.

What Can You Do with an Old Red Shoe?

By Anna Alter

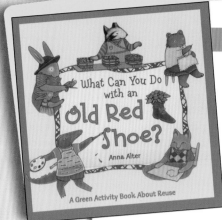

Story Line

An excellent book about reusing and repurposing, *What Can You Do with an Old Red Shoe?* contains thirteen "living green" craft and project ideas that will appeal to primary children. Some require adult assistance, such as cutting an old flip-flop to make it into an art stamp, sewing an old T-shirt into a pillow, or melting bits of crayons. Each craft idea begins with a story poem using a child's name and animal character. Each describes how the object became one that needed to be repurposed. The illustrations and directions are clearly stated and easy to follow. Each double-page spread is encircled with a border and brightly painted illustrations showing each of the steps of the project. Alter's inventiveness with reusing common objects for new purposes and her clever characters are certain to be child-pleasers.

Read-Aloud Presentation

Show the cover of the book and name the characters and their projects. They are Sarah and her flip-flop art stamp, Gertrude and her berry baskets, Ben and his raggedy T-shirt becoming a pillow, Jon making a new calendar from an old calendar, and Fred and his new painting apron from a shower curtain. Read about these projects for the children to get a sense of the content. Add Ruby's planting project, which answers the question, "What can you do with an old red shoe?" Without reading all of the other pages, show the pictures for children to see other possibilities. Announce that the STORY S-T-R-E-T-C-H-E-R-S will include some of the repurposing ideas from the book.

Art: From Flip-Flop to Art Stamp

What the children will learn
To follow directions and make something useful out of something that would have been discarded

Materials you will need
Old flip-flops, scissors, cookie cutters, marker, stamp pad

What to do
1. With the students, review the illustrations in *What Can You Do with an Old Red Shoe?*
2. The children can firmly push a cookie cutter into the bottom of the old flip-flops and then draw around the shapes with a marker.
3. With adult assistance, the children can cut out the shapes, leaving enough to use as a handle.
4. The children can then press the flip-flop shapes into a stamp pad and use them to create a picture.

Something to think about
Stamps have become quite popular with scrapbook makers. Consider inviting a parent who makes scrapbooks to come to your classroom and demonstrate how she or he uses stamps.

Art: Stamping Designs

What the children will learn
To use stamps in a variety of patterns

Materials you will need
Flip-flop stamps, paint trays, tempera paint, brushes, painting paper

What to do
1. Look at Alter's pictures of the Sarah flip-flop project. Notice how Sarah Rabbit makes a stamp of a carrot and stamps it across the page. Let the children suggest other ways Sarah could use her stamp, such as vertically, horizontally, overlapping, or with different colors.
2. Suggest that the children make pictures by using only one stamped shape and drawing or painting a picture around the stamped shape.
3. Display the stamp pictures in the art area of the classroom along with a sign, "What Can You Do with One Flip-flop?"

Something to think about

Consider adding some other art techniques along with stamping. For example, let the children draw with crayons, then stamp in between. The paint will not adhere to the crayon, creating another pattern.

Social Studies: Recycling Toys to Favorite Charities

What the children will learn

To recycle the toys they have outgrown and to be happy that other children now have toys to play with

Materials you will need

Large bins, labels, markers, volunteers

What to do

1. Contact parents and explain the toy-recycling plans. Ask for the names of the families' favorite charities.
2. Call the charities and determine if there are any special rules for their donations: Do they take used and refurbished toys and books? Do they want their donors and recipients to remain anonymous? Can your school name be used if individual names are not appropriate?
3. Plan a week of toy and book collections. You can start the collection so others will be inspired to give. If you have done this project in previous years, tell stories about what has happened in the previous years.
4. Plan for distribution of the toys using parent volunteers and, if possible, allow children to go along.

Something to think about

After distributing the toys to the charities, let the children talk about the experience.

Special Projects: Choose to Reuse and Repurpose

What the children will learn

To reuse an object by repurposing it

Materials you will need

Scissors; staplers; tables; parent volunteers; measuring tape; masking tape; double-sided tape; glue; paste; markers; crayons; pencils; paints; paintbrushes; paint trays; variety of art papers; Velcro dots; materials to reuse, such as old calendars, old wrapping paper and holiday cards, upholstery or heavy thread, twine, old crayons, ice trays, old flip-flops, shower curtain, old red or other color shoe, worn blankets, berry baskets, and tin cans.

What to do

1. Let the children decide which "Living Green—Reuse and Repurpose Projects" they want to do. Select the four or five most popular projects.
2. Set aside an afternoon to complete the projects.
3. Assign a parent volunteer to each table to work with the children making the project. Parents set up a table with enough supplies for their project and for the four or five children who want to do that project.
4. Display the children's projects for everyone to admire for a day before the children take them home.

Something to think about

Review the projects found in the book and help children decide on the next project they want to do at home.

Writing: Writing Instructions for Repurposing Projects

What the children will learn

To write with specificity

Materials you will need

Writing paper, pencils, tape

What to do

1. Ask the children to recall the steps in making their reuse and repurpose projects. What materials did they use? What were the steps?
2. After the children talk about the steps, have them write the instructions in their own words.
3. Tape the children's instructions to their projects.
4. When the children decide which project they want to do at home, have someone give them a set of instructions and go over the instructions with them.

Something to think about

Writing for clarity and precision is not easy to do. Listen to how the parents assist and direct the children with their crafts, and incorporate some of the parents' suggestions as recommendations to the children for their written instructions.

We Are Extremely Very Good Recyclers

By Lauren Child, based on a TV script by Bridget Hurst
Illustrations from the TV animation

Story Line

After a visit to a friend's brother's room that is terribly messy, Lola decides to throw her toys away to clean up her own mess. Her brother Charlie convinces her to recycle them to other children. The recycling message is cleverly conveyed through a contest. If Lola can recycle one hundred cans, one hundred plastic things, and one hundred paper things, she can win a tree to plant in the schoolyard. She only has two weeks and solicits help from her classmates who turn out to be "extremely very good recyclers." The contest motivates them, even the child whose brother has the messy room. The book comes with a poster of a tree with leaves to cut out for everything that is recycled. The endpapers contain some promises for children to make to help look after our planet, from riding bikes, to shutting doors to keep in heat. The illustrations are a combination of cartoon drawings of Charlie and Lola and friends, with scraps of collage materials that include pictures of real objects. The characters are endearing and child-friendly and the illustrations unique.

Read-Aloud Presentation

Ask the children what they like collecting. Discuss the difference between being a collector of a few things versus being a packrat. Talk about what can be done when we have too many things. Read *We Are Extremely Very Good Recyclers*. After reading, introduce the large tree chart and begin planning how the class could become "extremely very good recyclers." See the Recycle Zone website (www.recyclezone.org.uk) for vocabulary about recycling and some wacky facts.

Art: Collages of Recyclables

What the children will learn
To create pictures using scraps of other materials

Materials you will need
Art paper, glue, scraps of construction paper, magazines, scraps of other pieces of children's artwork

What to do
1. Look at the collage artwork in *We Are Extremely Very Good Recyclers*. Discuss how collages are made from parts of other materials that are no longer needed.
2. Provide collage materials with an assortment of textures.
3. Encourage the children to draw themselves recycling and add collage materials to make a new picture from something old.

Something to think about
Children can cut out pieces of their previous artwork, using only the best pieces. Adults often want to keep every piece of artwork a child does. Instead, help the children to pick out what they consider to be their best work to add to their personal art collections, not every picture.

Language Arts: Whisper, "Pass It On"

What the children will learn
To create excitement for a message

Materials you will need
Index cards, marker

What to do
1. Print on an index card the message, "I want to recycle. Pass it on." Do not show the children the message until it has been whispered from child to child around the room.
2. Have the children sit in a circle.
3. Whisper the message in the first child's ear.
4. Have the first child whisper the message to the second child and so on around the room.
5. Ask the last child to state what the message is, and compare it to the message on the index card.
6. Start another whisper with a second message, such as "We are starting Lola's tree contest tomorrow."

Something to think about

This activity is based on the old game of "Gossip" or "Telephone," where the message gets changed by the time it gets to the last person. If this occurs with the recycling message, you can also talk about listening and trying to get clear messages.

STORY S-T-R-E-T-C-H-E-R

Mathematics: Counting, Adding, and Subtracting One Hundred

What the children will learn
To count to one hundred and to add and subtract hundreds

Materials you will need
Tree poster with leaves

What to do
1. Read the pages of the book that describe the contest for which Lola must collect one hundred cans, one hundred plastic things, and one hundred paper things.
2. Write the equation $100 + 100 + 100 = 300$.
3. Count the leaves on the poster. There are one hundred. Write simple equations to show how many more leaves are needed.
4. Cut additional leaves from old newspaper or scraps of construction paper to add to the poster. Store the leaf cutouts for use with the recycling project. Consider making a tree of each type of material that is being recycled: cans, plastics, paper.

Something to think about
Primary-age children enjoy counting to one hundred, and the simplicity of adding and subtracting by hundreds is helpful as well. Consider counting other hundreds, like one hundred paper clips, one hundred crayons, and so on.

STORY S-T-R-E-T-C-H-E-R

Social Studies: Winning Our Tree Contest

What the children will learn
To conduct an extensive recycling project

Materials you will need
Whiteboard, marker, bins for recycling materials, poster and leaf cutouts, glue sticks, masking tape

What to do
1. Discuss Lola's recycling contest. Brainstorm some of the things the children could recycle in their classroom.
2. Introduce the bins and tape an aluminum can to one bin, a plastic drink bottle to another, and a piece of discarded paper onto the third bin.
3. Have the children look around their classroom and find things to recycle. For each thing found, glue a leaf onto the tree poster.
4. Call attention to the fact that there are not enough recyclables to have a $100 + 100 + 100 = 300$ things to win a tree contest.
5. The children will decide if they need help from other classes.
6. Plan a presentation to the other classes to enlist them in the recycling project.
7. Keep a careful tally or count of the objects until the classes reach one hundred cans, one hundred plastic things, and one hundred paper things.
8. Continue the recycling throughout the day.

Something to think about
Ask the students to bring things to recycle from home, to involve the student's parents and family members.

STORY S-T-R-E-T-C-H-E-R

Science: Planting Lola's Tree

What the children will learn
To plant a tree

Materials you will need
Tree, spades, watering hose, amended soil

What to do
1. Consult with the groundskeeper for your school for help on locating a good tree to plant as well as an appropriate site for the tree.
2. Visit a nursery or an arboretum and purchase a tree, or seek a donated tree.
3. Get explicit directions for planting and caring for the tree. If possible, have a professional from the nursery or arboretum help the class.
4. Plant the tree and continue to care for it over time.

Something to think about
Have a celebration of the recycling by having your poster on hand and telling about the project. Sing a song and read a poem about trees.

Dinosaurs Go Green! A Guide to Protecting Our Planet

By Laurie Krasny Brown and Marc Brown

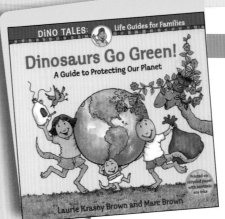

Story Line

The Dinosaur friends have become some of the most endearing characters in literature for primary-aged children. Slobosaurus is encouraged to live green, but he uses more instead of less, tosses things that he could use again, and chooses not to give back to the earth. The Dinosaur friends have to convince him to use less water and energy and to use things more than once instead of throwing them away. The three *R*s of reduce, reuse, recycle are the moral, and convincing Slobosaurus is the plot of the story. Children will learn the importance of protecting the planet and of making it more beautiful. Children will find many suggestions for living green; the characters and appealing Marc Brown illustrations work well with the message.

Read-Aloud Presentation

If your students have read other "Dinosaur friends" books, recall those titles. Introduce the book by reading the title, *Dinosaurs to the Rescue! A Guide to Protecting Our Planet*. Mention that one of the characters is Slobosaurus, and ask how the children think that Slobosaurus might act in the book. Read the book through from start to finish. At the end, check to see if the children's predictions about Slobosaurus were true. End by asking the children to recall the lessons Slobosaurus learned about reducing, reusing, and recycling.

Art: Protecting Our Planet Pictures

What the children will learn

To learn ways to "live green" and protect our planet

Materials you will need

Butcher paper; tape; painting paper; pencils; crayons; paintbrushes; blue, brown, white paints; cardboard pizza circle or pizza pan, scissors

What to do

1. Look at the cover of *Dinosaurs to the Rescue! A Guide to Protecting Our Planet*. On the cover, the Dinosaur friends are dancing around planet Earth with the shapes of the North and South American continents shown.
2. Fold a large sheet of painting paper in half.
3. Use a cardboard pizza circle or pizza pan to trace a circle onto the folded paper.
4. Cut out the circular shape, except for the last two inches on the fold. This makes it like a page that can open.
5. Have the children sketch the North and South American continents onto the paper, color the continents with brown crayon, and then paint the outside circle blue. The blue paint will resist the brown waxy crayon. Allow the paints to dry overnight.
6. Lift the outside blue painted circle, and let the children draw a picture or write a piece of advice for living green, such as "Turn off lights when you leave the room."

Something to think about

Compile a list of the students' advice for how to live green.

Mathematics: Measuring Liquid Quantities

What the children will learn

To measure large quantities of water and how much time it takes to fill each container

Materials you will need

One- and two-gallon buckets, half-gallon pitcher, quart and pint pitchers, sponges, stopwatch

What to do

1. Read the ideas for living green from the book. Wonder aloud how much water is used when brushing teeth.

2. Set up the containers: one- and two-gallon buckets, half-gallon pitcher, one-quart pitcher, one-pint pitcher.

3. Teach some children to use the stopwatches.

4. Let the children fill each of the buckets, pitchers, and containers with water and time how long it takes to fill each. Control the flow of water so that it is the same each time each container is used.

5. Allow different children to be the container fillers, the stopwatch users, and the guessers.

Something to think about

Announce the science experiment planned for later that will measure the amount of water we use when brushing our teeth.

STORY S-T-R-E-T-C-H-E-R

Science: An Experiment in Saving Water

What the children will learn

To conduct an experiment comparing how much water is used when brushing teeth while the water is running with how much is used when the water is used only briefly

Materials you will need

Toothbrushes, toothpaste, recyclable paper cups, one- and two-gallon buckets, half-gallon pitcher, one-quart and one-pint pitchers, sponges, marker

What to do

1. Place the containers from the mathematics STORY S-T-R-E-T-C-H-E-R in or near the sink.

2. Choose some children to be tooth-brushers and have them do their tooth-brushing routine. If they rinse their tooth brush first before putting on the toothpaste, turn on the water at that point.

3. Turn on the water and let it drain into the one- or two-gallon containers while the children are putting toothpaste onto their brushes and brushing their teeth. When each child stops brushing, turn off the water.

4. Measure the amount of water used in gallons, half gallons, quarts, and pints.

5. Repeat the exercise with other brushers. This time, turn off the water after rinsing the toothbrush, and do not turn it back on again until the children are ready to fill their paper cups to rinse out their mouths.

6. Measure the amounts of water used when water is turned off during tooth-brushing and when it is running.

Something to think about

Have the children write a message to their parents about what they want to do to help save water when they are brushing their teeth.

Social Studies: My Family Is Living Green

What the children will learn

To incorporate some of the ideas they have learned at school into their own family lives

Materials you will need

Writing paper, pencils, green crayons

What to do

1. Discuss some of the behaviors that Slobosaurus had to change to become an earth-friendly dinosaur.

2. Have the children write a list of what they could change at their own homes to be more earth-friendly, to reduce, reuse, and recycle. Write the list twice.

3. Send the list home and ask the families to read over the list and decide some routine changes they could make to live greener. Have them place a green crayon checkmark beside the behaviors they want to change.

4. Instruct the children to leave one copy of the list on the refrigerator or a bulletin board at home and return one copy of the list with the checkmarks to school.

5. Discuss the changes as a group at school.

Something to think about

Encourage parent involvement by also sending home a newsletter or referring them to a parent website for a discussion of the unit on living green.

STORY S-T-R-E-T-C-H-E-R

Writing: From Slobosaurus to Greenosaurus

What the children will learn

To write from their own experiences or imagined ones

Materials you will need

Writing paper, pencils, drawing paper

What to do

1. Have children fold a sheet of paper into thirds horizontally.

2. With a writing partner, have the children brainstorm what the beginning of the story might be and write these phrases on the top fold. For the beginning, let them think of a Slobosaurus they know or can imagine.

3. On the second horizontal fold, the children can write the middle of the stories they are telling. The children can imagine what changed Slobosaurus's behavior, such as he could not find his favorite toy because his room was so cluttered.

4. The children can use the last fold of paper for the end of their stories. Or, they can think about the end of the story when Slobosaurus's changed behavior and earned him a new nickname, Greenosaurus.

Something to think about

Young primary-age children may want to draw their ideas on each fold or dictate their thoughts to you or an older student.

References

Alter, Anna. 2009. *What Can You Do with an Old Red Shoe?* New York: Henry Holt.

Brown, Laurie Krasny and Marc Brown. 1992. *Dinosaurs to the Rescue! A Guide to Protecting Our Planet.* Boston: Little, Brown.

Child, Lauren and Bridget Hurst. 2009. *We Are Extremely Very Good Recyclers.* New York: Penguin Group (USA) Inc.

Gibbons, Gail. 1996. *Recycle! A Handbook for Kids.* Boston: Little, Brown.

Kroll, Steven. 2009. *Stuff! Reduce, Reuse, Recycle.* Illustrated by Steve Cox. Tarrytown, NY: Marshall Cavendish.

Additional References

Mariconda, Barbara. 2008. *Sort It Out!* Illustrated by Sherry Rogers. Mt. Pleasant, SC: Sylvan Dell. *Packy the Packrat's mother has had enough! It's time that he sorts through his ever-growing collection of trinkets and puts them away. Told in rhyme, the text leads the reader to participate in the sorting process by categorizing Packy's piles of things according to like characteristics.*

Siddals, Mary Kenna. 2010. *Compost Stew.* Illustrated by Ashley Wolf. Berkley, CA: Tricycle Press. *From eggshells to wiggly worms, this delightful recipe in bouncy verse features familiar items for the compost bin to nourish Mother Earth.*

Winter, Jonah. 2010. *Here Comes the Garbage Barge!* Illustrated by Red Nose Studio. New York. Schwartz & Wade. *Reduce, reuse, recycle. Teaching environmental awareness in a hilarious book that demonstrates that there are consequences to unlimited trash.*

Websites

1. Recycle Zone: www.recyclezone.org.uk
   - Resources for schools, teachers, and children
   - Fun games and activities
2. Environmental Kids Club: www.epa.gov/kids
   - Environmental kids club
   - Extensive teaching resources
   - Art and Game rooms
3. Eco Kids: www.ecokids.ca/pub/index.cfm
   - Games and activities
   - Lesson plans
   - Printables

Transportation

Cars and Trucks and Things That Go

By Richard Scarry

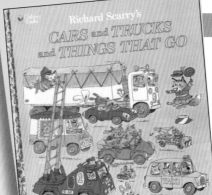

Story Line

The humorous Richard Scarry illustrations cover two-page spreads and are loaded with hundreds of vehicles, real ones and imagined ones. The story follows the Pig family on a picnic, with many types of mayhem along the way. Buried in the tiniest detail is Goldbug, which the children pore over the pictures to find, or they can follow Officer Flossy Fox as she seeks Dingo Dog in his red racing car. The story guides the reader to search the pages for the clues. Children will revisit the sixty-nine pages and giggle at the absurd, but learn about real transportation at the same time.

Read-Aloud Presentation

Show the cover of *Cars and Trucks and Things That Go,* point out the Pig family in the center of the page, and tell the children that they are the center of the story, or the main characters. Point out Goldbug, just below the Pig family in their car, and tell them that Goldbug is often hidden. Point out Officer Flossy Fox and Dingo Dog in his red racing car. Ask the children to predict what Officer Flossy Fox might do in the story and what Dingo Dog might do. Read the story, pausing occasionally to point out the characters, but not on every page, as you want the students to enjoy reading the text and finding the "almost hidden" characters on their own.

Art: Creating "Where's Goldbug?" Pictures

What the children will learn
To use colored pencils and to follow a style of illustration

Materials you will need
Drawing paper, colored pencils, pencils

What to do
1. Talk about the pages of *Cars and Trucks and Things That Go* and how they are illustrated with many different types of transportation on the same page.
2. Call attention to the way Richard Scarry drew illustrations with a pencil and then colored in the sketches with colored pencils.
3. Ask the children to draw a real car or truck and then a funny one. Point out some of the book's funny vehicles from the cover, like the alligator-shaped car on the front and the pumpkin-shaped car on the back.
4. Display the children's drawings around the room for everyone to enjoy.

Something to think about
Consider binding all of the drawings into *Our Class Big Book of Cars and Trucks and Things That Go.* Mark a one-inch margin along the left side of the drawing paper to leave room for the binding on the side.

Reading: Following Officer Flossy Fox

What the children will learn
To read the words *Officer Flossy* and to find them throughout the text, as well as in the illustrations

Materials you will need
Strips of poster board or construction paper, markers

What to do
1. Print the words, *Officer Flossy* and *Flossy* on strips of poster board or construction paper.
2. Show the children the first time the words appear on the pages of the book, and ask them to solve the mystery of how many times these words appear throughout the book (10).

3. Place the two strips, "Officer Flossy" and "Flossy" onto the word wall to read each day.
4. Search for how many times Officer Flossy appears in the illustrations in the book (10).

Something to think about
Complete the same exercise with the words *Goldbug, Pig Family,* and *Dingo Dog.*

STORY S-T-R-E-T-C-H-E-R

Science: Traveling in Different Temperatures

What the children will learn
To associate the ways vehicles look when traveling in different climates

Materials you will need
None needed

What to do
1. Discuss how it can be spring where you live, but when you travel to the mountains, it might be snowing and feel like winter, even though it is actually still spring.
2. With the children, leaf through *Cars and Trucks and Things That Go* find examples of vehicles, and decide what the location and the temperature might be. For example, look at the difference between the first pages when it looks like spring temperatures and pages 54 and 55 where it looks like summer at the beach, or pages 59, 60, and 61 where it looks like winter.
3. Notice what makes each picture look like a different season. Have the children dictate some words that are associated with the different temperatures and seasons. These words can become the science words for the day, such as *frozen, slippery ice; hot, blazing sun; chill in the air;* or *warm breezes.*

Something to think about
First graders may focus on the simple words—*hot, cold, warm,* or *freezing.* Older students may read the descriptive words more easily.

STORY S-T-R-E-T-C-H-E-R

Social Studies and Mathematics: Transportation at the Corner of Our School

What the children will learn
To organize information

Materials you will need
Notebooks, pencils, optional—video camera

What to do
1. Walk outside and notice the different types of transportation that go by.
2. Organize the transportation into different categories, such as cars, trucks, vans, and buses.
3. Separate the children into three or four groups and take them outside at different times during the day: beginning of the day, recess time, lunchtime, and end of the day.
4. Organize the children's data collection by having them write the time of day at the top of each group's page. Then, write the words *cars, trucks, vans,* and *buses* down the left side of their papers. Across from each word make a hash mark or tally mark each time they see different vehicles.
5. The next day, compare the different types of vehicles that each group saw. When were more buses seen? How many were counted?

Something to think about
Older students can classify the vehicles in more categories, such as sports car, family car, two-door, four-door, van, pick-up truck, trailer-truck, schoolbuses, and city buses.

STORY S-T-R-E-T-C-H-E-R

Special Project: Transportation Display

What the children will learn
To arrange a variety of toy cars and trucks by type

Materials you will need
Children's toy cars and trucks brought from their homes

What to do
1. Review the pictures in the book, noticing the variety of cars and trucks and things that go.
2. Ask the children to bring a toy vehicle to class. Make a display of the items.
3. Leave the display out for several days, and rearrange the toy cars and trucks by various categories, such as color, size, function, and other categories.

Something to think about
Select a few children each day to talk about their toys. Consider asking grandparents or an antique-toy collector to bring some samples for the children to see.

Trains: Steaming! Pulling! Huffing!

By Patricia Hubbell
Illustrated by Megan Halsey and Sean Addy

Story Line

Written as poetry, this story of many different kinds of trains includes double-page, full-color illustrations with mostly humans but a few animals sprinkled throughout, and inventive names for trains and their different cars. Page layouts enhance the concepts of the various trains, with most vertically and a few horizontally displayed. Clip art, etchings, and original drawings move the reader through the text. Action words drive the poem and the different train concepts, while adverbs add to the meaning and adjectives enhance the names of the trains. From *zooming, whooshing* streamlined passenger trains to *snorting, puffing* freight trains, every page is complete with pictures that illustrate the poem and rich content.

Read-Aloud Presentation

Take the dust cover off of the book and show the illustration of the streamlined passenger train. Ask what trains the students have been on. If children have traveled by subway, they may not think of these as trains. The trolley is shown as a train near the end of the book, which some may not think of with trains. Tell the children that because this book is written as a poem, you will read it through in its entirety and then go back through and show them the illustrations. Point out some humorous things in each picture, such as the mice with their newspapers and a load of thumbs with top hats for the Tom Thumb toy train. Notice the old-fashioned dress of some of the passengers: women with gloves and men with hats. See the Smithsonian's American history website (www.americanhistory.si.edu/onthemove) for a book on the history of train travel.

STORY S-T-R-E-T-C-H-E-R

Art: Crayon-Resist Night Pictures of Trains

What the children will learn
To use an art technique that can illustrate the night

Materials you will need
Dark red, purple, aqua, or black construction paper; crayons; black, dark brown, and dark blue thinned tempera paints; easels or tabletops; newspapers or butcher paper; masking tape; paint trays or plastic tubs

What to do
1. Show the children night scenes in the book. Have them notice the various colors that are still visible, even though the night looks very dark.
2. Prepare the easels, or use tabletops and tape down old newspapers to protect the tables.
3. Demonstrate how to make a crayon-resist night painting by taking a dark sheet of construction paper and drawing with the waxy crayons to make the trains and the background scene.
4. Wash the construction paper crayon drawings with paint. The watered-down paint will not adhere to the crayon drawing, and when it dries, it will allow the background colors from the construction paper and the crayon drawing to show through.

Something to think about
For older children, consider using watercolors, which are more difficult to manage in crayon resist than tempera paints.

STORY S-T-R-E-T-C-H-E-R

Art: Adding Humor to Pictures

What the children will learn
To interpret humor from the book and creatively add it to their drawings

Materials you will need
Drawing paper or construction paper, paper scraps, pencils, colored pens, markers, crayons, scissors, glue sticks

What to do
1. Point out the illustrations by Halsey and Addy that have something humorous about them. All the pages have humor; some subtler than others. Children will like the

animals as conductors and the unexpected animals mixed in with the humans.

2. Ask the children to draw a train and add something funny to the drawing. The children can draw the funny part separately and glue it onto their pictures or include it in the original drawing.

Something to think about

We have found that some younger children gravitated to the animals as the surprise engineers, while the third graders offered more subtle humor. All were adapting ideas from the illustrations.

STORY S-T-R-E-T-C-H-E-R

Mathematics: How Many Hubbell Trains?

What the children will learn

To count and to classify the trains in the book

Materials you will need

Chart tablet or whiteboard and marker

What to do

1. With a group of children, count the number of different trains in the book. Count toy trains and real-sized trains.
2. Let the children think of some possible categories of trains, such as passenger trains, freight trains, electric trains, steam trains, subway trains, and trolleys.
3. Count the trains in each category. Add them together and note if the number is the same as the total count. See how much the count is off by subtracting the categorized trains from the total count. If the numbers differ, it probably means some trains were not categorized.
4. Redo the categorization and add some categories, such as imaginary trains.

Something to think about

In sharing this book with children, we found the counts varied and could not figure out why until we realized some children were counting the trains on the cover and the dust jacket.

STORY S-T-R-E-T-C-H-E-R

Reading: Choral Reading of Trains

What the children will learn

To read the words of the book with fluency and to read the poetry while observing the punctuation

Materials you will need

Chart tablet or large sheet of poster board, markers

What to do

1. On a chart tablet or poster board, reprint the words of the book, which is a poem. Space the printing so that each verse has the pause needed. Print some of the words smaller and some larger for emphasis; for example, *ROAR* would be large. See the print in the book for examples.
2. Reread the book to the children, using the emphasis and cadence you want them to use.
3. Point out the punctuation in the poem: the period for complete stops, the exclamation point for emphasis, the ellipsis or three dots (. . .) for a pause, and the comma for a briefer pause.
4. Rehearse the poem as a choral reading with the whole class.
5. After the children are fluent and comfortable with reading the poem, assign different verses to groups of children—boys, girls, walkers, bus riders, long hair, short hair. Enjoy the groupings.

Something to think about

Choral reading is an excellent confidence builder for reluctant readers. Rehearse privately with some children who may be having reading difficulties, and give them a line to read with a special cue from you.

STORY S-T-R-E-T-C-H-E-R

Reading: Trains Poem Puzzle

What the children will learn

To pair rhyming words and place them in order

Materials you will need

Large index cards, markers

What to do

1. Reprint the poem onto large index cards, printing only one line on each card.
2. Have the children reassemble the poems by arranging the cards in order, using the rhyming words as clues.
3. Leave the Train Poem Puzzle in the classroom library area with the book. Younger children can use the book as a guide as they assemble the poem. Older students can put stanzas together then decide how to order them by referring to the book.

Something to think about

Getting children to revisit the text, as with the Train Poem Puzzle, helps them to read for information and to practice their reading.

Airplanes: Soaring! Turning! Diving!

By Patricia Hubbell
Illustrated by Megan Halsey
and Sean Addy

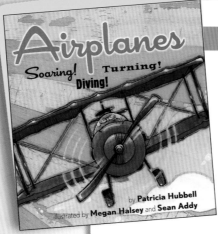

Story Line

Airplanes and their movements are shown on two-page spreads with rhyming poems and wordplay puns leading readers to get the message and the fun. Jumbo jets, cargo planes, crop dusters, single-engine planes, two- and four-motor planes, army and navy fighters, air-show planes, hydroplanes, banner-pulling planes, single-wing and biplanes, and model airplanes are the featured planes. The illustrations capture the planes and have funny interpretations, such as water buffalo seated behind a girl listening to her iPod, a rabbit pilot crop-dusting his carrot crop, and a cargo plane for a circus troop.

Read–Aloud Presentation

Let the children make airplane noises they used to make when they were little, flying around the room. Brainstorm a list of all the different types of planes the children know now. Read *Airplanes: Soaring! Turning! Diving!* After you finish the book, have the children add to the list of planes they know, including the ones in Hubbell's book. Announce the STORY S-T-R-E-T-C-H-E-R-S, and let the children choose whether they want to start by being artists or writers.

STORY S-T-R-E-T-C-H-E-R

Art: Collages of Airplanes

What the children will learn
To use a variety of materials to create a picture

Materials you will need
Scraps of paper, fabric, scissors, sturdy paper or poster board, glue sticks, optional—old calendars of airplanes

What to do
1. Show the children the illustrations by Halsey and Addy. Discuss that the illustrations are collage art, where shapes are glued on to a background.
2. Discuss the types of backgrounds that would be good for airplane pictures.
3. Let the children create airplane collages.

Something to think about
Look at the collage illustrations where a large object is prominent or is in silhouette, such as the weathervane showing directions, the Statue of Liberty, or soldiers saluting. Older children could think of the appropriate silhouette for the type of plane they want to feature in their collage.

STORY S-T-R-E-T-C-H-E-R

Poetic Voices: Choral Reading

What the children will learn
To read in unison

Materials you will need
Classroom copies of the text of the book

What to do
1. Read the text of the poem with the right emphasis at periods for stops, commas for pauses, and exclamation points for emphasis.
2. Let the children rehearse with you.
3. Mark what would be a stanza, such as after each exclamation point.

Something to think about
Orchestrate a background chorus. For example, have some children say, "Airplanes: Soaring! Turning! Diving!" after each stanza.

Special Visitor: Model Airplane Pilot

What the children will learn
To control a model airplane

Materials you will need
Remote control airplane brought by the special visitor

What to do
1. Invite a model-airplane enthusiast to class.
2. Ask him or her to demonstrate how to fly the model airplane.
3. Allow the children to fly the plane, if the controls are simple enough.

Something to think about
Often model-airplane enthusiasts are members of clubs and usually fly different models. See if several representatives of the club can share their planes.

Science: Paper Airplanes

What the children will learn
To fold different designs of paper airplanes

Materials you will need
Computer paper, electric fan

What to do
1. Demonstrate for the children how to fold paper airplanes with different wing formations.
2. Try flying the airplanes and see which wing designs will go the greatest distance.
3. Fly the different designs with the wind of an electric fan and compare the distances.

Something to think about
From a reference book on paper airplanes, fold and refine the models of planes. Ask some older children with more experience making paper airplanes to come to your class and teach the students how to fly the planes. Always invite brothers and sisters of your students.

Writing: Airplane Poetry

What the children will learn
To use descriptive words to explain design and movement

Materials you will need
Chalk, and chalkboard or markers and whiteboard, small slips of paper

What to do
1. Reread *Airplanes: Soaring! Turning! Diving!*
2. Notice the words in the title and in the book that describe the planes and their movements. For example, "the little planes with short wings that island hop make many short stops."
3. Write the names of types of airplanes on small slips of paper.
4. Have each child draw a slip of paper and read the type of airplane on the slip of paper. That plane becomes the plane he or she writes about for the plane poem.

Something to think about
Encourage the children to illustrate their poems. Group the poems about small planes together and bind them into a book. Group the poems about large planes together and bind them into another classroom book.

Toy Boat

By Randall de Sève
Illustrated by Loren Long

Story Line

A tiny toy boat made by a little boy is lost in a storm where it encounters various types of boats. Several boats almost destroy the tiny toy boat and brashly push it around and warn it to get out of their way. The tugboat, giant ferry, speedboat, sailboats, and sloops pass him by, but a little fishing boat guides the tiny toy boat back to shore. The little boatbuilder has been waiting, hoping to find his toy boat again. Loren Long's two full-page spreads and full-color illustrations show details of boats and capture the treacherous storm and the beautiful lakeshore.

Read-Aloud Presentation

Show the front and back covers of the book and ask the children what might happen to the little toy boat. Let the children brainstorm some types of boats that might be on a large lake, like one of the Great Lakes. Read the book through without stopping because the suspense moves the story along. At the end, have the children recall the types of boats the toy boat encounters.

Art: Stormy Weather Scenes

What the children will learn
To use tempera paints to shade and darken

Materials you will need
Tempera paints, brushes, easels or tabletops, painting paper

What to do
1. Reexamine Loren Long's illustrations in *Toy Boat* and notice the different shades of blue, when it is sunny, when the storm clouds are brewing, and when it is stormy.
2. Have the children paint their own versions of stormy seas or a sunny lakeshore.
3. Let the children experiment with mixing colors to lighten or darken the paints.

Something to think about
Ask the art teacher at the school to work on mixing paints to create a variety of shades of blue, similar to the ones in the book.

STORY S-T-R-E-T-C-H-E-R

Creative Dramatics: Voices to Match the Boat Characters

What the children will learn
To use their voices to demonstrate strength, authority, and power

Materials you will need
Recorder to capture the children's voices

What to do
1. Read *Toy Boat* again and practice the expressions of the tired tugboat, the bellowing ferry, the screaming speedboat, the warning voice of the sloop, and the humble helpful voice of the little fishing boat.
2. After the rehearsal, record the children reading the story with expression.
3. Place the recording in an area of the classroom library where children can enjoy the recording and the book together.

Something to think about

Consider adding sailors' hats and captains' hats for the children to wear while reading. It helps with the drama.

STORY S-T-R-E-T-C-H-E-R

Science: Making a Boat That Floats

What the children will learn
To follow directions as well as to improvise

Materials you will need
Cans cut in half, pencils, corks, white cloth, sticks, strong thread or twine, water table or children's plastic swimming pool, fan
Note: Cover any of the cans' sharp edges with duct tape.

What to do
1. Look at the illustrations and description of the toy boat that the little boy made.
2. Invite the children to work with the materials and experiment with making their own boats.
3. Try floating the boats in the water table or the plastic pool. Use a fan to simulate the wind.

Something to think about
After the children construct their boats, let them write directions for another class or for a younger group of children to follow their designs.

STORY S-T-R-E-T-C-H-E-R

Social Studies: Lakes Near Us

What the children will learn
To identify lakes within driving distance of the school

Materials you will need
Local maps, computer with internet access

What to do
1. Secure the maps and enlarge the legends of the maps so that the children can see the bodies of water.
2. By reviewing the maps with the children, decide on the most prominent lake nearby and chart how one would get there from the school.
3. Use a search engine to find websites about the lake and for the surrounding area.
4. Practice reading the map from near and from far.
5. Call attention to some markers one would see along the way if one were to drive from the school to the lake.

Something to think about

With GPS devices so commonplace, children may be familiar with maps, but they may not know the differences in land maps and charts for lakes, rivers, and bodies of water.

STORY S-T-R-E-T-C-H-E-R

Social Studies: Boat Safety Lessons

What the children will learn
To know the safety precautions for being on different types of boats

Materials you will need
Life preservers or life jackets, boating safety rules from a boating association or from a state park

What to do
1. Practice putting on life jacket or using life preservers.
2. Review the safety rules with the children.
3. Discuss how the safety rules may vary for different types of boats, but all boats require life preservers or life jackets.

Something to think about
Consider inviting a harbormaster or lake patrol professional to come to the school to speak. Emphasizing safety for children is paramount in this age group, who usually lack experience with boats. See safety tips also for walking and biking at the National Highway Traffic Safety website (www.nhtsa.dot.gov/people/outreach/safesobr/19qp/sect4/tips/index.html).

Always Got My Feet: Poems About Transportation

By Laura Purdie Salas
Illustrated by various photographers

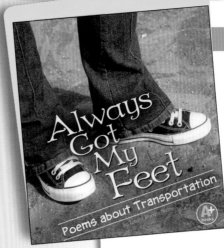

Story Line

Beautifully colorful photographs provide the pages for the superimposed poems. Types of transportation include *Air Force One*, the Staten Island ferry, school bus, skateboard, desert camel, bike, sailboat, monster truck, and one's own feet, to name a few. A mix of the familiar and unfamiliar transportation forms and six poetry forms make the book an extraordinary curricular find. A glossary, samples of poetry forms, and websites help teacher and reader stretch this book even more.

Read-Aloud Presentation

Ask the children to list all the types of transportation they have used to get to school today—car, van, bus, feet. Have the children think of other forms of transportation they have been on, such as an airplane, a train, or a subway train. Pause after each poem to add the name of the type of transportation to the class list. After reading the complete book, have the children think of the forms of transportation that were surprising, such as camel, monster truck, skateboard, sailboat, rowboat. Discuss safety tips for walking and biking to school. See the safety tips at www.nhtsa.dot.gov/people/outreach/safesobr/19qp/sect4/tips/index.html.

STORY S-T-R-E-T-C-H-E-R

Art: Cars, Trucks, and Vans of the Future

What the children will learn
To draw futuristic designs

Materials you will need
Photos of old cars or trucks, perhaps from classic car and truck calendars or from reference books; drawing paper; pencils; markers; crayons

What to do
1. Look at photos of old cars and trucks with the children.
2. Have the children describe how cars and trucks are different today—fewer fins, few two-tones, more vans, smaller cars, or two-cab trucks.
3. Discuss what cars of the future might be like—fold-up doors, bubble sunroofs, wings that appear, helicopter rotors, whatever the children can imagine.
4. Have the children use art materials to draw what they think the cars, trucks, and vans of the future will be.

Something to think about
Invite some older children from the fourth through sixth grades to bring their drawings of cars of the future to show to your class.

STORY S-T-R-E-T-C-H-E-R

Music: "Row, Row, Row Your Boat," Rewritten

What the children will learn
To rewrite a lyric to reflect new transportation information

Materials you will need
Chart tablet, markers

What to do
1. Write the words to "Row, Row, Row Your Boat" on a chart tablet:
   Row, row, row your boat, gently down the stream.
   Merrily, merrily, merrily, merrily, life is but a dream.
2. Suggest that the children rewrite the lyrics for a sailboat instead of for a row boat. For example,
   Wind, wind, catch the wind, as the sails unfurl.
   Merrily, merrily, merrily, merrily, sailing's but a dream.
3. Try other types of transportation, such as *Air Force One*,
   Fly, fly, fly around, fly around the world.
   Fly, fly, fly, fly, presi-dent on board.

Something to think about

Use other types of transportation with other descriptive words, such as *blasting monster trucks, rocking camels, swishing monorails.*

STORY S-T-R-E-T-C-H-E-R

Mathematics: Transportation Survey

What the children will learn

To represent results of a survey on a vertical bar graph

Materials you will need

Chart tablet or poster board; markers; glue sticks; construction paper cut in the shapes of car, truck, van, school bus, bike, and shoes or feet

What to do

1. Construct a bar graph with the shapes of the six types of transportation along the x-axis and the numerals from 1–25 or the number of children on the y-axis.
2. Begin the construction of the graph by asking each child which form of transportation he or she used to get to school. Place a hash mark or tally mark each time that form is mentioned, such as six marks beside the van, ten marks beside the bus, and so on.
3. Count the hash marks or tally marks for each form of transportation. Let the children find the point on the graph that is across from the form of transportation and count on the number line to find the right number.
4. Interpret the graph and answer the question of which forms of transportation your class used to get to school, and then rank the forms in order from the least used to the most used.

Something to think about

Simplify the graph for first graders. Use horizontal bars and simply place hash or tally marks directly on a chart. Let the children think of what types of transportation they would like to use to get to school, and graph those choices.

STORY S-T-R-E-T-C-H-E-R

Writing: Acrostic Transportation Poems

What the children will learn

To write a poem about a type of transportation using a poetry form

Materials you will need

Chart tablet or whiteboard, markers

What to do

1. Reread the acrostic poem, "The Trick," on page 7. It has the word *skateboard* written one letter at a time vertically down the page. Also read "Limo" on page 13.
2. Let the children select the type of transportation for you to demonstrate. For example, "Mono for Monorail." Print the letters *M-O-N-O* down the left-hand side of the page, then complete the poem. For example,
"Mono for Monorail"
Many people ride it
One is another word for mono
Number of rails
Over which the monorail runs.

Something to think about

Young children should start with simple short poems, but it also is a way for them to learn that not all poetry rhymes.

STORY S-T-R-E-T-C-H-E-R

Writing: Unusual Poetry Forms for Unusual Transportation

What the children will learn

To use a different poetry form and to use new knowledge of a form of transportation

Materials you will need

Chart tablet or board, chalk, markers, construction paper or drawing paper, pencils, colored pencils, slips of paper

What to do

1. Review the six types of poetry illustrated in the book.
2. Let children decide if they want to write a couplet, acrostic, concrete poem, diamonte, haiku, or sijo, which are all illustrated in the book.
3. Write the names of the different types of transportation mentioned in the book on small slips of paper.
4. Have each child draw a slip of paper from a paper bag, and then write a poem about that type of transportation using the type of poetry form he or she selected.

Something to think about

Select fewer poetry forms for first and second graders, such as rhymed couplet, acrostic, and concrete poem forms. See DLTK's Growing Together website (www.dltk-kids.com/transportation/index.html) for other transportation poems.

References

de Sève, Randall. 2007. *Toy Boat*. Illustrated by Loren Long. New York: Penguin Group (USA) Inc.

Hubbell, Patricia. 2005. *Trains: Steaming! Pulling! Huffing!* Illustrated by Megan Halsey and Sean Addy. Tarrytown, NY: Marshall Cavendish.

Hubbell, Patricia. 2008. *Airplanes: Soaring! Turning! Diving!* Illustrated by Megan Halsey and Sean Addy. Tarrytown, NY: Marshall Cavendish.

Salas, Laura Purdie. 2008. *Always Got My Feet: Poems About Transportation*. Mankato, MN: Capstone Press.

Scarry, Richard. 1974. *Cars and Trucks and Things That Go*. New York: Random House.

Additional References

Goodman, Susan. 2004. *Choppers!* Photographs by Michael Doolittle. New York: Random House. *Helicopters are amazing machines that go places other vehicles cannot. See daring jobs and rescues in full color.*

Potts, Aidan. 2010. *The Smash! Smash! Truck*. New York: David Fickling Books. *A truck speeds up the recycling process for glass bottles.*

Rex, Michael. 2002. *My Freight Train*. New York: Henry Holt. *A little boy, living out his fantasy of driving his own freight train, describes the different cars, what each carries, how they are connected, and more.*

Websites

1. National Highway Traffic Safety Administration, Child Transportation Safety Tips: www.nhtsa.dot.gov/people/outreach/safesobr/19qp/sect4/tips/index.html
   - Safety tips
   - Kids on the move—walking and biking safely
2. Smithsonian National Museum of American History, America on the Move: www.americanhistory.si.edu/onthemove
   - Games and learning resources
   - Extensive chronological exhibit of modes of transportation
3. DLTK's Growing Together: www.dltk-kids.com/crafts/transportation/index.html
   - Crafts, songs, poems, and posters
   - Links to other transportation-themed craft sites

Folktales, Fables, and Legends

Rainbow Crow

Retold by Nancy Van Laan
Illustrated by Beatriz Vidal

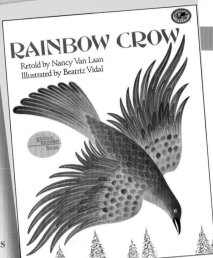

Story Line

Different tribes depict the crow as the creature that brings fire to the earth. *Rainbow Crow* is an adaptation of the Lenape tribe's legend of the fire bearer, as told by Elder Bill "Whippoorwill" Thompson and retold by Nancy Van Laan. Crow was once a beautiful bird with rainbow-colored feathers, who rescues the forest animals from a snowstorm by bringing fire to earth to melt the snow. In the process of bringing the fire from the Great Spirit, Rainbow Crow's feathers are burned and blackened. Beatriz Vidal's bright, colorful, full-page illustrations of the magnificent Rainbow Crow and the fire make this book excellent for reading to an entire class.

Read-Aloud Presentation

Ask the children what color feathers crows have. Show the cover of *Rainbow Crow* and have the children imagine how the crow's feathers turned from these beautiful colors to black. After a few children offer possible explanations, read the story. Pause at the scene in which the snow is getting higher and higher, and let the children predict what they think will happen to the animals. Read on, and have one or two children tell what might happen when Rainbow Crow approaches Great Spirit in the Sky. Continue reading until the end of the book. Then go back and read the author's note about when she first heard the legend of Rainbow Crow. Read the book again, and let the children join you in the chants and songs that the animals and Rainbow Crow sing.

Art: Feather Painting

What the children will learn
To use feathery strokes for painting

Materials you will need
Paper, feathers or construction paper, scissors, meat trays, tempera paints, brushes

What to do
1. If you do not have feathers available in a craft store, fold scraps of construction paper to make several thicknesses. Cut along one side in a curved line, and snip into the edge of the curve to make feathery wisps.
2. Pour bright colors of tempera paint into separate meat trays.
3. Gently float the real feathers on top of the tempera paint or dip the construction-paper feathers into paint.
4. Show the children how to place the paint-covered feathers on the paper and gently pull them along the paper to paint.
5. Continue painting with the feathers, or switch to brushes after the feathers become saturated with paint.

Something to think about
Leave the feather in the painting, and as it dries, it will adhere to the picture. (Idea adapted from one by Melissa Earl.)

Classroom Library: Storytellers— Keeping the Oral Tradition Alive

What the children will learn
To listen appreciatively

Materials you will need
None needed

What to do
1. Invite a Native American storyteller or a skilled storyteller from another cultural tradition to come to class and share a particularly exciting tale.
2. Select an animal story from an anthology for storytellers.
3. After a few practice sessions at home, tell the story to the class.
4. Invite children who are interested to learn a story to tell.

Something to think about

In addition to the importance of keeping the oral tradition alive for its own sake, teachers observe that improving children's listening skills improves their story comprehension, an important reading skill (Applebee, 1978; Isbell, et al., 2004; Raines & Isbell, 1994). Good storytellers are certain to have a profound effect on young children's desire to listen.

STORY S-T-R-E-T-C-H-E-R

Classroom Library: Geographic Native American Folktales and Legends

What the children will learn

The names of the Native American tribes or Indians who live or lived in your geographic region

Materials you will need

Reference books, map

What to do

1. Research the names and some interesting facts about the Indians who live or lived in your geographic region.
2. If possible, find a legend or an often-told tale that is credited to the native people of your area.
3. Invite a Native American to tell the story to the class.
4. With permission, record the story and transcribe it for the children to read.

Something to think about

Indians lived in all areas of the United States before the Europeans came, and many continue to live throughout the United States. Be sure to introduce the Native Americans from your area in terms of their ancient tales and customs and where they live now and their modern lives and homes. It is difficult for young children in the first and second grades to have a historical perspective, so treat the storytelling as just that—a story to be enjoyed—but also identify it as a story told by a certain people. See the American Folklore website (www.americanfolklore.net/index.html) for Native American tales from various states.

STORY S-T-R-E-T-C-H-E-R

Music and Movement: Rainbow Crow's Chant

What the children will learn

To chant and keep the rhythm in a spoken piece

Materials you will need

Chart tablet, marker, drum

What to do

1. Reprint Rainbow Crow's song to Great Sky Spirit and the animals' appreciation song on chart tablet paper.
2. Let the children practice reading the songs a few times.
3. Have the children hear the rhythm of the words and gently pat their knees or clap their hands together to keep the beat.
4. Chant the songs, keeping the rhythm, and then add a drum to keep the rhythm the children are making.

Something to think about

Ask the school music teacher to teach the children other authentic Native American rhythms, chants, and songs.

STORY S-T-R-E-T-C-H-E-R

Writing: An Animal Tale of a Great Feat

What the children will learn

To create their own folktale

Materials you will need

Chalkboard, chalk, scrap paper, writing paper, pencils, optional—art supplies for illustrations

What to do

1. Have the children recall that Native American folktales and legends are often about an element, such as fire or water, or about creation or animals with supernatural powers.
2. Discuss how Rainbow Crow performs a heroic deed and burns his beautiful feathers to save his friends.
3. Let the children brainstorm an idea they have for a story where an animal performs a heroic deed. When the group has generated enough ideas, ask the writers to draw what might happen at the beginning, middle, and end of their story on a scrap of paper and discuss it with a writing partner.
4. After the "prewriting" activity of drawing, let each child write his or her own piece for a classroom collection of animal tales.

Something to think about

Younger children can draw three illustrations: the first drawing showing the beginning of the story where the animal or animals are introduced; the second picture showing the problem that has to be solved; and the third drawing showing how one animal saves the others. Let the children write simple captions for their compositions and tell about their stories rather than write long pieces.

The Legend of the Indian Paintbrush

Retold by Tomie dePaola

The Legend of the Indian Paintbrush

retold and illustrated by Tomie dePaola

Story Line

Little Gopher is a young Plains Indian who paints pictures of the hills and meadows of what is now Texas and Wyoming. While Little Gopher has a great talent as a painter, he is small and wishes he could be like the other children and learn to hunt and be brave. After going into the hills to think about becoming a man, he has a vision that he will keep the stories of his people alive through his pictures. He strives to paint better and better pictures. As a reward for staying true to his talent, Little Gopher's paintbrush becomes the Indian Paintbrush flowers that emblazon the countryside every spring, and his people rename him He-Who-Brought-the-Sunset-to-the-Earth. Illustrated in classic dePaola style, the ancient legend comes to life with simple lines. Earthy tones, brilliant sunsets, and dramatic splashes of color are a beautiful complement to the book.

Read-Aloud Presentation

If possible, find a photograph of real Indian Paintbrush flowers. Show the children the pictures and let the children admire the flowers and read about where they grow and when they blossom.

Read *The Legend of the Indian Paintbrush* without pausing for discussion. At the end, look back through the illustrations, and let the children tell which pictures they like best and why. Talk about dePaola's use of line and color. Ask the children what they think it means when the author says that Little Gopher stays true to his gift or true to his talent. Do not belabor the point, but discuss talents as something we really enjoy doing and do well. Those things are our gifts, our talents.

Art: Painting on Paper Buckskin

What the children will learn
To paint pictures of scenes from nature

Materials you will need
Brown paper bags, scissors, tempera paints and brushes or crayons and markers

What to do
1. Look at dePaola's illustrations of Little Gopher painting on buckskin or leather.
2. Help the children make paper "buckskin" by cutting open a paper bag and cutting out an irregular shape that looks like a piece of leather.
3. Roll the paper up into a ball, crush it, and then open it. Repeat several times until the paper feels more pliable.
4. Spread the paper out flat, and let the children paint or draw scenes from nature that Little Gopher might have seen, such as landscapes, animals, and plants or natural things they enjoy.
5. Have the children write captions for their "Buckskin Paintings" and label them as painted by "[Child's first name] Little Gopher."

Something to think about
Make the paper even more pliable by wetting it and crushing it into a ball, then spreading it out to dry overnight. (Adapted from an idea by Kim Gerher, who was a student teacher at George Mason University.)

Classroom Library: Flannel Board Story of Little Gopher

What the children will learn
To retell the story using flannel board characters

Materials you will need
Chalkboard, chalk, felt, scissors, markers, flannel board, pieces of old emery boards, glue, large plastic sandwich bag, masking tape, marker

What to do

1. Look at *The Legend of the Indian Paintbrush,* and let the children decide which characters and landscapes are needed to retell the story. Print their list on the board and have the children practice retelling the story by recalling each person or scene.
2. Have the children draw the characters and landscapes on pieces of felt, cut them out, and glue a piece of old emery board onto the back of the felt to make the piece adhere to the flannel board easily.
3. Let the children use the flannel board pieces to retell the story.
4. Let one child read or retell the story while the other places the pieces on the flannel board.
5. Store the flannel board pieces in a plastic zipper-closure bag. Place the bag in the library area with a copy of the book. Write the title of the story on masking tape and place it on the outside of the storage bag.

Something to think about

Let the children make the flannel board pieces from construction paper by drawing and cutting out the characters. Laminate them, cut them out again, and glue the old emery board or a piece of sandpaper to the back.

STORY S-T-R-E-T-C-H-E-R

Science and Nature: Indian Paintbrush Flowers

What the children will learn
To recognize Indian Paintbrush and where it grows

Materials you will need
Photographs, reference books, map

What to do

1. Look at pictures of the Indian Paintbrush flowers.
2. Read about where the flowers grow, how they grow, when they blossom, the conditions under which they grow best, and whether or not the plant is endangered, as many wildflowers now are.
3. Locate on a map the areas of Texas and Wyoming where the Indian Paintbrush is indigenous.
4. Place the reference book in the science and nature center for children to look at the photographs.

Something to think about
Write to the tourism departments in Texas and Wyoming, and request brochures with pictures of the Indian Paintbrush.

STORY S-T-R-E-T-C-H-E-R

Science and Nature: Planting Wildflowers

What the children will learn
To read and follow planting directions

Materials you will need
Writing paper and pencils, chart tablet, marker, wildflower seeds, potting trays, potting soil, pots, hand spade, large plastic dishpans, science learning logs

What to do

1. After obtaining wildflower seeds, read aloud the directions for planting the seeds, and have the children list all the equipment that the class will need.
2. Have two children work together to write the planting directions in their own words and draw simple rebus illustrations of each step. Let these children make a chart of their directions and post it in the science and nature center for the other children to follow.
3. Plant the seeds and let the children record the growth of their plants by observing them each day.

Something to think about
Invite a local horticulturist to bring to class samples of wildflowers grown from seeds not taken from the wild.

STORY S-T-R-E-T-C-H-E-R

Writing: Two Stories from One Painting

What the children will learn
To interpret a painting in more than one way

Materials you will need
Writing paper, pencils

What to do

1. Look at Tomie dePaola's illustrations of Little Gopher's Dream-Vision. Discuss how Little Gopher's paintings tell the story of his people.
2. Have the children look at the buckskin paintings they did for the art STORY S-T-R-E-T-C-H-E-R and then write the stories their paintings tell.
3. Without reading their stories to each other, randomly pass out the children's buckskin paintings to each other, and let each child write a story for someone else's work.

Something to think about
Young children can dictate long stories to parents, who can type them on a computer. The children can see their spoken words becoming print.

One Fine Day

By Nonny Hogrogian

ONE FINE DAY
by Nonny Hogrogian

Story Line

This Caldecott Medal book published in 1971 is an Armenian folktale. An old woman sets down a pail of milk and gathers firewood. A fox comes along and drinks the milk, which makes the woman so angry she chops off his tail. The fox begs for his tail back, but the old woman will not put it back until the fox replaces the milk. So begins his journey to find the cow who will give the milk. But the cow will not give the fox the milk until he brings some grass, and so the tale continues. In the end, the old woman carefully sews the fox's tail back on so that none of his friends will laugh at him. With its vivid colors and stylized drawings of the bright orange fox, this book has become a favorite among young children and beginning readers.

Read–Aloud Presentation

Draw a large circle on the chalkboard. Write the title of the book in the middle of the circle, and make a slash mark on the circle for each scene of the story. At the top of the circle make a check mark for the beginning where the old woman chops off the fox's tail. Follow the outside curve of the story as you make the next check mark when you read about the cow, another for the fox talking to the grass, then the stream, and so on. Read the story through to the end where it returns to the top of the circle, and the old woman sews on the fox's tail. After completing the story, go back and write a key word beside each check mark, such as *tail, cow, grass, stream, jug, bead, peddler, egg, hen, grain*, and *tail* again. The story ends where it began, with the fox's tail. Tell the children this is a circle story.

Art: Picture Circle Stories

What the children will learn
To use graphic representations for scenes

Materials you will need
Pizza cardboard forms, pencils, scissors, construction paper or poster board, brad, crayons or markers

What to do
1. Trace the pizza cardboard form onto construction paper or poster board. Cut out the large circle.
2. Have the children mark off ten equal "pie pieces" around the circle and use these as the frames for small pictures or graphic representations that tell the story. For example, in the first frame the children can draw the fox's bushy tail; the second, the cow; and so on.
3. Make out another large circle, and cut an opening in it the size of one of the story frames.
4. Place the second circle over the circle story illustrations and hold it loosely in place with a brad.
5. The children can turn the picture frame with the cutout to the different illustrations and retell the story.

Something to think about
For first graders who may have difficulty drawing small pictures, eliminate the cover circle.

Classroom Library: Circle Stories

What the children will learn
To retell a story with graphic reminders

Materials you will need
Circle stories from the writing STORY S-T-R-E-T-C-H-E-R, other folktales and similar stories, chart tablet, marker

What to do
1. Have the children exchange circle stories and retell each other's story by looking at the story frames.
2. Let the children find other folktales, such as *Millions of Cats* by Wanda Gag and *It Could Always Be Worse* by Margot Zemach, and see if they are circle stories.
3. Display a collection of circle stories in the library area.

Something to think about

Try a variety of graphic representations of stories, for example a fan with a symbol for each scene drawn on its folds, or a sheet of paper folded to make three columns where the children can illustrate three-wishes tales.

Creative Dramatics: Readers' Theatre

What the children will learn
To read lines in unison and with expression

Materials you will need
None needed

What to do
1. Read *One Fine Day* as a readers' theatre piece by dividing the children into seven character groups: the cow, the grass, the stream, the maiden, the peddler, the hen, and the miller.
2. Ask another child to read the part of the fox, and you read the part of the old woman.
3. Read the book. Have the character groups read their lines together. Rehearse for expression.

Something to think about
Make paper bag masks to represent each character. Divide the class into character readers and mask wearers. As each group says its character's lines, the mask wearers can walk across the group-time area or stand in place. In the end, the mask wearers can take off their masks and say in unison, "And that is the story of how the red fox lost and found his tail on One Fine Day."

Music and Movement: Oh Where, Oh Where Can My Fox Tail Be?

What the children will learn
To sing the story by rewriting a familiar song with new lyrics

Materials you will need
Chart tablet, marker

What to do
1. Teach the children the old song, "Oh Where, Oh Where Has My Little Dog Gone?" and then print the words on a chart tablet.

Note: If you are unfamiliar with this song, the lyrics and tune are at http://kids.niehs.nih.gov/lyrics/doggone.htm.

2. After the children learn the tune, let them brainstorm how they might change the song to tell the story of *One Fine Day*. For example, for the first verse sing,
Oh where, oh where can I get some milk?
Oh where, oh where can it be?
Without the milk my tail is gone,
Oh where, oh where can it be?
3. Continue substituting for each item the fox must bring back: a jug for the water, a bead for the maiden, an egg for the peddler, and some grain for the hen.

Something to think about
One need not be an accomplished vocalist to sing with children. Choose simple songs with familiar tunes. Also, if you have a music specialist in your school, accompany the children when they go to their music lessons and learn along with them.

Writing: Writing Circle Stories

What the children will learn
To create a story that begins and ends in the same place

Materials you will need
Writing paper, pencils

What to do
1. Discuss the circle stories the children made in art and the additional ones they found and illustrated in the classroom library. Suggest that the children write their own circle stories, a story that begins and ends in the same place.
2. Let the children brainstorm in small groups or with a writing partner and then begin to write circle stories.
3. When the writers finish, let them draw their own illustrations of their stories.

Something to think about
Have the children read their stories in the author's chair, while their writing partners show the story circle. Place the children's circle stories in the classroom library, so the children can retell each other's stories.

Zomo the Rabbit: A Trickster Tale from West Africa

By Gerald McDermott

Story Line

Zomo the Rabbit is clever, but he wants more. He goes to Sky God and asks how he can become wise. Sky God tells him that to earn wisdom he must carry out three impossible tasks: capture the scales of Big Fish, the milk of Wild Cow, and the tooth of Leopard. Through a series of clever tricks, Zomo succeeds in each task. Sky God praises Zomo for his cleverness and offers him a gift of wisdom, meaning when he sees Big Fish, Wild Cow, and Leopard, it would be wise to run fast. McDermott's bold and comical graphics are bright in colors on sunny yellow and orange backgrounds. The patterns in Zomo's shirt, hat, and drum, as well as the plants and flowers, help the reader identify the tale's setting as West Africa.

Read-Aloud Presentation

Discuss the meaning of the word *trickster.* Note that in traditional tales, the rabbit is often a trickster. Some students may think of Bugs Bunny, who is always tricking his friends in the cartoons. Ask the children to listen for the three tasks Zomo must accomplish to prove himself. Read *Zomo the Rabbit: A Trickster Tale from West Africa*, pausing just once in the story when the Sky God tells Zomo the three things he must do to gain wisdom. After the reading, call attention to the fact that in many folktales, the trickster is the one who is tricked in the end. Explore other trickster tales at the Bright Hub website (www.brighthub.com/education/k-12/articles/9667.aspx).

Art: Zomo's Geometric Fabric Patterns

What the children will learn
To make beautiful geometric patterns

Materials you will need
Brightly colored poster board, pencils, scissors, glue

What to do
1. Cut large shirt-shaped pieces from poster board of different colors. Save the scraps.
2. Look closely at McDermott's illustrations of Zomo, and note the beautiful geometric patterns.
3. Encourage the children to trade scraps of poster board until they have each collected many different colors.
4. Ask the children to cut geometric shapes from the scraps.
5. Glue the geometric shapes to create a pattern on "Zomo's shirt."

Something to think about
Cut squares and triangles of brightly colored fabrics, and glue them onto Zomo's shirt. Invite a West African who has traditional clothing to wear a shirt or another garment with beautiful patterns.

STORY S-T-R-E-T-C-H-E-R

Classroom Library: Flannel Board Story of Zomo

What the children will learn
To retell the story of *Zomo the Rabbit: A Trickster Tale from West Africa*

Materials you will need
Flannel board, bright construction paper, laminating film, glue, old emery boards

What to do
1. Let the children create flannel board pieces out of construction paper upon which they have drawn with markers the following characters and props: Zomo, Drum, Fish, Fish Scales, Palm Tree, Cow, Rock, Tooth, and Sky God.
2. Cut the children's drawings out of construction paper.
3. Laminate the drawings and cut them again.

4. Cut old emery boards into small strips, and glue them onto the backs of the story pieces so that they will stick to the flannel board.
5. Let the children use their flannel board pieces to retell the story of Zomo the Rabbit.

Something to think about

Place the flannel board, story pieces, and *Zomo the Rabbit: A Trickster Tale from West Africa* in the classroom library for the children to use in retelling the story on their own.

STORY S-T-R-E-T-C-H-E-R

Music and Movement: Drums and Stories

What the children will learn

To play drums and create rhythms that tell a story

Materials you will need

Traditional drums

What to do

1. Ask a music teacher to bring traditional drums to the class.
2. Accompanied by the beat of the drum, retell the story of Zomo the Rabbit.
3. Distribute drums among the class members. Teach the children how to make different rhythms with their fingers, knuckles, heel of the hand, arms, even elbows.
4. After a few minutes of experimentation with creating sounds, decide how to beat the drum during different parts of the story.
5. Let the children accompany the story with their drums. Ask the music teacher to be the head drummer, and the children to follow the rhythms as you tell the story.
6. Explain that many cultures, such as African, Native American, Caribbean, and Asian, use drums for storytelling.

Something to think about

Invite a West African storyteller to your class to tell a drum story.

STORY S-T-R-E-T-C-H-E-R

Social Studies: Where Is West Africa?

What the children will learn

To locate West Africa and identify the countries there

Materials you will need

World map

What to do

1. Help the children locate Africa and decide which part is considered West Africa.
2. Note the shape of Africa. Call attention to the directions on the map of west, east, north, and south.
3. Read the acknowledgments in *Zomo the Rabbit: A Trickster Tale from West Africa,* and observe that the Zomo tale originated in Hausaland, Nigeria.
4. Locate Hausaland, Nigeria on a map, and help the children see that it is in West Africa.

Something to think about

Our goal for the children is not that they memorize the countries, but that they become aware of different continents and countries and begin to explore a world map.

STORY S-T-R-E-T-C-H-E-R

Writing: Tricksters and Morals

What the children will learn

To give Zomo advice

Materials you will need

Writing folders, bright collage materials

What to do

1. With a small group of writers, read *Zomo the Rabbit: A Trickster Tale from West Africa* again.
2. Discuss what *advice* means. Many trickster stories have morals that are meant to give readers and listeners advice.
3. Help the children think through the moral of the story of Zomo. One moral of the story is that he is not big and he is not strong, but he is very clever. Another is that tricksters often get tricked in the end. Another is to appreciate what one is, rather than wish to be something else. For example, Zomo is clever, but rather than appreciate his cleverness, he seeks to be something different.
4. Ask the children to write to Zomo and advise him about appreciating who he is and what he can do.

Something to think about

Children often have difficulty stating morals. Ask the children whether they think Zomo will take their advice.

The Lion and the Mouse

By Jerry Pinkney

Story Line

The winner of the 2010 Caldecott Medal, Jerry Pinkney makes this Aesop fable come to life through his detailed drawings and masterful use of watercolors and colored pens. Set on the African Serengeti, Pinkney illustrates the ferocious lion, the frightened mouse, and their unlikely friendship. The adventuresome mouse proves that even small creatures are capable of great deeds when a tiny mouse can rescue the King of the Jungle. The book is wordless, except for sound words, like *whoooo, grrr, screeeeech, squeak, scratch,* and *rrroaarrrr.* The exquisite illustrations make this wordless picture book a lively story, waiting for the reader's narrative.

Read-Aloud Presentation

Present the book to small groups of children. Show the cover of the book, and discuss the meaning of the Caldecott Medal as the best picture book of the year that tells the story well through illustrations. Discuss that the book only has a few sound-effect words, but the pictures tell the story, so we "read" the pictures. Select a very verbal child to explore the book ahead of time. At the small group presentation, ask him or her to tell the story as told by the pictures. Explain that everyone can "read" the illustrations and tell the story in his or her own words. Place the book in the classroom library in a featured spot for children to explore independently.

Art: Three-Medium Illustrations

What the children will learn
To use a combination of media to create details and color combinations

Materials you will need
Watercolors, watercolor paper, small brushes, watercolor palette or plastic dishes, paper towels, scraps of paper, colored pens, pencils

What to do
1. Look at Pinkney's illustrations closely, and have the children notice the lines that appear to be pencil lines, the watercolor washes, and the details drawn by colored pencils.
2. Suggest that the students practice creating some layered drawings with pencils and colored pencils.
3. Let the children practice using watercolors to help them improve their control of the medium. The children can explore the medium by wetting the brush, dipping it in the watercolor, and dabbing off the excess until the paintbrushes are almost dry.
4. After practicing on the scrap paper, have the children create their own drawings to illustrate their favorite scenes from *The Lion and the Mouse.*

Something to think about
First graders may need to use the pencils and colored pencils without the watercolors, but encourage their experimentation. Some second and most third graders will accept the challenge of creating three-medium illustrations.

Drama: Acting out Aesop's Fable "The Lion and the Mouse"

What the children will learn
To listen for implied movements, emotions, and sound-effect words

Materials you will need
None

What to do
1. Create groups of children and assign each group a major scene from the story: mouse being chased by the owl; mouse running into the path of the lion; poachers capturing the lion; lion roaring for help; mouse racing

to the scene and gnawing the rope; lion escaping and lion and mouse being friends.

2. Practice dramatizing scenes from *The Lion and the Mouse*. Have the children only use the sound-effects words as you tell the scene and they creatively move and show emotions evoked by the scene.

3. After rehearsing their scenes, let each group dramatize the scenes in order to tell the whole story.

Something to think about
You do not have to assign roles. You may have more than one lion or mouse. Another way to conduct the drama is to assign half of the class as the audience and the other half as the actors, then reverse them for a second performance.

STORY S-T-R-E-T-C-H-E-R

Mathematics: Comparing Sizes

What the children will learn
To compare sizes of the mouse and the lion

Materials you will need
Measuring tape or meter stick, ruler

What to do
1. Look at the cover page and notice that the tiny mouse can sit in the lion's paw print. Ask the children to estimate the size of a mouse and the size of a fully grown lion.

2. Reveal that a usual field mouse is about three inches long, while a lion can be six to seven feet long.

3. Cut a strip of paper about three inches long, then lay two measuring tapes on the floor to show the length of the lion and then the length of the lion plus his tail.

4. Solve several comparison problems, such as, "How many field mice can fit on the back of the lion?" "How long is a mouse's tail in comparison to a lion's tail?" "How tall is a lion, and how tall is a mouse?"

Something to think about
For younger children, it is not necessary to know the exact dimensions of each animal. For older children, look up the height and length dimensions in a reference book.

STORY S-T-R-E-T-C-H-E-R

Reading: Versions of Aesop's Fables

What the children will learn
To recognize that stories may vary and the moral will be the same

Materials you will need
Several sources for Aesop's Fables, including "The Great Lion and the Tiny Mouse," retold by Shirley Raines and Rebecca Isbell in *Tell It Again! 2*

What to do
1. Discuss the moral in *The Lion and the Mouse*, which can be interpreted as, "One good turn deserves another."

2. Read at least two versions of the story, and discuss whether or not the moral stays the same. For example, read "The Great Lion and the Tiny Mouse," the retold story from Raines and Isbell, as well as versions from the school or local library. Consider using Ash and Higton's *Aesop's Fables*.

Something to think about
Select two or three additional Aesop's fables, such as "The Hare and the Tortoise" and "The Ants and the Grasshopper," and compare versions from different books.

STORY S-T-R-E-T-C-H-E-R

Writing: The Class Version of "The Lion and the Mouse"

What the children will learn
To author several versions of the story and make each a story true to Pinkney's wordless story

Materials you will need
Computer with projector, screen, and printer, or chart tablet and markers

What to do
1. Have small groups of children each dictate a story using the illustrations in Pinkney's *The Lion and the Mouse*.

2. Type each story on the computer, projecting the story as the children tell it. Print the story, and let the students add illustrations. If a computer, screen, and projector are not available, use chart paper and markers.

3. Let each child in the group have a page to illustrate.

Something to think about
Consider copying the children's illustrated pages and binding them into a book for each group. Place the books into the classroom library for children to take home. (See Appendix page 234 for an illustration of how to bind a book.)

References

dePaola, Tomie. 1988. *The Legend of the Indian Paintbrush*. New York: Penguin Group (USA) Inc.

Hogrogian, Nonny. 1971. *One Fine Day*. New York: Simon and Schuster.

McDermott, Gerald. 1992. *Zomo the Rabbit: A Trickster Tale from West Africa*. New York: Houghton Mifflin Harcourt.

Pinkney, Jerry. 2009. *The Lion and the Mouse*. New York: Little, Brown.

Van Laan, Nancy. 1989. *Rainbow Crow*. Illustrated by Beatriz Vidal. New York: Random House.

Additional References

Applebee, Arthur. 1978. *The Child's Concept of Story: Ages Two to Seventeen*. Chicago: University of Chicago Press.

Ash, Russell and Bernard Higton. 1990. *Aesop's Fables*. San Francisco: Chronicle Books. *A selection of Aesop's fables with illustrations from older editions, featuring such artists as Randolph Caldecott, Arthur Rackham, Walter Crane, and Alexander Calder.*

Isbell, Rebecca, Joseph Sobol, Liane Lindauer, and April Lowrance. 2004. "The Effects of Storytelling and Story Reading on the Oral Language Complexity and Story Comprehension of Young Children." *Early Childhood Education Journal*, 32(3): 157–163.

Raines, Shirley and Rebecca Isbell. 1994. *Stories: Children's Literature in Early Education*. Clifton Parks, NY: Thomson Delmar Learning.

Websites

1. Scholastic: Myths, Fairytales, and Folktales:
   www.teacher.scholastic.com/writewit/mff
   - Links to folktale, myths, and fairy-tale sites
   - Numerous folktale- and legend-themed lesson plans
   - Extensive teaching resources
2. American Folklore:
   www.americanfolklore.net/index.html
   - Folktales, myths, and legends from all fifty states
   - Web resources
   - Folklore books
3. Bright Hub Fairytales and Folktales Lesson Plan: Exploring Imagination:
   www.brighthub.com/education/k-12/articles/9667.aspx
   - Six-part lesson plan: Exploring fairy tales, folktales, and legends
   - Links to related articles

Chapter 15

Poetry Children Want to Read

The New Kid on the Block

Button Up! Wrinkled Rhymes

Dirt on My Shirt

If You're Not Here, Please Raise Your Hand: Poems About School

Where the Sidewalk Ends

The New Kid on the Block

By Jack Prelutsky
Illustrated by James Stevenson

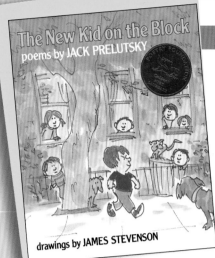

Story Line

Filled with surprises, jokes, riddles, and giggles, Prelutsky's 107 poems range from rhymed couplets to long narratives, and lure primary-age children into poetry.

The funny animal poems are only surpassed by the funny people poems. The simple, cartoonlike drawings support the text without overshadowing it. The collection is a good one for read-aloud sessions and for children to read independently.

Read-Aloud Presentation

Read the title poem, "The New Kid on the Block." Have the children tell you which line surprises them. Select six or seven other poems about people to read at the first of many poetry sessions: "Clara Cleech," "Mabel, Remarkable Mabel," "Euphonica Jarre," "Sneaky Sue," "Dainty Dottie Dee," and "Stringbean Small." At another session, read several poems about animals, such as "An Alley Cat with One Life Left," "My Dog, He Is an Ugly Dog," "I Toss Them to My Elephant" and "A Wolf Is at the Laundromat." Plan still another poetry reading session about relationships among children and their parents and brothers and sisters. Read "I Wonder Why Dad Is So Thoroughly Mad," "My Baby Brother," "My Brother's Head Should Be Replaced," "My Sister Is a Sissy" and "My Mother Says I'm Sickening." No celebration of Jack Prelutsky's poetry would be complete without reading the uproariously funny verses about body parts. Read "Be Glad Your Nose Is on Your Face," "Louder than a Clap of Thunder" (a poem about snoring), "I've Got an Itch," "You Need to Have an Iron Rear," and "Baloney Belly Billy." End with "I'm the Single Most Wonderful Person I Know."

STORY S-T-R-E-T-C-H-E-R

Art: Illustrate a Giggle

What the children will learn
To portray a funny poem visually

Materials you will need
Drawing paper, colored pencils, charcoals, markers

What to do
1. Have the children look at James Stevenson's illustrations in *The New Kid on the Block* and discuss why the simple line drawings are so effective. Point out how the drawings allow the reader or the listener to add color or additional scenes to the poem through their own mind's eye rather than the artist's.
2. Ask the children to select one of their favorite poems.
3. Have them read their poems aloud and think of ways to illustrate the poems by showing what the poems visualize.
4. Display the poems and illustrations in the classroom library. Arrange the display with the title, "Illustrations of Giggles."

Something to think about
Some children's literature specialists think that all poetry should be read without showing children the illustrations so that the child interprets the meaning for herself or himself.

STORY S-T-R-E-T-C-H-E-R

Classroom Library: A Week of Prelutsky Poetry Readings

What the children will learn
To enjoy reading aloud

Materials you will need
Poster board, marker

What to do
1. Make posters for poetry readings from *The New Kid on the Block*. Make a separate poster for each category. Let the children sign up to read poems about animals, families, people, creatures, or events. Ask the children to write the titles of the poems they want to read so that there are no repeats.
2. Schedule Monday for "Animal Poems," Tuesday for "Family Poems," Wednesday for "Funny People Poems,"

Thursday for "Creature Poems" and Friday as "It Can Happen Poems."

3. Have the children who are scheduled to read poetry aloud on other days become the audience for the readers.

Something to think about
Young children can practice the short four-line verses or poems with repeated phrases.

STORY S-T-R-E-T-C-H-E-R

Classroom Library: Partners Read Prelutsky

What the children will learn
To read in unison

Materials you will need
CDs and CD player or tapes and tape recorder

What to do
1. Let reading partners decide on poems they would like to read aloud.
2. Try various ways to read the poems. For example, one child reads the first verse, the other reads the second verse, and they both read the third verse together, or they might alternate lines and read the last lines in unison.
3. Have the children record different ways of reading the poem and use the recording to decide which way they would like to read the poem to the class.

Something to think about
Try choral readings of the poems with several verses and have the entire class read the poems together.

STORY S-T-R-E-T-C-H-E-R

Writing: Poems with a Laugh

What the children will learn
To try humorous writing

Materials you will need
Writing paper, pencils, optional—art supplies

What to do
1. Read a number of Prelutsky's funny poems, such as "Be Glad Your Nose Is on Your Face."
2. Let the children brainstorm some topics that they think are humorous and they could write about. For example, "Be Glad Your Knee Is a Part of Your Leg."

3. Other children may want to write funny poems based on their own experiences. Have them read Prelutsky's "Homework! Oh, Homework!" and "Michael Built a Bicycle" for inspiration.
4. For the students who are interested in writing about feelings, have them read "Ma! Don't Throw That Shirt Out," "Today Is Very Boring," "I'm Thankful" and "I'm in a Rotten Mood." They can write about their own feelings or try writing a poem that expresses the opposite feeling than the poet wrote in the original poem.

Something to think about
Encourage lots of experimentation. Avoid giving children the idea that they must always follow the pattern set by another poet. As primary learners, keep the children writing, experimenting, and enjoying the experience of finding their voices in print. See the Poetry Teachers website (www.poetryteachers.com) for other poems.

STORY S-T-R-E-T-C-H-E-R

Writing: Happy Birthday, Dear Animals

What the children will learn
To use the poet's model to restructure a poem

Materials you will need
Chalkboard, chalk, writing paper, pencils, drawing paper, art supplies

What to do
1. Read "Happy Birthday, Dear Dragon."
2. Have the children think of animals to whom they would like to wish a happy birthday.
3. Using the frame of Prelutsky's poem, ask the children to write the poem as if they were saying happy birthday to the animals. For example, if the children choose a bear, they might begin by describing the bear's den, instead of the dragon's lair.
4. Let the children reprint their poems on drawing paper and add illustrations.
5. Publish the children's verses in a class book of poetry. (See Appendix page 234 for book-binding directions.)

Something to think about
For young children, work in small groups and write the poems together. Encourage the children to try their own poetry style without following the poet's model.

Button Up! Wrinkled Rhymes

By Alice Schertle
Illustrated by Petra Mathers

Story Line

"Do the clothes in your closet have a life all their own?" Each poem is written from the garment's perspective. The owners' names are used and their activities described. The "duds" have personalities like their owners. The clever poems include ones about shoelaces, hiking hats, galoshes, undies, bicycle helmets, shoes, jammies, T-shirts, swimsuits, jerseys, dress-up clothes, sweaters, costumes, sweatshirts, and jackets. Mathers's illustrations match the funny text, and animal friends act like children in this book of poems that will delight primary students.

Read-Aloud Presentation

Wear a favorite sweater, blouse, or shoes to school on the day you read *Button Up! Wrinkled Rhymes*. Tell the children about your piece of clothing and why you like it. Mention that if this favorite sweater could talk, it would say, "I've been to school, shopping, church, visiting, to movies, and out to lunch with your teacher." Discuss some of the children's favorite pieces of clothing that they like to wear. Read several poems at each sitting so the children can begin to understand the structure of the poems. The title of each poem contains a child's name and when the garment was worn.

Art: Our Favorite Pieces of Clothing

What the children will learn
To draw themselves and express special feelings and activities

Materials you will need
Drawing paper, construction paper, scissors, glue sticks, markers, crayons, colored pencils

What to do
1. Refer to Petra Mathers's illustrations in the book.
2. Notice the ways Mathers draws the animal characters behaving like humans, wearing human clothing and shoes.
3. Ask the children what they would be if they could be any animal.
4. Have the children draw themselves as those animals, doing their favorite activities and wearing their favorite clothes. For example, Brian might be a bear wearing his favorite blue cap.
5. Display the pictures in an art area and let the children talk about their favorite pieces of clothing.

Something to think about
Select poems that go with certain seasons to read together, such as the sweater, jacket, and galoshes for the fall.

Creative Dramatics: Not too Old for Dress-Up Clothes

What the children will learn
To enjoy dressing up in costumes and playing the parts

Materials you will need
Costumes and dress-up clothes

What to do
1. Let the children select a costume or dress-up clothes they would like to wear.
2. Have the children pretend to be the characters they have selected—a clown, a princess, an action hero.

Something to think about

Have older children who are acting in a play come to the classroom and show off their costumes for the play. Ask the older children to talk about how dressing like the characters help them to act out their parts.

STORY S-T-R-E-T-C-H-E-R

Reading: Matching People in Poems with Their Wrinkle Rhymes

What the children will learn

To recall the poem and the words and phrases that help them remember

Materials you will need

Shoes, galoshes, shoelaces, unworn underwear, cap, bicycle helmet

What to do

1. Collect the garments and footwear in a box.
2. Begin reading the poem and let three or four children stand near the box. When they recognize which article of clothing the poem is describing, one child pulls it out until there are no articles of clothing left.
3. Continue by reading key phrases from other poems and letting the children guess the garments.

Something to think about

Collect some favorite garments from the adults around the school, such as the custodian's cap, cook's apron, and the art teacher's smock. Let the children make up poems to go with each garment. Give the poems to the school helpers as a gift.

STORY S-T-R-E-T-C-H-E-R

Reading: Choral Readings from Button Up! Wrinkled Rhymes

What the children will learn

To practice reading with fluency and expression

Materials you will need

CDs and CD player or tapes and tape recorder, chart tablet, markers

What to do

1. Allow the children to select five of their favorite poems from Button Up! Wrinkled Rhymes.
2. Print the poems on chart tablet paper.
3. Have groups of four or five children choose one of the poems to present as a choral reading.
4. Decide which lines the group of children will say collectively and which lines an individual will read. For example in "Bertie's Shoelaces," everyone says the opening two lines, child one could do the next two lines, child two the next two lines, and the entire group could do the last two lines together. For "Violet's Hiking Hat," consider having one group of children be the Hat speaking, and another group of children can be Violet speaking.

Something to think about

Choral reading is an excellent means for children to practice fluency and for proficient readers to lead others who are learning. See the Education World website (www.educationworld.com) for additional ideas to integrate poetry into other curriculum areas.

STORY S-T-R-E-T-C-H-E-R

Special Event and Writing: Button Up! Favorite Clothing Day

What the children will learn

To speak with clarity and expressively

Materials you will need

Note to parents to explain the Button Up! Day, favorite clothes children bring from home

What to do

1. Help the children compose a note to parents through a group writing exercise.
2. Explain that on the designated day, everyone wears a special piece of clothing. At group time in the morning, one half of the children share their stories, and in the afternoon, the other half share.
3. Match the piece of clothing to the poem in the book that is about a similar story. For instance, "Jack's Soccer Jersey" goes with a child's favorite jersey. "Clyde's Costume" goes with Melinda's costume, and so on.

Something to think about

There are an equal number of poems with boys' names as there are with girls' names in Button Up! Make a list of all the children's names in the book and let the children look for names on the list that begin with or contain the same letters as their own names. First graders will especially enjoy this.

Dirt on My Shirt

By Jeff Foxworthy
Illustrated by Steve Bjorkman

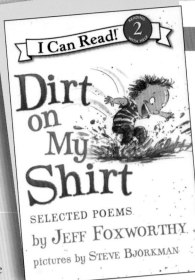

Story Line

Foxworthy, the famous comedian, has teamed up with Steve Bjorkman, the famous children's book illustrator, to create *Dirt on My Shirt*. The thirty-four hilarious poems are the stuff of childhood friendships and curious observations of the world. The poems about relatives, "What Do You See?," "In the Night," and the title poem, "Dirt on My Shirt," receive rave reviews. Mostly rhymed couplets, these are poems that boys will enjoy especially, and all will laugh and savor the rhythm and the terrific comic illustrations.

Read-Aloud Presentations

Read the title poem, "Dirt on My Shirt," and ask the children if they think the poems will be funny ones or serious ones. Show the back cover of the picture of Jeff Foxworthy, the comedian. Ask the children if they would like to hear funny poems about relatives or about animals. Based on the children's answers, choose one set of poems to read at the first sitting and wait to share other subjects on the next day.

Art: Comic Features, Caricatures

What the children will learn
To draw caricatures

Materials you will need
Sample caricature drawings, drawing paper, pencils, charcoals, colored pencils

What to do
1. Look at the caricatures of the children, animals, and relatives depicted by Bjorkman in *Dirt on My Shirt*. Notice the enlarged heads, exaggerated eyebrows, or bushy red hair.
2. Let the children draw pictures of themselves, in which they exaggerate some feature. If a child has a beautiful smile, that child might draw an exaggerated large smile. If a girl walks like a ballerina, she might draw tiny ballet shoes on her feet, but with a larger body. If someone has terrific arm strength for batting a baseball, that child might draw the arms much larger.

Something to think about
If the children are hesitant to begin drawing, let them experiment with a caricature of you, and then laugh and enjoy their work. The children can also choose to draw of a funny relative, if you think drawing a caricature of themselves is too much for their self-esteem.

Game: What Do You See? I Spy

What the children will learn
To play a game that encourages using descriptions

Materials you will need
Regular classroom objects

What to do
1. Show the children the double-page illustrations of the poem, "What Do You See?"
2. Read the poem to a small group of children, and let them find the almost-hidden object in the very busy illustration.

3. Tell the children that the poem reminds you of the game, "I Spy." Teach the children how to play the game by looking around the room and saying, "I spy a metal object that is used to hold things together, and it makes a clicking sound when it works. What is it?" (a stapler), or "I spy a metal object that makes things sharp. What is it?" (a pencil sharpener).

4. Have several different students take turns being the describers while others guess.

Something to think about

First graders may need more help with this game, so it is all right to whisper some hints. Second and third graders can also play "I Spy," describing class members, but remember to keep all of the descriptions positive. For example, "I spy someone who has on a yellow and blue striped shirt."

STORY S-T-R-E-T-C-H-E-R

Reading: Descriptive Word Match

What the children will learn
To recognize phrases and associate them with subjects of poems

Materials you will need
Chart tablet or poster board, markers, strips of paper, markers, tape or glue stick

What to do
1. Read some of the short poems that are descriptions, such as "Deer," "Spare Hair," "True Love," "Uninvited Guests," and "Roly Poly."
2. Write the names of the poems on chart paper or poster board.
3. On strips of paper, write each of the following descriptive phrases from the poems, such as "gone in a dash," "no hair," "tails they cannot see," "birds are concerned," and "walked away."
4. Let the children match the name of the poems with the descriptive phrases.

Something to think about
Do a similar exercise with descriptive phrases from the poems about relatives.

STORY S-T-R-E-T-C-H-E-R

Reading: Finish the Rhyme

What the children will learn
To complete a rhyming couplet

Materials you will need
Recording of the poems, paper and pencil

What to do
1. Make a recording of several of the poems in *Dirt on My Shirt*. Omit the last word in each rhyming couplet. For example, read "Staring Contest," and leave out the second rhyming words, such as *eye (bye)* and *blink (wink)*.
2. Have the children listen to the recordings, and then think of a word that would complete the rhymes.
3. Record other poems, such as "Bumblebee Breakfast," "Friends," and "What Do You See?"

Something to think about
Practice with groups of first graders. Second graders and third graders will be able to manage listening to a recording and then writing responses, if you have modeled what is expected of them.

STORY S-T-R-E-T-C-H-E-R

Writing: Concrete Foxworthy Poems

What the children will learn
To write poems about concrete forms or shapes

Materials you will need
Pencils, scissors, construction paper to cut in shapes of squirrel, deer, bear, turtle, bumblebee, frog, and car

What to do
1. Remind the students that one way a poem can be described as "concrete" is when it describes the shape of something.
2. Look through the poems in *Dirt on My Shirt,* and select some that would be good concrete poems.
3. Illustrate this concept using the poem about squirrels, "The Uninvited Guests."
4. With the children, look at other illustrations of poems and decide what shapes would fit them.
5. Let the children draw and cut out shapes and write their poems about the shapes.

Something to think about
Older students might be able to compose their own poems to fit the shapes. First and second graders will enjoy copying Foxworthy's poems and taking them home to share with family members.

If You're Not Here, Please Raise Your Hand: Poems About School

By Kalli Dakos
Illustrated by G. Brian Karas

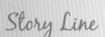

Story Line

Humorous poems are children's favorite poetry, and there is a lot to laugh about in this collection of thirty-eight poems about school. Some favorites among children include "Math Is Brewing and I'm in Trouble," "I Brought a Worm," "Substitute Teacher," "It's Inside My Sister's Lunch," "Hiding in the Bathroom," and "Budging Line-Ups." While most of the poems are funny, there are a few very serious ones, including "The Cry Guy," "J.T. Never Will Be Ten," and "A Lifetime in Third Grade." Karas illustrates the book with comically twisted, childlike, black-and-white drawings for each poem.

Read-Aloud Presentation

Begin by reading the title poem "If You're Not Here, Please Raise Your Hand." Practice reading while yawning, like the sleepy teacher who is trying to wake up. Read the dust jacket of the book, which explains that the poet is a teacher. Another good poem to read is "They Don't Do Math in Texas." In addition to reading from the book during read-aloud time, schedule several poetry readings throughout the day. Select poems to match the time of day. Read "Hiding in the Bathroom" before or after the children go to the bathroom. Read "It's Inside My Sister's Lunch," before you collect money for books or pictures or a special event. Read "Caleb's Desk Is a Mess" before clean-up time.

Art: The Poems Remind Me

What the children will learn
To illustrate poems

Materials you will need
Paper, crayons, colored pencils

What to do
1. Tell the children that people have described poetry as pictures that dance in our heads. Ask the children to draw and color the pictures that dance in their heads when they hear a poem read.
2. Since Karas creates sparse illustrations, the children may think of more elaborate pictures.
3. Bind the illustrations into a book or place them in a large scrapbook.
4. Place the book of illustrations in the library area of the classroom.

Something to think about
Let the children choose which poems they want to illustrate.

Classroom Library: Recording Poems

What the children will learn
To read with expression

Materials you will need
CDs and CD player or tapes and tape recorder

What to do
1. Let readers who do not participate in the creative dramatics STORY S-T-R-E-T-C-H-E-R read poems on tape.
2. Rehearse with the children to help them read the poems with expression.
3. Introduce the tape and each poem by telling the listener the appropriate page number in *If You're Not Here, Please Raise Your Hand,* so that listeners may read with the tape, if they wish.
4. Group the poems about teachers, such as "Substitute," "The Mighty Eye," "Dancing on a Rainbow," and "A Teacher's Lament." Other groupings might include poems about homework, being sick or embarrassed, or exaggerated tales.

5. End the recording by reading "I'm in Another Dimension" yourself, substituting your name for Ms. Digby's.

Something to think about
Select a narrator to read the dust jacket information about the poet, Kalli Dakos.

STORY S-T-R-E-T-C-H-E-R

Classroom Library: Other Funny Poets

What the children will learn
To begin recognizing poets by their works

Materials you will need
Children's favorite poetry books, slips of paper, pencils, fishbowl or glass salad bowl

What to do
1. Display all the poetry books from this unit, along with books by the children's other favorite poets, like Bill Martin Jr., Jack Prelutsky, Shel Silverstein, Diane Siebert, and Karla Kuskin.
2. Ask each student to write on a slip of paper the title and first line of a favorite poem. On the opposite side of the paper, ask the students to write the title of the book where the poem can be found.
3. Invite other students to draw slips from the fishbowl and guess which poet wrote that poem, or think of other lines from the same poem.

Something to think about
Do not make this STORY S-T-R-E-T-C-H-E-R a competition, but keep it an opportunity for the children to see how many poems they enjoy. Some poems will also be liked by other children, and some are individual favorites. With older children, try categorizing the poems by type, such as free verse, acrostic, ballad, blank verse, chant, cinquain, concrete, couplet, or list poem. See the Education World website (www.educationworld.com) for additional poetry forms.

STORY S-T-R-E-T-C-H-E-R

Creative Dramatics: Humor Comes to Life

What the children will learn
To dramatize funny events

Materials you will need
Dress-up clothes, props from the classroom

What to do
1. Let the children select the poems that they want to dramatize.
2. Try various approaches. Some children may want to pantomime while you read the poem. Other children may want to recite a short poem and act it out. Small groups of children might want to work together.

Something to think about
Involve as many children as possible, but do not insist that everyone perform. Costumes that somewhat disguise the players often help children relax and be more free in their actions.

STORY S-T-R-E-T-C-H-E-R

Writing: Diary of Funny Times at School

What the children will learn
To tell, write, and share funny stories that encourage laughing at ourselves

Materials you will need
Writing paper, pencils, art supplies

What to do
1. Encourage the children to remember something funny that happened to them. Talk about how important it is to learn to laugh at ourselves.
2. After the children remember a few events, ask individual storytellers to write their stories. Let others work as partners.
3. Encourage older children to write the story as a narrative and rewrite it as a poem.
4. Plan on having several sharing sessions, and compliment the children on learning to laugh at funny things that happen to them.
5. Provide art supplies for illustrations. Children always want to illustrate funny stories and poems.

Something to think about
Avoid making jokes at the expense of others.

Where the Sidewalk Ends

By Shel Silverstein

Story Line

A collection of 109 poems, this thirtieth-anniversary edition contains Silverstein-inspired giggles, imagination, musings, and terrific child connections. His simple line drawings are humorous and almost childlike. The title poem, "Where the Sidewalk Ends," is a tribute to the places and imaginary spaces that children occupy. Favorite poems that are the focus of this unit are: "Jimmy Jet and His TV Set," "For Sale," "Sarah Cynthia Sylvia Stout Would Not Take the Garbage Out," "Colors," "Smart," "Boa Constrictor," "Spaghetti," and "Open-Close."

Read-Aloud Presentation

Select a few of your favorite Shel Silverstein poems, such as "Jimmy Jet and the TV Set," "For Sale," and "Snowman," and tell the children why you like them. Be sure to show the illustrations, which are childlike yet humorous. Read the focus poems, "Colors," "Boa Constrictor," "Sarah Cynthia Sylvia Stout Would Not Take the Garbage Out," "Spaghetti," and "Smart." Announce the STORY S-T-R-E-T-C-H-E-R-S associated with each poem.

STORY S-T-R-E-T-C-H-E-R

Art: The Colors That I Am

What the children will learn
To mix colors

Materials you will need
Paints (black, white and primary colors), paper plates, coffee stirrers, small art paintbrushes, large class mirror or small handheld mirrors

What to do
1. Read the poem "Colors," in which the poet describes all the colors of his skin, eyes, and hair.
2. Let the children try mixing the paints to match the colors of their skin, hair, and eyes.
3. Compare the colors the children mixed to the colors they see in the mirrors.
4. After the children mix the paint samples, ask them to draw and paint self-portraits.

Something to think about
Read "Who," which is also a self-awareness poem filled with imagination. Let the children illustrate this poem with drawings and descriptions of themselves.

STORY S-T-R-E-T-C-H-E-R

Cooking and Snack Time: Silverstein Spaghetti

What the children will learn
To follow cooking directions

Materials you will need
Pasta pot, measuring cup, pasta, timer, strainer, spaghetti sauce, plates, forks, spoons, napkins, serving spoons, large printed version of the recipe to cook the pasta and to heat the already-prepared sauce.

What to do
1. Read Shel Silverstein's "Spaghetti."
2. Either in the classroom or the school cafeteria, have the children prepare pasta and heat prepared spaghetti sauce.
3. Print on a large chart the directions for preparing the pasta.
4. Involve as many children as possible, from opening the pasta boxes to measuring the water, watching the timer, and printing the directions.

5. Eat and enjoy, and then suggest that the children write a poem about the spaghetti-cooking experience.

Something to think about
If one of the parents enjoys cooking Italian food, ask him or her to prepare special sauces and special pastas.

Mathematics: Counting Money

What the children will learn
To associate the values of different bills and coins: dollars, quarters, dimes, nickels, and pennies

Materials you will need
Play money, shoebox lids, paper, pencil

What to do
1. Read "Smart," where a little boy swaps his one dollar for two quarters, two quarters for three dimes, three dimes for four nickels, and four nickels for five pennies, thinking he is smart to keep getting more money.
2. Let the children manipulate the play money by placing a dollar bill on a box lid and counting out four quarters to equal one dollar. Write the problem on their paper: $1 = 4 quarters.
3. Write a problem adding 25 + 25 + 25 + 25 = 100 or 1 dollar ($1).
4. How much money did the little boy lose when he traded $1 dollar for 2 quarters?
5. Place the 4 quarters on the lid and subtract the 2 quarters. $1 dollar = 4 quarters. 4 quarters – 2 quarters = 2 quarters or 50 cents.
6. Place two quarters on the lid and have the children write 25 + 25 = 50. Place 3 dimes on the lid and have the children write 10 + 10 + 10 = 30. How much money did the little boy lose when he swapped the two quarters, 50 cents, for the 3 dimes? 50 – 30 = 20 cents.
7. Place the 3 dimes on the lid, 10 + 10 + 10 = 30, and the 4 nickels, 5 + 5 + 5 + 5 = 20. How much did the little boy lose when he swapped the three dimes for the 4 nickels? 30 – 20 = 10 cents.
8. Place the 4 nickels on the lid, 5 + 5 + 5 + 5 = 20, and the 5 pennies, 1 + 1 + 1 + 1 + 1 = 5. How much did the little boy lose when he swapped the 4 nickels for the 5 pennies? 20 – 5 = 15 cents.
9. How much did he lose all together? How much did he have after he swapped all the money? (5 pennies or 5 cents) What was the dollar worth at the beginning? (100 cents) 100 cents – 5 cents = 95 cents.

Something to think about
Vary the mathematical problems depending on the ages of the children. First graders may be making associations of how much each coin is worth, while second graders may do the simple addition and subtraction, and third graders may be able to write the equations as multiplication and subtraction problems. See the Poetry Archive (www.poetryarchive.org) for children to read some other number poems or to submit their own.

Music and Movement: I'm Being Swallowed by a Boa Constrictor

What the children will learn
To associate a poem with chant and movement

Materials you will need
Chart tablet, markers

What to do
1. Print the first two lines of "Boa Constrictor" on a chart tablet and teach children to chant or sing it.
2. The phrase is repeats two more times, and the boa constrictor starts nibbling body parts from toes up to the neck.
3. Chant the poem once and then let the children join in. Let them help you devise movements that emphasize the words.

Something to think about
Add more body parts than are mentioned in the poem, and think of possible rhymes, such as *belly* and *jelly*. Write the new class version on your chart tablet for fun breaks throughout the day.

Writing: Our Version of "Open-Close"

What the children will learn
To write poetry using a model

Materials you will need
Large printed copy of "Open-Close," pencil, paper, art paper, choice of markers, crayons, colored pencils

What to do
1. Read "Open-Close." The poem asks the reader to open his mouth, close his eyes, and wait for a surprise. Silverstein goes on to tell the reader he will receive a surprise, and then there are various types of foods mentioned.

2. Let the children brainstorm what kind of food they would like to have as a surprise.
3. Rewrite the poem with the children's surprise foods, and make accompanying rhymes. Point out the rhyming pattern in the original poem.

Something to think about

After the class writes their version of "Open-Close" together, ask them to try individual versions of "Eighteen Flavors," a poem about ice cream flavors, or "Who," which the children can use to brag about things they can do and describe the things they wish they could do.

References

Dakos, Kalli. 1990. *If You're Not Here, Please Raise Your Hand: Poems About School*. Illustrated by G. Brian Karas. New York: Simon and Schuster.

Foxworthy, Jeff. 2008. *Dirt on My Shirt*. Illustrated by Steve Bjorkman. New York: HarperCollins.

Prelutsky, Jack. 1984. *The New Kid on the Block*. Illustrated by James Stevenson. New York: HarperCollins.

Schertle, Alice. 2009. *Button Up! Wrinkled Rhymes*. Illustrated by Petra Mathers. New York: Harcourt.

Silverstein, Shel. 1974. *Where the Sidewalk Ends*. New York: HarperCollins.

Additional References

Kennedy, X.J. and Dorothy Kennedy. 1992. *Talking Like the Rain: A Read-to-Me Book of Poems*. Illustrated by Jane Dyer. Boston: Little Brown. *An illustrated collection of poems for very young children, including works by Robert Lewis Stevenson, Edward Lear, and Jack Prelutsky.*

Martin, Bill Jr. and John Archambault. 1998. *Listen to the Rain*. Illustrated by James Endicott. New York: Henry Holt. *Describes the changing sounds of the rain, the slow soft sprinkle, the drip-drop tinkle, the sounding pounding roaring rain, and the fresh wet silent after-time of rain.*

Prelutsky, Jack. 2005. *It's Raining Pigs and Noodles*. Illustrated by James Stevenson. New York: Greenwillow. *More than one hundred Prelutsky poems populate this book of humor, nonsense poetry, and clever wordplay.*

Websites

1. Education World: www.education-world.com/a_lesson/lesson262.shtml
   - Several lesson plans
   - Links to other poetry sites
   - Online student poetry publishing links
2. Meadowbrook Press/Poetry Teachers.com: www.poetryteachers.com
   - Games
   - Lesson plans
   - Poetry theatre
3. The Children's Poetry Archive: www.poetryarchive.org/childrensarchive/home.do
   - Poem and poet search engine
   - Ask the poet section
   - Poetry links

Chapter 16

Jokes, Riddles, and Fun with Words

Eight Ate: A Feast of Homonym Riddles

The King Who Rained

Teach Us, Amelia Bedelia

Silly Knock-Knocks

Wise Crackers

Eight Ate: A Feast of Homonym Riddles

By Marvin Terban
Illustrated by Giulio Maestro

Story Line

The line drawings illustrate a collection of original riddles with each homonym as the answer, such as *bear* and *bare*, *foul* and *fowl*, *tee* and *tea*, and other similar pairs of words. Children enjoy the absurd, the obvious, and the clever riddles, which are appealing to primary-grade children's humor.

Read-Aloud Presentation

About a week before reading the book to the children, ask them to collect homonyms and compose questions to go with them as the riddles. For example, "What is rabbit fur? Hare hair." Have the students print their jokes on index cards and place them on a bulletin board. Each morning begin group time by selecting a child's homonym card to read. Read *Eight Ate: A Feast of Homonym Riddles*, reading a few selections a day. Encourage reluctant and beginning readers to participate in reading by scheduling a few practice sessions before they perform for the class. See www.brownielocks.com/jokes.html for tips on telling a joke.

STORY S-T-R-E-T-C-H-E-R

Art: Make Me Laugh Pictures

What the children will learn
To represent homonym riddles in picture form

Materials you will need
Drawing paper, markers, crayons, colored pencils

What to do
1. Let each child select a homonym riddle to illustrate, one from the book or one from the class collection.
2. Help each student decide how many scenes are necessary to illustrate the joke.
3. Fold the papers so that each section represents a scene. Make greeting card folds, tri-folds, or accordion folds.

Something to think about
Post the illustrated homonym riddles on a bulletin board at the children's eye level.

STORY S-T-R-E-T-C-H-E-R

Classroom Library: Pause for a Homonym Riddle

What the children will learn
To use clues to solve homonym riddles

Materials you will need
Collection of riddles, poster board or large index cards, scissors, markers, paper, large brown envelope

What to do
1. Collect homonym riddles from books and children's magazines.
2. Print the questions and the answers on different strips of poster board or large index cards.
3. Shuffle the cards and have the children make matches with the questions and the homonym riddle answer.
4. For example, "What is rabbit fur?" is printed on one card, and the answer, "Hare hair," is printed on another card.

Something to think about
For first graders, have five to seven cards for them to match. For second and third graders, increase the numbers.

Drama: Class Comedy Club

What the children will learn

To read riddles with the proper timing and inflection

Materials you will need

Index cards, markers, thumbtacks or tape

What to do

1. From the collection of knock-knocks, jokes, and riddles that the children have brought to class, select homonyms to read aloud.
2. Have the reading partners rehearse their presentation of the riddles, with one posing the questions and the other providing the answers.
3. Assemble an audience for the riddle tellers. Have the reading partners perform their riddles.
4. On other days, let the partners try their riddles with audience participation.

Something to think about

Every form of text has a certain rhythm to the way it should be read. The pauses, stops, and anticipation in the voices of the readers are what make the riddles work. Help the children rehearse their timing and inflection.

Mathematics: Funny Survey Results

What the children will learn

To represent combined data graphically

Materials you will need

Chart tablet, marker, scissors, construction paper, tape, sticky notes

What to do

1. Select three children to poll the class on whether they like homonym riddles or knock-knock jokes better.
2. When the pollsters have finished surveying all of the students, have them meet again and decide how to present their findings to the rest of the class. They can tally the results and simply post the winner, or rank them, or state the results in terms of the likes of the boys versus the girls.

3. Have the surveyors decide whether to make a horizontal or vertical bar graph to show the results. They can cut strips of construction paper for each child's vote and tape the pieces to the chart tablet or use sticky notes.

Something to think about

Older students might try a more complicated process of surveying the class before they have read books of knock-knock jokes and funny homonym riddles. They can compare whether or not the class preferences change after they learn more jokes and riddles.

Writing: Homonym Riddle Book

What the children will learn

To select homonym riddles they think would make good illustrations

Materials you will need

Typing paper; ruler; cardboard; contact paper; masking tape; art supplies such as pencils, colored pencils, markers, crayons

What to do

1. Have each child construct two blank books. (See the directions on Appendix page 234 for binding books.)
2. As the children read knock-knock jokes and homonym riddles they want to remember, ask them to print the jokes and riddles in the appropriate books.
3. When the children finish their books, have them sign up for a day to share their very favorite knock-knock jokes or riddles. However, make one rule. If one student shares a second student's favorite when it is the second student's turn, tell the class what your favorite is, and then read your next favorite. The process keeps the children returning to their texts over and over.
4. Keep a tally of what the children's favorites are, and which are clear winners. Print the children's favorites on posters and display them in the hallway to inform passersby.

Something to think about

Younger children might make one book with two sections—knock-knock jokes and homonym riddles, rather than two separate books. Extend the activity by having children cut out favorite cartoons and make a collection of these.

The King Who Rained

By Fred Gwynne

Story Line

A little girl imagines what her parents mean when they say phrases such as "bear feet" for "bare feet." When her father says there are forks in the road, the child imagines huge silverware forks connecting the highways. A collection of nineteen phrases and illustrations, the book is an excellent way to introduce homonyms and idioms. The hilarious full-page illustrations make it a favorite for group or partner reading.

Read-Aloud Presentation

Show the children the cover of *The King Who Rained* and tell them the little girl in the story gets things mixed up, but she has a terrific imagination. She visualizes in funny ways what her parents tell her. Read the book and stop on each page for every child to see the illustrations clearly. Plan for lots of giggles. Wait for the children to say it is time to turn the page. At the end, the children will immediately say, "Read it again!" Go through the book a second time, and let the children interpret what the parents really meant.

STORY S-T-R-E-T-C-H-E-R

Art: Draw What You Say

What the children will learn
To draw interpretations of sayings and homonyms

Materials you will need
Chalkboard; chalk; drawing paper; choice of crayons, markers or colored pencils; stapler; masking tape

What to do
1. Brainstorm a list of sayings that can be interpreted literally. For the example, "It's raining cats and dogs," the children can draw cats and dogs falling from a cloud in the sky. There are many other possibilities, such as "danced my feet off," "elephant ears," "eyes like a hawk," and "elbow grease."
2. Brainstorm a list of homonyms, words that have the same sound but are spelled differently and have different meanings, such as *see* and *sea,* and *right* and *write*. Children can choose some of these words to illustrate humorously.
3. After the children complete their pictures, have them print their homonyms or phrases on a cover sheet and staple it over the top of their pictures.
4. Place the pictures in the classroom library or tape them along a chalk railing for the children to read the phrase or words, visualize how the artist might have interpreted it, then look underneath at the picture.

Something to think about
Younger children can select one of the homonym pairs or phrases in the book and draw a picture placing themselves or their families in a situation similar to that in the book.

STORY S-T-R-E-T-C-H-E-R

Classroom Library: What It Really Means

What the children will learn
To interpret homonyms, idioms, and funny phrases

Materials you will need
Chalkboard, chalk, CDs and CD recorder or tapes and tape recorder, stapler or xylophone

What to do
1. Read *The King Who Rained* again. Have the children say what the parents really mean instead of what the little girl visualizes.
2. Tell the students you would like to make a recording of *The King Who Rained*, but you are concerned that some children might not understand the real meanings. Ask the children what could be done to be sure that everyone understands the real meanings.
3. Tell the children that the introduction to this recording will be very important. Ask them to decide what needs to be said, and then write what they say on the chalkboard. Let one student read the introduction on the recording.

4. Make a recording of the book. Read the book, and let the children record what the phrases mean.
5. After each phrase you read, the children can say together, "That's so funny," and then one child can tell what the phrases really mean.
6. Click a stapler or play one note on a xylophone as the page-turning signal.

Something to think about
Record the children's book from the writing center STORY S-T-R-E-T-C-H-E-R.

STORY S-T-R-E-T-C-H-E-R

Creative Dramatics: Improvised Sayings

What the children will learn
To dramatize and interpret phrases

Materials you will need
Index cards, pencils, chalkboard, chalk

What to do
1. Let each child work with a partner.
2. On index cards, print the homonyms, idioms, and funny phrases from the art center activity and from the book.
3. Give each set of partners a card and secretly ask them how they will interpret the phrase. Let them plan any props or costumes they need and bring them to school the next day.
4. The partners improvise a scene that illustrates their phrase, and the audience tries to guess the phrase.
5. Print the phrases on the board after the children have guessed them.

Something to think about
Randomly assign partners or pair children who are already reading or writing partners.

STORY S-T-R-E-T-C-H-E-R

Writing: Partner Writing

What the children will learn
To write interpretations of homonyms, idioms, and funny phrases

Materials you will need
Drawings from the art STORY S-T-R-E-T-C-H-E-R, writing paper, pencils

What to do
1. Pair children who have painted or drawn illustrations of homonyms and funny phrases at the art center.
2. Let each student take his or her partner's drawing and write about a situation in which this saying might be heard, and what the saying really means.
3. Have the partner whose picture was written about add information and help edit the description.
4. Place the partners' drawings and descriptions in the classroom library.

Something to think about
Writing partners often help children write better.

STORY S-T-R-E-T-C-H-E-R

Writing: Binding Our Own Class Book

What the children will learn
To write and publish a book of funny phrases

Materials you will need
Typing paper, pencils, ruler, colored pencils, cardboard, contact paper, stapler, masking tape

What to do
1. Give each child two sheets of typing paper. Have them draw a margin of about one-half inch along the right-hand edge of one page and along the left-hand edge of the other page. Show the children that when these two sheets are stapled together they will look like facing pages in a book.
2. On the left-facing pages, have the children print their funny phrases. On the right sheet, have the children draw the illustrations.
3. Assemble all the children's writing into a book. Bind the book by following the directions provided on page 234 of the Appendix.
4. Place the book in the classroom library.

Something to think about
If binding all the children's writing into one book makes it too thick, make several smaller books. For schools with computers, have the children use word processing and computer graphics to print their funny phrases. Some students can type their own, while younger children will enjoy seeing their words become print as someone else types them.

Teach Us, Amelia Bedelia

By Peggy Parish
Illustrated by Lynn Sweat

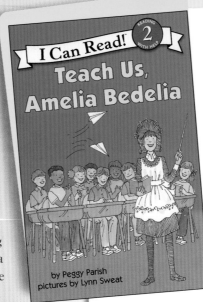

Story Line

A favorite funny character for beginning readers, Amelia Bedelia, who is usually a housekeeper, is mistaken for a substitute teacher. Following the teacher's lesson plan, Amelia takes everything on the list quite literally. She calls the roll by taking a roll from a boy's lunch box and calling to it. And so the zany, wacky day begins. Endearing, confused Amelia Bedelia becomes the children's favorite substitute teacher, but Amelia thinks she prefers housekeeping, even though she loves children. Lynn Sweat's illustrations of Amelia, quaintly dressed in her uniform, have become synonymous with the series.

Read-Aloud Presentation

At the mere mention of an Amelia Bedelia book, children often cheer. They like the outrageous situations, and Amelia's literal nature is close to their own interpretations of the world. Read *Teach Us, Amelia Bedelia,* and pause to let the children make predictions about what Amelia Bedelia will do in each situation. Survey the children for other Amelia Bedelia books they like, and place those books in the library. Let the children make recordings of the books.

STORY S-T-R-E-T-C-H-E-R

Art: Mixed-Up Pictures

What the children will learn
To illustrate with a sense of humor

Materials you will need
Chalkboard, chalk, choice of art media: paints, crayons, markers, pastels, painting or drawing paper

What to do

1. Look through the illustrations of *Teach Us, Amelia Bedelia,* and have the children decide what makes each scene funny.
2. Make a list of other literal interpretations that Amelia Bedelia might make. For example, she might interpret *library book* as a book about libraries or "putting up pictures" as holding them in the air.
3. Fold sheets of paper in half. On the left side, let the children draw or paint a picture of their favorite Amelia Bedelia mix-ups.
4. On the right side of the paper, have the children illustrate how Amelia Bedelia should have interpreted the situation.
5. Display the students' artwork on a bulletin board, and enjoy the humor in the illustrations.

Something to think about
Young children may not be able to think of other Amelia Bedelia misinterpretations because they think of the world in literal terms as well.

STORY S-T-R-E-T-C-H-E-R

Cooking: Amelia's Taffy Apples

What the children will learn
To follow recipe directions

Materials you will need
Saucepan, hot plate, caramel sauce, wooden spoon, measuring cup and spoons, water, apples, Popsicle sticks, marker, waxed paper, trays

What to do

1. Melt caramel sauce from a jar in a saucepan, stirring continually with a wooden spoon so the mixture does not stick. Add teaspoons of water to the mixture to keep it from thickening too quickly.
2. Have the children write their names on Popsicle sticks and insert the sticks into the stem end of apples. Caution the children to make one stab and not to wiggle their sticks, because then they would be too loose to stay in the apples.
3. Help the children twirl their apples in the warm caramel (taffy) sauce.
4. Cool the apples on a tray covered with waxed paper, and then enjoy the apples as a snack.

Something to think about

Give each child a piece of waxed paper to hold their apple if it falls off the stick.

STORY S-T-R-E-T-C-H-E-R

Creative Dramatics: Amelia Bedelia, Come to Our School

What the children will learn

To think of literal interpretations

Materials you will need

Housekeeper's uniform

What to do

1. Dress up like Amelia Bedelia.
2. Have another teacher tell the children they will have a substitute teacher today.
3. Come to class and introduce yourself as Amelia Bedelia.
4. Ask for help throughout the day with what you are supposed to do next.
5. Interpret everything literally. For example, if a child asks to call his mother, ask, "What do you want to call her?" When you say, "Take a seat," have the students pick up their chairs and take them to another place in the classroom.
6. Enjoy the humorous situations that arise.

Something to think about

Teachers of younger children might have "Amelia" in the classroom for a short period of time.

STORY S-T-R-E-T-C-H-E-R

Mathematics: Amelia Bedelia Story Problems

What the children will learn

To interpret mathematics problems literally

Materials you will need

Apples, oranges, play money, index cards, pencils

What to do

1. Read the mathematics problems the children solved in *Teach Us, Amelia Bedelia*.
2. Solve the problem using real apples.
3. Read some mathematics problems from the math book you use in the classroom. Select some story problems that are easy to interpret with apples, oranges, play money, and items found in the classroom.

4. Divide the class into groups of three or four children.
5. Write the story problems on index cards, and randomly distribute the cards.
6. Have the groups of children dramatize their story problems. One child can read the problem and the other two or three can act out the problem.
7. While the children are dramatizing the story problem, write the mathematical problem on the board. For example if Jim and Brian took one apple each for snack on Monday, how many apples would be left in the fruit bowl if their mother had bought two apples for each day of school that week? On the board write $1 + 1 = 2$; $2 \times 5 = 10$; $10 - 2 = 8$. The multiplication could be written as repeated addition for younger students.

Something to think about

Collect as many examples of real life mathematics as possible so that children use mathematics routinely for solving problems.

STORY S-T-R-E-T-C-H-E-R

Music and Movement: Amelia Bedelia's Song

What the children will learn

To compose some zany lyrics that fit the character

Materials you will need

Chart tablet, marker

What to do

1. Tell the students you have written the beginning of a song for Amelia Bedelia.
2. Write the lyrics based on the tune of "Mary Had a Little Lamb." For example,

   A-me-lia went to school one day, school one day, school one day.
   A-me-lia went to school one day, to sub-sti-tute teach.
   She made the children laugh and play, laugh and play, laugh and play.
   She made the children laugh and play, when Amelia went to school. (Raines, 1991)

3. Have the children continue writing lyrics for each of the funny situations in the story.

Something to think about

The title of this unit is "Jokes, Riddles, and Fun with Words." Discuss how a lyricist, a songwriter, has fun making words fit the pattern of a tune.

Silly Knock-Knocks

By Joseph Rosenbloom
Illustrated by Steve Harpster

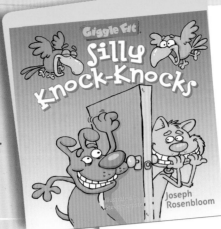

Story Line

Primary-grade children love knock-knock jokes. Part of the Giggle Fit series of books, Rosenbloom has found the children's funny bones. Simple yet artful, the jokes focus on the "ear" of primary-grade children to decide what is funny. The children's mistakes become simple goofs, instead of big mistakes, when they learn to laugh at the language. For example, "Knock, knock." "Who's there?" "Flea." "Flea who?" "Flea blind mice." There are also some of the old traditional knock-knocks we all learned as children: "Knock, knock." "Who's there?" "Boo." "Boo, who?" "You don't have to cry about it." Rich with language and richer with humor, Rosenbloom's collection and Harpster's illustrations will become staples.

Read-Aloud Presentation

Ask the children if anyone knows a knock-knock joke he or she could tell. If not, be prepared to tell one of the first knock-knock jokes you learned as a child. Look at the table of contents of the book and let the children select a section of the book. Go to that section, and read a knock-knock joke. Read with expression as this modeling will help the students when they prepare to read and dramatize their own knock-knock jokes.

STORY S-T-R-E-T-C-H-E-R

Art: Who's Behind the Door?

What the children will learn
To illustrate using a sequence

Materials you will need
Large sheets of drawing paper, rulers, crayons, markers

What to do
1. Model how to fold a large sheet of drawing paper so that it has five sections. Leave a large margin about the size of one of the folds along one side of the sheet. Then, fold into fourths to create a five-fold sheet of paper.
2. Read a knock-knock joke, and let the children count the scenes. For example, first scene—"Knock-knock"; second scene—"Who's there?" Third scene—"Boo"; fourth scene—"Boo who?" Fifth scene or punch line—"You don't have to cry about it."
3. Have the children think through what they will draw on each fold and then create their illustrations and writing.
4. Refold the five-fold fan. Let children enjoy unfolding and reading each other's jokes.

Something to think about
For children who have difficulty drawing in small spaces or matching the sequence of the joke, fold a sheet of paper in half, but be sure the punch line is hidden and the illustration for the punch line is hidden.

STORY S-T-R-E-T-C-H-E-R

Drama: Knock-Knocks on Stage

What the children will learn
To dramatize a scene and memorize some lines

Materials you will need
Knock-knock jokes, large index cards, markers

What to do
1. Rehearse a knock-knock joke with one of the students. Dramatize the joke to the children.
2. Assign partners.
3. Let the partners choose a knock-knock joke to dramatize for the class. Have each pair print the partner's joke on a large index card for rehearsal.
4. Choose a few children a day to tell their jokes.

Something to think about
For painfully shy children, let them use puppets and a puppet theater to tell their knock-knocks. Then the attention is on the puppet and not on them.

Drama: Knock-Knock Surprise Visitors

What the children will learn
To participate in a surprise dramatization

Materials you will need
Cooperation of school staff

What to do
1. Arrange for school personnel to make "surprise visits" to your classroom. Have these visits begin with a loud "Knock-knock." Rather than answer the door, let the children call your attention to the knocking.
2. Plan the sequence with the school personnel. Have each person learn a knock-knock joke and come to the class. Play out the joke by you serving as the answerer, saying, "Who's there?"
3. Include as many school personnel as possible.

Something to think about
Ask the librarian to help the school personnel find knock-knock jokes that go with their professions, if possible. If not, let the jokesters tell knock-knock jokes they enjoyed as children.

Mathematics: Survey Results Are a Knockout

What the children will learn
To record results and make comparisons

Materials you will need
Paper, pencil, chart tablet or whiteboard, large index cards, markers, masking tape, graph paper

What to do
1. Tell the children your favorite knock-knock jokes.
2. Have the children ask their parents their favorite knock-knock jokes from childhood. If parents cannot remember any, ask older brothers or sisters their favorite knock-knock jokes. Let the children have a day or two to complete this assignment, as the families may need some time to recall jokes from their childhood.
3. Ask the children to write their parents' or family members' favorite knock-knock jokes on large index cards or sheets of paper and bring them to school.
4. Collect all the knock-knock jokes. Read through the jokes and then have the children help you sort them into stacks of ones that are the same, then ones that are similar. Try other categories, as animals, food, or nursery-rhyme characters.

5. Count the number of knock-knock jokes in each category. Make a graph of the jokes by taping them with masking tape onto a wall or board.
6. See which categories have the most knock-knock jokes. Let the children make a graph on graph paper of the knock-knock joke comparisons.

Something to think about
For younger children, just count the jokes and make the wall graph. For older children, let them graph by two characteristics, such as favorite animal knock-knocks from dads on yellow cards, favorite animal knock-knocks from moms on green cards.

Writing: Our Class's Favorite Knock-Knock Jokes Book

What the children will learn
To read and think critically and to practice penmanship

Materials you will need
Knock-knock joke books, chart tablet, corrugated or heavy cardboard, masking tape, paper, contact paper, stapler

What to do
1. Assemble the materials for making a demonstration book. See page 234 in the Appendix for directions on how to construct a blank book.
2. Tell the students that they have been such good knock-knock-joke tellers that you want to keep their favorite jokes and that they can use this book to learn more knock-knock jokes.
3. Let each child select his or her favorite knock-knock joke. Have the children use key words to say what their knock-knock joke is about when they sign up on the chart tablet. For example, *Flea* for "Flea blind mice."
4. Distribute sheets of paper, at least two per child, and let the children write and draw their knock-knock jokes. Make sure the punch lines are on the second page.
5. Collect the knock-knock jokes and bind them into the sturdy bound version, using the directions on Appendix page 234 of this book.

Something to think about
Consider putting a child's favorite knock-knock joke into the parent newsletter or website. Indicate the child's name. Parents will begin to look for their child's joke.

Wise Crackers

By Michael Dahl

Story Line

The latest in the series of super funny joke books from Michael Dahl, *Wise Crackers* has the subtitle of "Riddles and Jokes about Numbers, Names, Letters and Silly Words." The collection of jokes and riddles contains some old childhood favorites as, "What did one math book say to the other math book? Man have I got problems!" and some new ones, "What did the spider say to the other spider? See you on the web." The 79 page books is divided into "Nutty Names: Name Jokes," "Mind Knots: Silly Riddles," and "Laughing Letters and Nutty Numerals." There are two jokes or riddles per page and each is graphically bold with different colors to show the joke and the punch line. Dahl ends with a page of suggestions about "How to be Funny." The vibrantly colored acrylic paints fit the style of the text and draw the individual readers onto the next riddle. See the AZ Kids Net website (www.azkidsnet.com/jsknockjoke.htm) for riddles and brainteasers.

Read-Aloud Presentation

Choose a child who tells jokes and ask him or her to tell a silly name riddle, such as "What do you call a girl who lives in France? Paris." If the child does not know a funny riddle, but has the timing to tell riddles, have the child tell one of the jokes that will be easy for the students, such as, "What letter of the alphabet buzzes and stings? B." Choose a few different types of jokes riddles to read from the book. Place the book in the library corner or on a book table for a few days and announce the STORY S-T-R-E-T-C-H-E-R-S associated with the book.

STORY S-T-R-E-T-C-H-E-R

Art: Illustrating Riddles

What the children will learn
To draw comically

Materials you will need
Drawing paper, crayons, markers, scissors, scraps of construction paper, brads

What to do
1. Riddles are questions that have witty answers, so the children need to find ways to keep surprises in these drawings, such as something that is opened or a page that is turned.
2. Model for the children several different ways to expose the answer or surprise. A simple one is to fold drawing paper in half and write the question on the first page, open it up and draw and write the answer to the riddle on the second page. Another option one is to write and illustrate the question on a larger sheet and connect a smaller sheet on top with a brad. The smaller sheet can then rotate and the answer can be exposed behind the cover.
3. Display children's artistic illustrations of the goofy riddles and their ways of hiding the answers.

Something to think about
Parents who are scrapbookers may have some inventive ways they can show children to make riddle art.

STORY S-T-R-E-T-C-H-E-R

Art: Drawing Cartoons

What the children will learn
To draw in a cartoon style

Materials you will need
Newspapers or magazines with cartoons, scrap practice paper, drawing paper, colored pencils, markers or crayons

What to do
1. Look at cartoons from newspapers or children's magazines. Notice how the dialogue appears above the scene, usually in a bubble.
2. Select a few examples from *Wise Crackers* and divide the riddles into a dialogue sequence. Add characters when necessary. For example, "How many feet are in a yard?" could have a drawing of a yardstick. The second frame could show people's legs and feet, which

provides a hint to the answer, "It depends on how many people are standing in the yard."

3. Have children practice framing the riddles with some of their favorite ones and adding themselves, their friends, or family members to the drawings.

Something to think about

If your local newspaper has a cartoonist or the high school paper has a cartoonist, invite him or her to class to demonstrate some drawing ideas.

STORY S-T-R-E-T-C-H-E-R

Language Arts: Alliterations, Say This Sentence Three Times

What the children will learn

To hear alliterations and tongue twisters

Materials you will need

Collection of tongue twisters, large index cards, markers, hole-punch, notebook ring or large plastic bag

What to do

1. Select some tongue twisters from ones you know and others in joke and riddle books. Teach the children some of the traditional tongue twisters, such as "How much wood would a woodchuck chuck, if a woodchuck could chuck wood?"

2. Write individual tongue twisters on large index cards. Have a child draw a cover page. Punch holes in one corner of the cards, then secure the cards with a large metal ring or store them in a large plastic bag.

3. Have each child select a tongue twister to memorize and to say at different speeds.

4. Teach the children that tongue twisters are the repetition of the same sounds in a succession of words. For example, "She sells seashells by the seashore."

Something to think about

Have a tongue twister week where children are called on to say their tongue twisters.

STORY S-T-R-E-T-C-H-E-R

Language Arts: Funny Vocabulary

What the children will learn

To use expressive language and synonyms

Materials you will need

Chart tablet or whiteboard, markers

What to do

1. At the top of the chart tablet or the whiteboard, write the question, "How many different ways can we say 'funny'?" Highlight *funny* using color or shape.

2. Let the children think of words that mean the same or similar meanings as *funny*. Tell the children these words are synonyms.

3. Read the title of the book, *Wise Crackers*. Ask the children what they think "wise crackers" means? They will probably say funny jokes. Write funny on the list and continue the list: *silly, hilarious, side-splitting, humorous, laughable, chuckles, guffawing,* and so on.

4. Ask the children to choose some of their favorite riddles from *Wise Crackers*.

Something to think about

Check two of the websites at the end of the reference list for word games.

STORY S-T-R-E-T-C-H-E-R

Writing: Our Favorite Jokes Book

What the children will learn

To practice reading, penmanship and making critical selections

Materials you will need

Joke and riddle books, writing paper, pencils, colored pencils or markers, poster board, masking tape, stapler, contact paper

What to do

1. Let children tell some of their favorite jokes and riddles. Then ask them to find at least one more joke or riddle that they think will be funny to their classmates. Discuss how they could decide if their classmates might like the joke or the riddle. For example, the children could try out the joke on one of their friends who they think has a good sense of humor.

2. Ask the children to print their jokes, riddles, or tongue twisters on a sheet of paper and add illustrations, making sure the reader has to turn a page or lift a flap to find the answer to the joke or riddle.

3. Combine the children's printed jokes, riddles, and tongue twisters into a bound book. See the Appendix for directions on binding a sturdy book.

4. Choose a fitting title for the book using one of the synonyms from the "Funny Vocabulary" exercise.

Something to think about

Wise Crackers is a part of a series of *Super Funny Joke Books,* from Michael Dahl. Help the children to think of what they may want to call their bound books of humor.

References

Dahl, Michael. 2011. *Wise Crackers*. Mankato, MN: Capstone.

Gwynne, Fred. 1970. *The King Who Rained*. New York: Simon and Schuster.

Rosenbloom, Joseph. 2002. *Goofy Riddles*. Illustrated by Steve Harpster. New York: Sterling.

Rosenbloom, Joseph. 2002. *Silly Knock-Knocks*. Illustrated by Steve Harpster. New York: Sterling.

Terban, Marvin. 1982. *Eight Ate: A Feast of Homonym Riddles*. Illustrated by Giulio Maestro. New York: Sandpiper.

Additional References

Maestro, Marco. 1997. *What Do You Hear When Cows Sing? And Other Silly Riddles*. Illustrated by Giulio Maestro. New York: HarperCollins. *Twenty-two outrageous original riddles targeted to beginning readers, with zany illustrations.*

Kessler, Leonard. 1991. *Old Turtle's 90 Knock-Knocks, Jokes, and Riddles*. New York: Greenwillow. *An illustrated collection of animal jokes and riddles.*

Pfeffer, Susan Beth. 1995. *The Riddle Streak*. Illustrated by Michael Chesworth. New York: Henry Holt. *Since her older brother always wins at ping-pong, checkers, and everything else, Amy decides to learn riddles in hope of finding some way she can beat him.*

Websites

1. BrownieLocks & The 3 Teddy Bears: www.brownielocks.com/jokes.html
   - Numerous categorized jokes and riddles
   - Tips for joke telling
2. AZ Kids Net: www.azkidsnet.com/JSknockjoke.htm
   - 170 knock-knock jokes
   - Riddles and brainteasers
   - Silly rhymes
3. Fun Brain.com: www.funbrain.com/words.html
   - Fifteen fun word games for kids
   - Teacher and parent resources
   - Links to free lesson plans

Chapter 17

Favorite Characters in a Series

Flat Stanley

Nate the Great Goes Undercover

George and Martha Rise and Shine

Ramona Quimby, Age 8

Encyclopedia Brown's Book of Strange but True Crimes

Flat Stanley

By Jeff Brown
Illustrated by Macky Pamintuan

Story Line

A terrifically silly adventure that lures the young listener into imaginary possibilities, *Flat Stanley* is an excellent read-aloud selection for class or for primary readers. A huge bulletin board falls on Stanley while he is asleep, and when he awakes, he is flat. His parents, though distressed, find Stanley's unusual size most convenient. He helps his mother find a ring that has dropped into a street grate, and Stanley himself enjoys entering rooms by sliding under the door. His most daring feat is helping capture art thieves at the museum. Complete with sibling rivalry, the story ends on a happy note when Stanley's brother helps him return to normal shape by pumping him up with a bicycle-tire pump. The comic illustrations are just the right touch for Stanley's peculiar predicament.

Read-Aloud Presentation

Have the children look at the cover of *Flat Stanley* and notice that he is tall and wide, but he is not very thick. Let the children imagine how Stanley might have gotten so thin. Read the book, and at the end let several children tell what they thought the most exciting parts of the story were. Ask when the children felt sorry for Stanley. Discuss the importance of not making fun of other people's appearances when they look different from us.

STORY S-T-R-E-T-C-H-E-R

Art: Flat and All That, Paper Dolls

What the children will learn
To follow directions for cutting

Materials you will need
Typing paper, scissors, crayons or colored pencils, optional—lightweight cardboard

What to do
1. Remind the children that Flat Stanley looks like a paper doll.
2. Demonstrate how to fold the paper and cut paper dolls. If the children have difficulty visualizing your directions, cut one example and then show the children how you did it.
3. Place the paper horizontally and fold it in half, then fold again.
4. Hold the paper together and draw the outline of one half of a doll, leaving the base and the arms extending all the way to the folded edge. Cut on the outline.
5. Let the children practice the folding, drawing, and cutting. When they get shapes they like, have them decorate their Flat Stanleys.

Something to think about
Put the children's paper dolls in envelopes and mail them to their homes. List the return address as Flat Stanley, the school street address, city, state, and zip code.

STORY S-T-R-E-T-C-H-E-R

Science and Nature: Bicycle Pump

What the children will learn
To observe the effects of air under pressure

Materials you will need
Bicycle pump, balloons, inflatable rafts, beach balls and other inflatable toys

What to do
1. Show the children how a bicycle pump works. If any children have bicycle tires with inner tubes, bring one to school and pump up the tube.
2. Demonstrate how to blow up balloons, inflatable toys, beach balls, and rafts by attaching the end of the pump hose to the valves.
3. Have the children continue pumping so they can feel the resistance as they depress the pump handle.
4. Take some items off the hose and let the children feel the air coming out.

Something to think about
Do not let children put balloons in their mouths; do not release balloons into the environment because they can harm wildlife.

Science and Nature: Stanley Kites

What the children will learn
To construct and fly a kite

Materials you will need
Strips of balsa wood, butcher paper, tempera paint, paintbrushes, crayons or markers, stapler, masking tape, string, fabric or crepe paper streamers

What to do
1. Make a two-by-three-foot cross of balsa wood, and staple it together in the middle or bind tape around it to hold the wood in place.
2. Cut butcher paper about two inches longer and wider than the kite shape. Let the children decorate the paper.
3. Fold the edges of the paper several times to strengthen them and make the butcher paper fit the wood frame.
4. Staple the paper to the balsa wood. Tape over the staples so they do not come loose.
5. Make a tail for the kite with strips of lightweight fabric or crepe paper streamers, and then attach it to the bottom of the balsa wood.
6. Staple one end of the string to the middle of the kite where the wood crosses. Place masking tape over the staple and continue wrapping the masking tape around the center of the crosses to attach it firmly.
7. Fly the kites on a windy day. Teach the children the safety rules about kite flying, such as staying away from power lines, traffic, and trees.

Something to think about
Let the children make self-portrait kites of themselves as Flat Stanleys.

Writing: Another Stanley Adventure

What the children will learn
To write a story appropriate for the main character

Materials you will need
Chalkboard, chalk, writing paper, pencils, large brown envelopes, optional—art supplies

What to do
1. Read again the part of the story where Flat Stanley is put into an envelope and mailed to California.
2. Let the children discuss some places they would like to be mailed if they were Flat Stanley. List these on the board as the children tell the beginning of an adventure that might occur when they arrive at their destination. Tell the children to keep the rest of their ideas a secret.
3. Have the children write very secretively and seal their stories in large brown envelopes. The children can add illustrations if they like.
4. Each day, open several large brown envelopes, and let the writers read their Flat Stanley adventures aloud.

Something to think about
Mail some of the children's Flat Stanley adventures to another classroom, and let the children take turns reading their stories to the other class. Visit the Flat Stanley Books website (www.flatstanley.com) to put the students' stories online.

Writing: Newspaper Account of Stanley's Heroics

What the children will learn
To review their writing for who, what, when, where, why, and how information

Materials you will need
Newspapers, chalkboard, chalk, writing paper, pencils, optional—art supplies

What to do
1. Select a few brief newspaper articles of interest to the children and read them aloud.
2. After reading each article, print the following on the chalkboard: who? what? when? where? why? how? Let the children recall the answers to these questions from the article.
3. Read again the account of Flat Stanley's heroic deed of helping to stop the art thieves.
4. Ask the children to write an account of Stanley's adventure in the museum.
5. Suggest they critique their writing to determine if it is a thorough account by reading their articles and checking that they have written answers to the questions: who? what? when? where? why? and how?

Something to think about
Let the children read their newspaper accounts to each other and have the listeners check off the answers to the good reporting questions.

Nate the Great Goes Undercover

By Marjorie Weinman Sharmat
Illustrated by Marc Simont

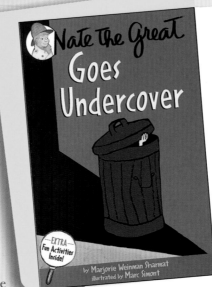

Story Line

Nate the Great takes on his first nighttime case. Characters are Nate's dog, Sludge, who loves pancakes; Oliver, his pesky neighbor; Rosamond and her cats; Esmeralda, a girl who provides good clues; and a mysterious someone or something who turns over the garbage cans at night. The young sleuth assembles the clues, eliminates possibilities, is thrown off by events, and ultimately, solves the mystery. Marc Simont alternates black-and-white charcoal drawings with illustrations to which a bit of color is added. His illustrations make Nate the Great memorable.

Read-Aloud Presentation

Ask the children if their family has ever found their garbage cans overturned at night. Invite the children to think about how they might solve the mystery of the overturned garbage cans. Show the children the cover of the book and ask them to predict what the story is about. Read *Nate the Great Goes Undercover*.

STORY S-T-R-E-T-C-H-E-R

Art: Night Scenes in Nate's Neighborhood

What the children will learn
To make crayon etchings

Materials you will need
Heavy construction or art paper, crayons, black or dark navy tempera paints, brushes, liquid detergent, plastic margarine tubs, plastic knives

What to do
1. Pour black or dark navy tempera paint into margarine tubs. Mix a drop of liquid detergent into the paint.
2. Invite the children to cover their construction paper with different colors of crayon.
3. Paint over the entire sheet of paper with the paint. Lay the papers flat and allow them to dry overnight.
4. Show the children how to use the edge of a plastic knife to "etch" or scratch shapes into the paint.

Something to think about
The liquid detergent in the tempera paint allows the paint to adhere to the waxy crayon.

STORY S-T-R-E-T-C-H-E-R

Classroom Library: Night Animals Reports

What the children will learn
To read about the night animals mentioned in *Nate the Great Goes Undercover*

Materials you will need
Encyclopedias or picture dictionaries, chalkboard and chalk, or chart tablet and markers, writing paper, pencils

What to do
1. Ask the students to recall the night animals that Nate reads about when he is at the library. Make a list on the chalkboard or chart paper.
2. Reread the section of the book where Nate goes to the library.
3. Read about nocturnal (night) birds to the children from the encyclopedia.
4. Read about cats, rats, bats, mice, shrews, skunks, raccoons, opossums, and moles.
5. Ask the children to describe the animals. List their descriptions on the chalkboard or chart tablet. Use key words and phrases.
6. Invite the children to decide whether or not Nate should be suspicious of each animal.

Something to think about
Some children may be able to read from picture dictionaries or children's encyclopedias and write their own descriptions.

Cooking and Snack Time: Mystery Pancakes

What the children will learn
To read and follow recipe directions

Materials you will need
Mixing bowl with a pouring spout, pancake mix, eggs, vegetable oil, wooden spoon, tablespoon, electric skillet, spatula, plates, plasticware, butter or margarine, syrup, variety of fresh or canned fruits, cartons of milk

What to do
1. Review the responsibilities with the children. The recipe reader reads the recipe from the package, prepares the electric skillet, and sets out the ingredients. The mixer-pourer measures and mixes the ingredients, then pours the batter onto the hot electric skillet. The pancake turner watches the pancakes until small bubbles begin to form, then flips the pancake. The server-mystery maker places a pancake in the plate, spoons on fruit, then places another pancake on top, making a mystery.
2. Divide the children into groups of four or five. Let the children decide who will do each job.
3. The children can eat and enjoy their mystery pancakes with servings of cold milk.

Something to think about
Closely supervise the children using the hot electric skillet.

Special Project: Follow-the-Clues Mystery Treasure Hunt

What the children will learn
To read and follow instructions

Materials you will need
Index cards, pencils, recycled envelopes, notepaper, box of pancake mix, encyclopedia, badge maker, badges

What to do
1. Organize the Treasure Hunt. Have teams of four or five detectives take turns reading and following the clues.
2. Write clues on index cards and seal them inside envelopes. Distribute the envelopes and props throughout school.
3. On the first envelope, print "Clue #1: Go to the office and ask everyone there if he or she knows Nate the Great. When you ask the right person, he or she will give you something found in the story."

4. When the detectives ask the right person, he or she will give the detective team the envelope marked "Clue #2: Go to the cafeteria and find the person who has the next clue."
5. Have the cafeteria worker give the detectives the pancake mix or a pancake recipe and an envelope marked "Clue #3: Go to the library and find the next clue."
6. At the library, the clue is hidden in the encyclopedia under *N* for Nate the Great. The librarian may give clues, including: "Remember where Nate looked in the library to help solve the mystery."
7. When the detectives go to the *N* in the encyclopedia, they will find directions to go to the library workroom.
8. In the workroom, a parent volunteer helps the children make a "Nate the Great" badge.
9. The detectives put their badges on and return to the classroom. Warn the detectives not to tell anyone else about their clues and how they solved the mystery.

Something to think about
First graders will probably need an adult to help them.

Writing: Another Nate the Great Mystery

What the children will learn
To write a story in a sequence and leave clues for the reader

Materials you will need
Writing paper, pencils, folders

What to do
1. Have the writers recall a mystery (a lost watch or car keys) that happened in their home.
2. Ask the children to write the end of the story—the discovery of the lost object. Explain that mystery writers often know the beginning of a story (the mystery) and the ending of a story (the solution). To write their story, they must construct clues for the middle of the story.
3. Let the children write the middle of the story—the clues needed to solve the mystery.
4. Encourage the children to illustrate their stories and bind them into a collection of class mysteries. (See page 234 of the Appendix for instructions to bind books.)

Something to think about
As an alternative, read only the beginning and the ending of another Nate the Great mystery. Let the children write the middle of the story.

George and Martha Rise and Shine

By James Marshall

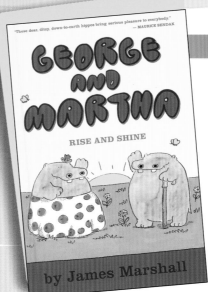

Story Line

George and Martha are hippos who happen also to be the best of friends. In *George and Martha Rise and Shine*, the two friends tease and then forgive each other. They decide that telling fibs is dangerous, have a silly misadventure with fleas, appreciate Martha's talent as a saxophonist, go to a scary movie, and discover the potential for hurt feelings when Martha is excluded from George's secret club. Each episode provokes laughter and relief that the friendship survives their antics. James Marshall's cartoon renditions of the hippos are as famous as their friendship. The sparse line drawings are overlaid with lime, bright yellow, tangerine, and of course, the gray of hippos.

Read-Aloud Presentation

Collect all the George and Martha books you can find. Show the children the covers and see whether they recognize the series. If any children have read any of the George and Martha books, ask them to tell the others something about George and Martha. Write their descriptions on the chalkboard or on chart paper. Children often describe George and Martha as hippos who are friends. Engage the children in a discussion of what friends do together. Read at least two stories from *George and Martha Rise and Shine*. After reading the stories, invite the children to add to the description of George and Martha. Use the term *characterization*. Ask the children how they would characterize George and Martha. During other read-aloud sessions, complete the book and continue adding to the characterizations.

STORY S-T-R-E-T-C-H-E-R

Art: Make a George and Martha Fan Club Poster

What the children will learn
To interpret a friendship visually

Materials you will need
Variety of art materials, poster board, markers, poster paints, construction paper, glue, crepe paper streamers

What to do
1. Decorate the art area or another area of the classroom with crepe paper streamers.
2. When the children ask about the streamers, announce that this area of the classroom is for the George and Martha Fan Club.
3. Ask the children to make posters of their favorite George and Martha stories from any of the books.

Something to think about
Allow children to work together if they choose. Find two of the newest class members or the least popular children and work with them to make the first poster. Brainstorm ideas for materials and scenes for the poster to help them succeed in working together.

STORY S-T-R-E-T-C-H-E-R

Classroom Library: Books and Videos

What the children will learn
To create a catalog system for books and videos

Materials you will need
Index cards, markers, paper, pencils, storage space, videos from the writing STORY S-T-R-E-T-C-H-E-R

What to do
1. After the children write and perform several George and Martha book reports, talk about the importance of cataloging their reports so that they can locate particular reports easily.
2. Let interested children brainstorm ways to organize the display and cataloging of the videos.
3. After the students devise a system, have them explain the system to the class and ask for ideas to improve it.
4. After the class members use the system for a while, again ask the inventors to solicit suggestions from their classmates for changes to improve the system.

Something to think about

Although it would be easier for the teacher to organize a simple card catalog for books and videos, encouraging the children to think about how to organize the materials and to try out their ideas promotes higher levels of thinking. Having the inventors solicit suggestions from the class for improving their system avoids criticism and promotes listening and critical thinking.

STORY S-T-R-E-T-C-H-E-R

Cooking and Snack Time: George and Martha, Friends' Picnic

What the children will learn
To prepare foods that their friends will like

Materials you will need
Picnic supplies (coolers, picnic baskets, serving dishes, and utensils), sandwiches, juices, fruits

What to do
1. Survey the children to learn their favorite sandwiches for picnics. Note everyone's choices.
2. Encourage children from different cultures to talk about picnic foods that their families like.
3. Select the top three sandwich choices from among the children's favorites.
4. Ask the cafeteria manager to provide the bread, sandwich fillings, and condiments.
5. Have three or four children prepare the sandwiches.
6. Let the children serve each other at the picnic.

Something to think about
If time does not allow for a picnic, have a George and Martha popcorn party and watch a videotape of a favorite picture-book character.

STORY S-T-R-E-T-C-H-E-R

Mathematics: George and Martha Surveys

What the children will learn
To collect, analyze, display, and interpret data

Materials you will need
Notepads, pencils, chalkboard and chalk or markers and chart paper

What to do
1. Sort the entire class into pairs of data collectors, or draw names from a hat to select a small group of data collectors.

2. Work with the groups to decide what questions they want to be answered.
3. Conduct a variety of surveys inspired by George and Martha by asking class members questions: "What is your favorite story from *George and Martha Rise and Shine*?" or "What is your favorite story from all the George and Martha books?"
4. Ask the children to write their questions at the top of a survey sheet. List all the children's names down the left margin of the paper. Write their answers on the lines beside their names.
5. Give the raw data to a group of data analysts. Let them decide how to collapse the answers and create a graph or some other display of the results.
6. Suggest that the students create a display of the information.

Something to think about
Consider having older reading buddies from other classrooms become mathematics buddies. Experienced data collectors, analysts, and interpreters can help younger ones.

STORY S-T-R-E-T-C-H-E-R

Writing: Producing a Video of a George and Martha Story

What the children will learn
To script, read, and film a short book report

Materials you will need
Paper and pencils or computers and word processing program, video camera or videotape

What to do
1. Invite interested children to write and produce their own video book reports.
2. Divide these class members into script writers, readers, filmmakers, and set producers. Ask the children to work as teams.
3. After the children complete the videotaping, schedule one video book report per day.

Something to think about
Show the videos at parent meetings to demonstrate how a developmentally appropriate language and reading program works: by involving children in reading, writing, listening, and speaking in ways that are meaningful to them.

Ramona Quimby, Age 8

By Beverly Cleary
Illustrated by Tracy Dockray

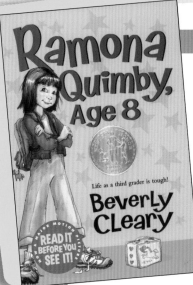

Story Line

Ramona enters third grade feeling misunderstood in a new school, on a new bus, and with a new teacher who has new expectations. Told from Ramona's perspective, a playground feud with "Yard Ape," requires standing up to a bully. Forced to stay at a neighbor's house, Ramona feels neglected, and she's angry at having to play games with four-year-old Willa Jean. Stressed by the new requirements of being in third grade, Ramona is embarrassed when she throws up at school. Frustrated and angry inside, Ramona has to deal with a changed family where Mother has to work while Father goes to school. Eventually, she understands life at school and at home, while making temporary peace with her friends, teachers, and family.

Read-Aloud Presentation

Chances are someone in the class has read some of the Ramona books. If this is the first Ramona book you have read to the children, make a display of the other Ramona books by Beverly Cleary. Talk about how some children worry about starting a new grade or a new school. Some children cry and others get mad and act stubborn when they do not know what to do. Read a few chapters each day, and pause at the end to discuss how Ramona is acting and what she is feeling. Let a child predict what they think Ramona may do next in the following chapters.

STORY S-T-R-E-T-C-H-E-R

Art: Favorite Ramona Book Cover

What the children will learn

To choose favorite books and favorite art materials

Materials you will need

Tempera, watercolor, and acrylic paints; markers; chalks; charcoals; crayons; colored pencils; variety of papers; glue; scissors

What to do

1. Have the children recall some of their favorite Ramona books or look at the ones from the classroom display.
2. Ask the children to choose their favorite Ramona book and browse through the book, remembering some of the details of the story.
3. Turn the books covers down and ask the children to think of what they want to draw on the cover that would make others want to read the book.
4. Let the children choose their art media to create their very special covers. Some covers may be larger than the book and can be described as posters for their favorite Ramona book.

Something to think about

Allow the children to make large posters and then photocopy the posters and shrink them to the size of a book cover.

STORY S-T-R-E-T-C-H-E-R

Mathematics: How Many Children Do You Know from Your Old School?

What the children will learn

To compare using numbers and graphing the responses

Materials you will need

Chart tablet, markers, ruler

What to do

1. Read the part of the book where Ramona realizes that she will be going to school with a lot of children she does not know.
2. Write each child's name down the vertical side of the chart tablet.

3. Have each child in the classroom count the number of children they knew from last year by recalling who was in their classroom last year.
4. Make marks at the bottom on the horizontal axis for the graph.
5. Call each child's name and let them tell you how many children they knew from last year.
6. Mark the graph by counting off the spaces across from each child's name.

Something to think about
Recall all the teachers who returned to the school from last year, the number of teachers you knew, and the number of teachers who were new to the school this year.

STORY S-T-R-E-T-C-H-E-R

Reading: DEAR—Drop Everything and Read

What the children will learn
To select and enjoy books

Materials you will need
Collection of library books for the classroom, index cards, pencils

What to do
1. Institute a program of DEAR or "Drop Everything and Read." At approximately the same time each day, declare it is DEAR time.
2. Allow ten to fifteen minutes of time to read a book without any interruptions. Have no requirements except to read and enjoy the book.
3. Have children write the names of the authors, illustrators, and titles of the books they have read on index cards.

Something to think about
First graders who are learning to read may complain about not knowing how to read well enough to read a book, but talk with them about reading a story using both the pictures and the words. For second and third graders, extend the time when children begin wanting more time to read.

STORY S-T-R-E-T-C-H-E-R

Social Studies: Where Is Ramona's School?

What the children will learn
To identify states on a map

Materials you will need
Atlas, map of the United States, computer with Internet access

What to do
1. Read again the section of the book that tells how from Ramona's school yard, she could see Mt. Hood.
2. With the students, look in an atlas and find where Mt. Hood is located in Oregon.
3. Use an Internet search engine to find information about Mt. Hood, and then read the information.
4. Decide where Ramona might live if she could see Mt. Hood from her school yard.

Something to think about
Explore other facts discovered from reading the Internet source about Mt. Hood.

STORY S-T-R-E-T-C-H-E-R

Writing: Commercial for Favorite Ramona Quimby Book

What the children will learn
To write using convincing language

Materials you will need
Computer with Internet access, book covers

What to do
1. Read the inside book flaps of the Ramona books and emphasize the positive words.
2. Read reviews of Ramona books from the publisher, HarperCollins, and from websites that feature children's books.
3. Have the children identify words that make them want to read the book that is being reviewed.
4. Let the children try "selling" the book to children who might be interested in reading the book.

Something to think about
Plan to write commercials advertizing the Ramona books that might be a part of a book fair, or think of key words to use as a part of a submission to a website. See http://edhelper.com/books/Ramona_Quimby_Age_.htm for additional ideas for Ramona activities.

Encyclopedia Brown's Book of Strange But True Crimes

By Donald J. Sobol and Rose Sobol
Interior Illustrated by John Zielinski

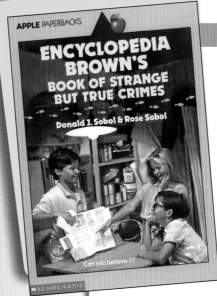

Story Line

The combination of humor and mystery is irresistible to third graders who are Encyclopedia Brown fans. *Encyclopedia Brown's Book of Strange But True Crimes* is a scrapbook of the child-sleuth's newspaper clippings of wacky but true crimes. The highlights include a burglar who has to be rescued by the police after he gets caught in a window, safecrackers who set the money on fire while blow-torching a safe, an elephant who snatches a purse at the zoo, and a bridegroom who gets arrested to avoid his wedding. Third-grade sleuths will especially enjoy solving "the case of the two-headed toothbrush," but they will laugh at the absurdity of all the stories in Encyclopedia Brown's scrapbook of wacky crimes. The small interior line drawings on every third or fourth page are by John Zielinski.

Read–Aloud Presentation

Display a large collection of Encyclopedia Brown mysteries. No doubt some children will already know this famous character. If reading to second graders, discuss the meaning of the word *mystery*. If reading to children unfamiliar with Encyclopedia Brown, read one of the famous early mysteries. Ask the children to talk about things that they or their family members clip from newspapers. Call attention to the cover of the book, which shows children looking at Encyclopedia Brown's scrapbook. Read a few of the very humorous stories, like those about the elephant purse-snatcher or the cactus thieves. Read at least two wacky stories that involve money.

STORY S-T-R-E-T-C-H-E-R

Art: Encyclopedia Brown's Scrapbook Bulletin Board

What the children will learn
To illustrate the strange but true crimes

Materials you will need
Fine-point markers, old newspaper, used business envelopes, staples, stapler, white construction paper, copying paper, scrapbook, scissors

What to do
1. Ask children who come to the art center to select a few of the wacky stories from the book.
2. Fold construction paper in half vertically, and then draw a line along the fold. Unfold the paper. To the left of the line, have the students retell the wacky story in their own words. To the right of the line, ask the students to illustrate the story.
3. After photocopying the students' rewrites and illustrations, cut along the vertical line, separating the stories from the illustrations.
4. Cover a bulletin board with old newspaper. Make a heading that reads, "Solve the mystery." Print "Match the wacky illustrations to the strange but true crimes" on drawing paper and staple it to the bulletin board.
5. Staple the wacky stories onto the bulletin board. Below each of the stories, staple a recycled business envelope with the back side of the envelope facing out to form a pocket.
6. Invite mystery solvers to look through the illustrations, read through the wacky stories, and then place the correct illustration into the envelope pocket of the matching story.

Something to think about
See the Encyclopedia Brown website (www.kidsread.com/series/series-brown.asp) for a characters trivia game.

STORY S-T-R-E-T-C-H-E-R

Classroom Library: Mystery in a Mystery File

What the children will learn
To locate information using the table of contents and other clues

Materials you will need

Pens or pencils, ten file folders and ten dividers, marker, plastic file bin or tray

What to do

1. Place the file folders and dividers into a plastic file bin, tray, or tub.
2. On the first divider, print the title of the first chapter of the book. Continue with the remaining chapters.
3. Select one wacky story from each chapter. Print the story on the inside of a folder.
4. Shuffle the ten folders.
5. Have the children read the stories printed on the inside of the folders and decide in which chapters the stories probably appeared.
6. Ask the children to place the file folders behind the appropriate dividers. For example, if the story selected was the one about the elephant who snatched a woman's purse at the zoo, then the reader would place that file folder behind the divider marked, "Wacky crimes."
7. The file-folder sleuths can check their answers by looking up the cases in the book.

Something to think about

Extend this STORY S-T-R-E-T-C-H-E-R by choosing new stories from each chapter.

Cooking and Snack Time: Snack Sleuths

What the children will learn

To recognize fruits by their smells, textures, and tastes

Materials you will need

Variety of fruits, knives, serving bowls, napkins, spoons, paper bags, blindfold

What to do

1. Place several different fruits in a paper grocery bag.
2. Ask one child to close his or her eyes, or blindfold him or her.
3. Direct the blindfolded child to reach into the bag, feel the fruit, and remove the fruit that he or she wants to eat.
4. Be sure that the children wash the fruits before eating .

Something to think about

With older children, have a group of snack preparers wash the fruit and make a fruit salad.

Mathematics: Money Mysteries

What the children will learn

To arrange stories involving money in order based on the amount of money the stories mention

Materials you will need

Three or four paperback copies of the book, paper and pencil and markers or computer and printer, small sticky notes or index cards, file folders

What to do

1. Observe that many crimes in *Encyclopedia Brown's Book of Strange But True Crimes* involve money. Invite the students to recall the stories about money that they heard during the read-aloud time.
2. Place sticky notes on the pages of the book where the money stories appear.
3. Ask the children to write on the sticky note the amount of money mentioned in the story and the page number on which the money was mentioned.
4. After the children finish reading the book and locate all the money mysteries, the readers should take their sticky notes and arrange them in order from the lowest amount of money mentioned to the highest.

Something to think about

Let the children tell or read a story about money. Ask the file-folder sleuths to look at their sticky notes and say which page the story appears on.

Writing: Wacky Stories, Truth or Fiction?

What the children will learn

To interpret meaning from drawings and words and to recall stories they have read

Materials you will need

Photocopies of the illustrations, paper, pencils, large index cards, small index cards, marker, push pins, bulletin board

What to do

1. Photocopy the illustrations from the book. Distribute one illustration to each pair of students.
2. Ask the writers to recall the story that went with the illustration and rewrite the story in their own words. These stories become the "true wacky stories."
3. Using the same illustrations, let the writers compose a

fictional story to go with the drawings. These stories become the "fictional wacky stories."

4. Ask the students to print each story on a large index card, and then attach the cards to the bulletin board.
5. Print "Truth" on a few small index cards and "Fiction" on others.
6. Ask other students to read the stories on the bulletin board and decide whether they are truth or fiction. Once the children decide, they pin the small "Truth" or "Fiction" index cards to the story.

Something to think about

Place a solution book or key nearby so that the students can check their "Truth" or "Fiction" assessments.

References

Brown, Jeff. 2003. *Flat Stanley*. Illustrated by Macky Pamintuan. New York: HarperCollins.

Cleary, Beverly. 1992. *Ramona Quimby, Age 8*. Illustrated by Tracy Dockray. New York: HarperCollins.

Marshall, James. 2009. *George and Martha: Rise and Shine*. Illustrated by James Marshall. New York: Houghton Mifflin Harcourt.

Sharmat, Marjorie Weinman. 1974. *Nate the Great Goes Undercover*. Illustrated by Marc Simont. New York: Random House.

Sobol, Donald J. and Rose Sobol. 1991. *Encyclopedia Brown's Book of Strange But True Crimes*. New York: Scholastic.

Additional References

Howe, Deborah and James Howe. 1979. *Bunnicula: Rabbit-Tale of Mystery*. Illustrated by Alan Daniel. New York: Simon and Schuster. *Though scoffed at by Harold the dog, Chester the cat tries to warn his human family that their foundling baby bunny must be a vampire.*

O'Connor, Jane. 2009. *Fancy Nancy: Explorer Extraordinaire*. Illustrated by Robin Preiss Glasser. New York: HarperCollins. *Nancy and her best friend Bree explore the fascinating world of birds and insects in their exclusive and glamorous Explorer Extraordinaire Club.*

Willems, Mo. 2008. *The Pigeon Wants a Puppy*. New York: Hyperion. *The incorrigible bird returns in his fourth book. He argues like a child for a puppy in hilarious text and images.*

Websites

1. edHelper.com: Ramona Quimby, Age 8 Literature Unit: www.edhelper.com/books/Ramona_Quimby_Age_.htm
   • Reading Journal
   • Book Report
   • Analogies
   • Chapter Reviews and Activities
2. FlatStanleyBooks.com: www.flatstanleybooks.com
   • Numerous classroom activities
3. KidsRead.com: www.kidsreads.com/series/series-brown.asp and www.kidsreads.com/series/series-nate.asp
   • Encyclopedia Brown and Nate the Great trivia games
   • Fact Sheets
   • Character descriptions

Chapter 18

Fractured Fairy Tales and Stories with a Twist

The True Story of the 3 Little Pigs! by A. Wolf

The Paper Bag Princess

The Stinky Cheese Man and Other Fairly Stupid Tales

Waking Beauty

Once Upon a Cool Motorcycle Dude

The True Story of the 3 Little Pigs! By A. Wolf

As told to Jon Scieszka
Illustrated by Lane Smith

Story Line

Wolf tells his side of "The Three Little Pigs," beginning with a birthday party for dear Granny Wolf, a sneeze, and a cup of sugar. Wolf goes over to the little pig's house to borrow sugar for Granny's cake, but he has such a terrible cold that, just as the pigs are about to open the door, he sneezes a giant sneeze, which causes him to huff and puff. The great sneeze does all the damage to the little pig's straw house. Of course, the same thing happens at the next house, made of sticks. The third little pig rather rudely refuses to let Wolf come into his brick house. The police come and arrest Wolf for making a commotion after the third pig says something bad about Wolf's granny. According to Wolf, the two reporters who write the newspaper story about the events jazz up the story and make him sound like a Big Bad Wolf. Smith's hilarious sepia-toned illustrations have a surreal quality that fits this fractured fairy tale.

Read-Aloud Presentation

Without referring to "The Three Little Pigs," read *The True Story of the 3 Little Pigs! By A. Wolf.* Draw the children's attention to the cover of the book, which is printed like a newspaper. Also point out the pig reading the newspaper, holding the paper with his foot, as if the foot were a hand. At the end of the story, encourage the children to laugh about the surprises in the story. Discuss the viewpoint of this story, and observe that every story is told from a particular point of view.

Art: Newspaper Artists

What the children will learn
To create a cartoon storyboard

Materials you will need
Cartoons from the newspaper, drawing paper, pencils, colored pencils, markers or crayons, scissors, glue, sheets of newspaper

What to do
1. Let the children look at the sequence of events in one of their favorite cartoons in the newspaper.
2. Cut the cartoon panels apart. Have the children reassemble them in the correct order.
3. Show the children how to fold a sheet of art paper in half three times: one fold creates halves; two folds create fourths; three folds, eighths.
4. Unfold the paper. Using the fold lines as guides, cut the sheet of paper into eight small rectangles.
5. Read *The True Story of the 3 Little Pigs! By A. Wolf* and ask the children to decide the story's eight main scenes.
6. Suggest that the children print a few words that signify one scene on each rectangle, like "wolf–no sugar," meaning that the wolf is baking a cake for his granny and discovers he has no sugar.
7. On the reverse side of each of the rectangle, have the children draw and color a picture of the scene.
8. When all the scenes are illustrated, the artists glue their storyboards in the correct sequence on sheets of newspaper. Display the storyboards in the art center.

Something to think about
With younger children, form partnerships in which each child is responsible for four scenes. For larger cooperative projects, more children can work together.

Classroom Library: Collecting Fractured Fairy Tales

What the children will learn
To compare and contrast the original fairy tale with the fractured or retold fairy tale

Materials you will need
A collection of three little pigs books from school library

What to do

1. Pair the children with reading partners.
2. Ask the partners to read the original story of *The Three Little Pigs* and then read their favorite parts of *The True Story of the 3 Little Pigs! by A. Wolf.*
3. Discuss the similarities and differences.
4. Vote on the class favorites among these stories.

Something to think about

Connecting reading and writing through STORY S-T-R-E-T-C-H-E-R-S is very natural in this unit.

STORY S-T-R-E-T-C-H-E-R

Cooking and Snack Time: An Upside-Down Birthday Cake

What the children will learn

To follow the directions for making a pineapple upside-down cake

Materials you will need

Large baking pan, vegetable oil, flour, cake mix, eggs, water or milk, powdered sugar, canned pineapple, red cherries, measuring cups, spoons, mixing bowls, oven, plates, napkins, candles

What to do

1. Because *The True Story of the 3 Little Pigs! By A. Wolf* is an upside-down story, and because all the trouble starts when innocent Wolf just wants to make his poor granny a birthday cake, bake a pineapple upside-down cake.
2. Bake the cake according to the package directions. Before pouring the batter into the pan, cover the bottom of the pan with pineapple rings and place red cherries in the center of each ring.
3. Pour the batter into the pan.
4. Bake the cake and serve it so that the side with the pineapples and cherries is on the top.
5. Add candles and sing, "Happy Birthday, Granny Wolf."

Something to think about

Remember that adding humor and frivolity to your classroom motivates children. Do not be afraid to show your comic side, but never poke fun at the children.

STORY S-T-R-E-T-C-H-E-R

Writing: Newspaper Accounts of Other Fairy Tales

What the children will learn

To rewrite stories as if they had appeared in the newspaper

Materials you will need

Chart tablet paper and markers or chalk and chalkboard

What to do

1. Explain to a group of writers that newspaper accounts are supposed to answer who, what, when, where, why, and how in their stories.
2. Brainstorm a list of questions that the newspaper reporter might have asked the Wolf. For example, "What where you doing outside Third Pig's house?"
3. Let the children work with their writing partners. One child asks the questions; the other writes the answers. Together they compose the newspaper story, asking and answering the who, what, when, where, why, and how questions.

Something to think about

If you have access to a computer software newspaper program, lay out the children's stories and print them.

STORY S-T-R-E-T-C-H-E-R

Writing: Wolf's Version of Other Fairy Tales

What the children will learn

To write from a different point of view

Materials you will need

Writing folders, paper, pencils, optional—art supplies for illustrations

What to do

1. Let the children select other stories that they could tell from a different point of view: "Goldilocks and The Three Bears" from the Little Bear's perspective, "The Three Billy Goats Gruff" from the troll's point of view, or "The Little Red Hen" from the dog's or cat's.
2. Form writing partnerships, and let the children brainstorm a beginning for their stories. Once the children have a beginning, they can usually continue through to the ends of their stories.

Something to think about

Point-of-view writing is a good exercise for writing partners across grade levels; try pairing third graders with first graders, for example.

The Paper Bag Princess

By Robert Munsch
Illustrated by
Michael Martchenko

Story Line

A read-aloud favorite, *The Paper Bag Princess* takes the damsel-in-distress, prince-charming-to-the-rescue story and twists it into the princess to the rescue of prince in distress. Captured by a dragon, Prince Ronald is rescued by Princess Elizabeth. When she tries tricking the dragon through flattery to perform dragon feats, she finds her clothes burned off and has to don a paper bag while she continues her quest to rescue Prince Ronald. When rescued, he tells her how awful and not so princess-like she looks with ashes in her hair and her paper bag dress, and he tells her not to return until she is dressed appropriately. Obviously, the story has a happy ending, but not the married-and-lived-happily-ever-after ending. The feisty female, Princess Elizabeth, prevails. Martchenko's comical pen-and-ink drawings with watercolor washes help children understand the twisted elements of the tale and the tongue-in-check quality of the humor.

Read–Aloud Presentation

Help children to make some of the associations with themes in fairy tales. Point out that if there is a prince, there is usually a princess. How are the princess and the prince often dressed? What fire-breathing animal is often found in fairy tales? Who is usually the person rescued in the fairy tales? Talk with the children again about fractured fairy tales and stories with a twist. Ask them to listen to the reading of *The Paper Bag Princess* and decide if this is a usual or a fractured fairy tale. See the Read Write Think website (www.readwritethink.org) for several prince and princess variations.

Art: Designing Paper Bag Shirts

What the children will learn
To follow directions and add their creative ideas to a group project

Materials you will need
Paper grocery bags, scissors, crayons or markers, stapler, paper bag scraps

What to do
1. Design your own paper bag shirt as a model. Fold a grocery bag flat. Use the bottom of the grocery bag as the top of the paper bag shirt. Cut a neck hole large enough for your head to fit through. Slit the sides to within three inches of the bottom of the bag.
2. Decorate your paper bag shirt with some colors and shapes that are your favorites. If a paper bag is too small for you, cut it all the way and attach it by stapling paper bag strips across the shoulders and letting it hang loose. This method will also be appropriate for some larger children.
3. Invite the children to create their own paper bag shirts. Have the children decide what their favorite colors are and some of their favorite patterns. They can also draw a favorite scene from *The Paper Bag Princess* as their design for their paper shirts.

Something to think about
Wear the paper bag shirts for the drama STORY S-T-R-E-T-C-H-E-R below.

Art: Drawings of Major Scenes in *The Paper Bag Princess*

What the children will learn
To select major scenes that help tell the plot of the story

Materials you will need
Whiteboard, paper grocery bags, scissors, staplers, crayons, markers, paper bag scraps

What to do
1. Look through *The Paper Bag Princess* with a group of children, helping them to identify the major scenes of the story. Write the list of scenes on the whiteboard.
2. Have children sign up for the scene they want to draw.
3. Demonstrate how to make the paper bag T-shirts from the directions above.

4. After everyone finishes making their T-shirts, let the children arrange themselves in the order of the story.
5. Have a child or two "retell" the story by interpreting the drawings on the paper bag T-shirts.

Something to think about
For younger children, read the story aloud again, and let the children arrange themselves in order as you read.

STORY S-T-R-E-T-C-H-E-R

Drama: Paper Bag Princesses to the Rescue

What the children will learn
To listen for their cues, say their lines, and do the actions

Materials you will need
Chart tablet or whiteboard, markers, large index cards or scraps of poster board

What to do
1. Reread *The Paper Bag Princess*. Decide with the children who the characters are in the story—Princess Elizabeth, Prince Ronald, and the Dragon. Ask the children who is telling the story (the narrator)—another character. Assign children to each role.
2. Copy some of the dialogue from the beginning and some from the end of the book onto large index cards. Have groups of children rehearse these lines.
3. Choose the first set of characters and let them read their lines from the large index cards.
4. Decide on a cue that indicates when the children should say their lines. After a few groups perform *The Paper Bag Princess*, ask for volunteers to memorize the lines from the beginning and end of the story.

Something to think about
Consider performing *The Paper Bag Princess* for younger students at the school. It is a sure to be a hit.

STORY S-T-R-E-T-C-H-E-R

Reading: Scene Shuffle Game

What the children will learn
To place scenes from the story in sequence

Materials you will need
Large index cards, markers, plastic sandwich bag

What to do
1. With a smaller group of students, leaf through the book and list the scenes on large index cards. Use their words to title the scenes.

2. Shuffle the scenes, let the children place the scenes back into order, and then demonstrate the Scene Shuffle to the other members of the class.
3. Place the Scene Shuffle Game into a plastic sandwich bag. Place *The Paper Bag Princess* book and the "Scene Shuffle Game" cards together on a reading table or in the classroom library.

Something to think about
Sequencing is both a reading and a mathematics concept. One can count the scenes and the number of characters in each scene and assign a number to each scene. Scene One can have the equation of N + PR + PE = 1: Narrator plus Prince Ronald plus Princess Elizabeth equals Scene One. The children can then write an equation for each of the major scenes.

STORY S-T-R-E-T-C-H-E-R

Social Studies: Geography: A Map to Find the Dragon

What the children will learn
To create a simple map

Materials you will need
Whiteboard, drawing paper, scissors, poster board, markers, glue sticks

What to do
1. Talk about using maps to get from one place to the other.
2. Recall the scenes from *The Paper Bag Princess* where Princess Elizabeth has to go in search of the dragon. Write the scenes on the board from the beginning of the search until the end of the search for Dragon. Emphasize the "where" question.
3. On poster board, draw an imaginary map following the path to find Dragon. Mark on the map *North, South, East,* and *West*.
4. Ask the children to draw a small scene for each of the stops along the path in the search for Dragon.
5. Let the children cut out those scenes and glue them onto the poster board.

Something to think about
Consider taking a familiar board game, such as *Candy Land,* and marking the board with *North, South, East,* and *West*. Let the children practice telling the directions of their moves.

The Stinky Cheese Man and Other Fairly Stupid Tales

By Jon Scieszka
Illustrated by Lane Smith

Story Line

Winner of a Caldecott Honor Medal, *The Stinky Cheese Man and Other Fairly Stupid Tales* provides the funny adaptations of ten familiar stories. Meant to be enjoyed as a compilation, the surprises in the print, illustrations, and layout of the book add to the creativity. Children's favorites appear to be "The Little Red Hen," "Chicken Licken," "The Princess and the Bowling Ball," "The Really Ugly Duckling," and "The Stinky Cheese Man," although there are many laughs in all of the stories. The book is funny from beginning to end, even with the author and illustrator pictured as George Washington and Abe Lincoln. It can be shared with the whole class, but must be looked at individually for children to appreciate its full creativity.

Read-Aloud Presentation

Help the children recall one of the original tales, such as "The Little Red Hen," and then read the fractured fairy tale version from *The Stinky Cheese Man and Other Fairly Stupid Tales*. Ask them which parts they found the funniest. Discuss that these tales are called fractured fairy tales or tales with a twist. Mention that we could not enjoy the funny parts of the new tales, the fractured fairy tales, if we did not know the originals.

STORY S-T-R-E-T-C-H-E-R

Art: Design Your Own Literary Medal

What the children will learn
To use the Caldecott Honor Medal from *The Stinky Cheese Man and Other Fairly Stupid Tales* as a model for their own designs

Materials you will need
Copies of the Caldecott Medal, reference materials on the Caldecott, aluminum foil or gold holiday foil, retractable ball point pen, small pizza pans

What to do
1. Look at the Caldecott Honor and other medals that appear as stamps on children's books.
2. Have the children brainstorm ideas about what they would put on a medal. For example, their names might be part of the medal or they might include a drawing.
3. Help the children cover their small pizza pans with aluminum foil or gold holiday foil and smooth it out.
4. Using a retractable ball point pen without the point out, demonstrate how to draw the images on their medals.

Something to think about
Let the children display their medals with a book that would be a medal winner in their eyes.

STORY S-T-R-E-T-C-H-E-R

Cooking and Snack Time: Green Jell-O Frogs

What the children will learn
To follow simple directions for making Jell-O

Materials you will need
Gelatin molds, Jell-O, mixing bowl, measuring cup, water, microwave, refrigerator, plastic knives, spoons, paper bowls or plates, jelly roll pan

What to do
1. Read the story of "The Other Frog Prince" in *The Stinky Cheese Man and Other Fairly Stupid Tales*.
2. Make green slime or green Jell-O, following the directions on the package.
3. Pour the Jell-O into a frog- or other-shaped mold, or pour the Jell-O onto a jelly roll pan.

4. Refrigerate. Once the Jell-O sets, let the children use plastic knives to carve out frog shapes for their snacks. Serve the Jell-O in paper bowls or on paper plates.
5. Eat and enjoy green frogs or green slime for snack.

Something to think about

For safety purposes, let an adult heat and pour the water to dissolve the Jell-O. Green slime can be created by not allowing the Jell-O to fully set and can be eaten from a paper cup or bowl. Older children can carve frogs from the green set Jell-O, adding marshmallow eyes or other decorations.

STORY S-T-R-E-T-C-H-E-R

Drama: Fracturing Chicken Licken

What the children will learn

To organize themselves and act like the characters

Materials you will need

Copies of "Chicken Little" and the fractured tale "Chicken Licken"

What to do

1. Read "Chicken Little."
2. Plan a dramatization of the story by selecting children to read and act out the parts of the narrator and the characters: Chicken Little, Ducky Lucky, Goosey Loosey, Cocky Locky, Foxy Loxy, and the king.
3. Have the narrator read his or her part. Each time a new character is introduced, repeat the former characters until the entire story is told.
4. Next, plan to dramatize how each character will act.
5. Dramatize the story for the class.
6. Redo the story and dramatize it this time as presented in the fractured tale of "Chicken Licken" in *The Stinky Cheese Man and Other Fairly Stupid Tales*.

Something to think about

Ask the children to redo the story and change it, giving it a twist, such as going to see the president, or having each of the characters desert Chicken Licken.

STORY S-T-R-E-T-C-H-E-R

Snack Time: Cheese Man Cutouts

What the children will learn

To carve the shape of a gingerbread man or the "Stinky Cheese Man"

Materials you will need

Slices of cheese, plastic knives, gingerbread man cookie cutters, napkins, crackers, juice

What to do

1. Read "The Stinky Cheese Man," which is a twisted tale of "The Gingerbread Man."
2. Distribute cheese slices to the children.
3. Let the children decide if they want to cut their cheese into the shape of the Gingerbread Man or the shape of the Stinky Cheese Man.
4. Serve the cheese slices with crackers for snack.

Something to think about

If some of the children's parents are bakers, invite them to make gingerbread men with the class.

STORY S-T-R-E-T-C-H-E-R

Writing: Combining Fairy Tales to Give Them a Twist

What the children will learn

To recall two fairy tales and to write with originality

Materials you will need

Copies of books with fairy tales, whiteboard, marker, paper, pencil

What to do

1. Read "Cinderumpelstiltskin or the Girl Who Really Blew It," and have the children recall the stories "Cinderella" and "Rumpelstiltskin." While many children will know "Cinderella," they might not know "Rumpelstiltskin."
2. Call attention to the things in the fractured fairy tale that were in the original stories.
3. Have the children write other fractured fairy tales that combine elements from other stories. "The Little Red Hen" might have an additional two characters, such as the tortoise and hare from the story "Tortoise and the Hare," instead of having the dog, cat, and mouse. "The Three Bears" could be visited by "Snow White and the Seven Dwarfs." The "Gingerbread Man" could chase the "Frog Prince" into a pond instead of being eaten by a clever fox.

Something to think about

Have the children leaf through fairy tale books for ideas. Let younger children draw their stories and help them to add text to their illustrations.

Waking Beauty

By Leah Wilcox
Illustrated by
Lydia Monks

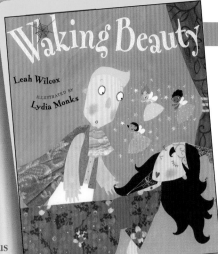

Story Line

Wilcox and Monks have turned a famous fairy tale on its ear, and that's just Prince Charming's problem. He doesn't use his ears to listen to the fairies guarding Sleeping Beauty. He tries many methods to wake her: shouting, "Lazy bones," dumping water on her, shooting her from a cannon, and—finally listening to the fairies—with a kiss. When she awakes she punches him out, and the story ends with a sleeping prince, until she wakes him with a kiss. The rhyming text and the colorful, humorous illustrations draw the listeners in, and the read-aloud sessions are sure to have children predicting the ends of phrases. The book is also a state award winner in several states.

Read-Aloud Presentation

Discuss fractured fairy tales, which are sometimes called twisted fairy tales. Let children recall what they know about the original Sleeping Beauty story, especially the part about what will awaken Sleeping Beauty—the kiss. Read the story, which is written in rhyme, but tell the children that you want them to just listen at the first reading and that during the second reading, you will show the pictures and pause for them to help fill in the blanks. Read, pausing where there is a rhymed couplet, such as those ending in *fair* and *hair, snout* and *out,* and *miss* and *kiss.* Place the book in the classroom library for children to enjoy during choice reading time.

STORY S-T-R-E-T-C-H-E-R

Art: Funniest Scenes

What the children will learn
To depict humor in their illustrations

Materials you will need
Drawing paper, pencils, markers, crayons, colored pencils

What to do
1. Look through Lydia Monks's illustrations in *Waking Beauty*. Ask the children, "What in the pictures makes the story funny?"
2. Draw attention to how Monks shows humor, such as the princess snoring with her mouth wide open (not the way princesses are usually seen), or describing the prince with his eyes popping out of his head (not the way princes are usually drawn). Also, talk about the funny antics, like the fairies pulling on the prince's ears.
3. Ask the children to draw the scenes in the story that they think are the funniest.

Something to think about
Create a bulletin board by removing the dust cover from the book and placing it on a board. Have the children add their drawings to create the bulletin board.

STORY S-T-R-E-T-C-H-E-R

Art: Fabric Collage

What the children will learn
To make collages using fabric

Materials you will need
Swatches of cloth, scissors, glue sticks or white paste, pencils, colored pens, markers, printer paper, heavy drawing paper or drawing paper

What to do
1. Look through the book of Lydia Monks's illustrations. Notice the patterns on the prince's and princess's clothing, as well the fairies' clothes and the draperies.
2. Show the children how to draw their pictures, without coloring in the clothing, then place a thin sheet of paper over their drawing and trace a pattern for the clothing in their pictures.
3. The children can cut out the pattern, place it on a piece

of fabric, draw around the pattern with a marker, and then cut around the pattern to create the fabric for the piece of clothing.

4. The children can glue or paste the fabric to the heavier paper to create a collage.

Something to think about
Ask parents or a fabric store to donate scraps of fabric for the children to use.

STORY S-T-R-E-T-C-H-E-R

Reading: Rhyming Word Matches

What the children will learn
To hear rhyming words and complete the rhymes

Materials you will need
Large index cards, markers

What to do
1. Look through the entire story of *Waking Beauty,* and copy down all of the rhyming words.
2. Make sets of rhyming word cards, with one word on each card.
3. Shuffle the cards and let the children find the rhyming word matches.

Something to think about
For young readers, provide a checklist in the library or reading area for the children to reference.

STORY S-T-R-E-T-C-H-E-R

Reading: One of the Versions of *Sleeping Beauty*

What the children will learn
To compare literature versions

Materials you will need
Copies of *Sleeping Beauty* found in your school library or in anthologies

What to do
1. Read one of the older versions of "The Sleeping Beauty," such as the one in the Charles Perrault book *The Complete Fairy Tales*, a reprint of the 1697 French tale. If the really old copies are not available, read a more recent version.

2. After reading the story aloud, reread *Waking Beauty.*
3. Let the children compare the two versions of the story, starting with the beginning, the main scenes, and the ending.

Something to think about
Many different cultures have sleeping-beauty-and-an-evil-spell tales. Consult with your school or public librarian and try to find stories from other cultures to compare to *Waking Beauty.* See the Education World website (www.educationworld.com) for other fractured fairy tale reading ideas.

STORY S-T-R-E-T-C-H-E-R

Writing: Change the Ending

What the children will learn
To write within a context but to use their imaginations to create an alternative story

Materials you will need
Writing paper, pencils

What to do
1. Reread the ending of *Waking Beauty.* Pause before the last page and discuss how the story could have ended with the fairies not caring anymore about a sleeping prince.
2. Let the students discuss some possible endings.
3. Cut sheets of writing paper the same size as *Waking Beauty.*
4. Encourage the children to write new, alternative endings.
5. Place the different endings in the back of *Waking Beauty.* The children will be eager to reread the ending with their versions.

Something to think about
For young primary children, let them draw their ending and tell the ending to a teacher or a reading-writing partner from another grade, with the partner writing what the young primary children have drawn. For younger writers, consider asking them to add a scene, such as another way to wake Sleeping Beauty.

Once Upon a Cool Motorcycle Dude

By Kevin O'Malley
Illustrated by Scott Goto and
Carol Heyer

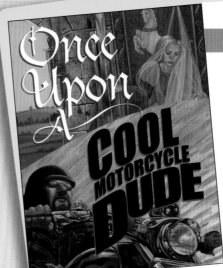

Story Line

Primary-grade children request that teachers and librarians read *Once Upon a Cool Motorcycle Dude* often. The laugh out-loud tale alternates between a boy and a girl who are assigned to tell a fairy tale together. The girl has the Fairy Princess's voice, and the boy tells about the Motorcycle Dude, but as they alternate telling the story, the reader also learns what the children are saying to each other and what they are thinking, not just the tale they invent. The gender stereotypes are evident at the beginning when the fairy tale falls along these expected lines. Then, the Fairy Princess has enough of the Motorcycle Dude making all of the decisions, so she takes over the action and breaks the stereotype. The contrasting styles of the characters are reflected in the art with the fairy-tale-type sweetness of the princess and the comic book style of the Cool Motorcycle Dude. Sure to be a hit among listeners and one that children will want to read on their own.

Read-Aloud Presentation

Show the cover of *Once Upon a Cool Motorcycle Dude*. Encourage a comparison of the two artistic styles and the two characters: the blonde, long-haired princess in fairy-princess dress in a castle, and the dark, helmeted motorcycle dude with his big gloves and dark visor. Tell the children that this book is full of stereotypes and discuss what that means. How do they expect the princess to act? How do they expect the motorcycle dude to act? Read the book, and at the end, surely there will be a request to read it again. Read it a second time, and pause to explore some of the more surprising pages.

Art: Cardboard Castle

What the children will learn
To use cardboard as a creative resource material and to work as teams, performing various roles

Materials you will need
Chart tablet, markers, variety of shoeboxes, corrugated cardboard, small sturdy gift boxes, thin poster board, pencils, markers, tempera paint, brushes, scissors

What to do
1. Have the children describe what a castle should look like. Look at the cover of *Once Upon a Cool Motorcycle Dude*. Notice the shapes of the stones of the castle, the turret, and the colors of the castle.
2. List the students' descriptive words on a chart tablet. Display it during the group castle construction.
3. Decide to make one castle or have teams of children construct several castles.
4. Choose an architect(s), who will draw up the plans; contractor(s), who will assemble the materials; and building boss(es). Break out of stereotypes.
5. Assign one lead from each group.
6. Have the architects draw a picture of the castle; the contractors assemble the materials the builders will need; the boss decides how to store and access the materials and how to begin building. The other builders will follow the lead of their head builder.
7. Allow the students several days to construct the castles and then paint and add details to their work.

Something to think about
Assembling the materials will take several days. As children begin their construction, they will decide on different types of materials they will need.

Art: Model Motorcycle Display

What the children will learn
To appreciate following directions and the skills of model building

Materials you will need
Simple model motorcycle kits, safe glue, volunteer, collections of models from other builders

What to do

1. Ask an experienced model builder to bring his or her model motorcycles to the classroom. Be certain each model can be handled.
2. Help the builder choose a simple motorcycle model kit for the children to build. Buy multiples of the kit, if possible.
3. Let individual children decide if they want to build a motorcycle model or not. Form teams of builders from the group of children who want to be builders. One member of the team can be in charge of the instructions for a day, another the gluer, and another the painter and decorator. Change the roles the following days.
4. Construct the motorcycle models and place them on display in front of the cardboard castles from the art center STORY S-T-R-E-T-C-H-E-R.

Something to think about

Partner with an older classroom and see if the model-building volunteers who help children learn how to build model motorcycles can come from that classroom.

Language Arts: May I Introduce

What the children will learn

To make introductions and use descriptive language

Materials you will need

Large index cards, different colored markers

What to do

1. Ask the children to describe what Fairy Princess and Motorcycle Dude are like at the beginning of *Once Upon a Cool Motorcycle Dude* and at the end.
2. Demonstrate how to introduce one child to another. For example, following the protocol, say the person's name to whom you want to introduce the other. "Brian, may I introduce my friend, Riley. Riley enjoys playing soccer and singing." "Riley, this is Brian. He is a writer, and he enjoys rebuilding houses."
3. Using this protocol, write an introduction for both Fairy Princess and Motorcycle Dude.
4. Let the children break into groups of three. One is the introducer and the other two students are Fairy Princess and Motorcycle Dude. Introduce Fairy Princess to Motorcycle Dude first, then change the order and introduce Motorcycle Dude to Fairy Princess first.

Something to think about

Princess could curtsey and Motorcycle Dude could offer a high-five slap or a low-five touch of hands. Help the

children to get into character. Then, have the students come up with a surprising reaction from their characters, such as having Motorcycle Dude bow and Princess high-five.

Social Studies: Challenging Gender and Social Stereotypes

What the children will learn

To think about gender and social stereotypes in books and in life

Materials you will need

None needed

What to do

1. Discuss how we usually describe a princess and how we usually describe a motorcycle dude. Talk about the usual descriptions and that they are called *stereotypes*.
2. Discuss stereotypes that may appear in the school. For example, most of the teachers may be female, and the principal or the custodian, males, but there are male teachers and female principals and custodians.
3. Talk about times in the story when the students knew that there were going to be some surprises about the roles—that the princess was not going to act how we thought a princess would act, and the motorcycle dude was not going to act how we thought the motorcycle dude would act.

Something to think about

Invite people who break gender stereotypes, such as a male nurse, a female construction worker, a male secretary, or a female pilot, to visit the class.

Writing: What Next for Princess and Motorcycle Dude?

What the children will learn

To write a next scene for *Once Upon a Cool Motorcycle Dude*

Materials you will need

Writing paper, pencils, drawing paper, markers, computer, scanner

What to do

1. Have the children brainstorm some ideas of what Princess and Motorcycle Dude might do after reading the ending in the book. Encourage several different variations.

2. Let the children draw and color pictures of their next scenes, using either fairy-tale-type drawings or comic-book-type drawings.

3. Scan the drawings into the computer, and show them to the class. Let the children take drawings that are not their own and write a story based on the drawings.

4. Edit the stories and scan the edited stories into the computer.

5. Print the drawings and scanned stories on the same size paper as *Once Upon a Cool Motorcycle Dude*. Insert the new versions into the back of the book.

Something to think about

Young primary-age children may have difficulty with writing outside of their stereotypes.

References

Munsch, Robert. 1992. *The Paper Bag Princess*. Illustrated by Michael Martchenko. Toronto: Annick Press.

O'Malley, Kevin. 2005. *Once Upon a Cool Motorcycle Dude*. Illustrated by Carol Heyer and Scott Goto. New York: Walker Books.

Scieszka, Jon. 1989. *The True Story of the 3 Little Pigs! By A. Wolf*. Illustrated by Lane Smith. New York: Penguin.

Scieszka, Jon. 1992. *The Stinky Cheese Man and Other Fairy Stupid Tales*. Illustrated by Lane Smith. New York: Penguin.

Wilcox, Leah. 2008. *Waking Beauty*. Illustrated by Lydia Monks. New York: Penguin.

Additional References

Lechner, Jack. 2008. *Mary Had a Little Lamp*. Illustrated by Bob Staake. New York: Bloomsbury. *Updating the classic rhyme,* lamp *instead of* lamb *gives this book a hilarious twist. Mary has a little lamp that she takes everywhere: to school, the movies, the circus, the zoo, and even a wedding. When she goes off to summer camp, she learns she can leave her little lamp on a shelf.*

Minters, Frances. 1997. *Cinder-Elly*. Illustrated by G. Brian Karas. New York: Puffin. *In this rap version of the traditional fairy tale, the overworked younger sister gets to go to a basketball game and meets a star player, Prince Charming.*

Scieszka, Jon. 1994. *The Frog Prince Continued*. Illustrated by Steve Johnson. New York: Puffin. *After the frog turns into a prince, he and the Princess do not live happily ever after, and the Prince decides to look for a witch to help him remedy the situation.*

Websites

1. Fractured Fairy Tales: www.readwritethink.org/files/resources/interactives/fairytales
   - Fractured fairy tale samples
   - Template for students to create their own fractured fairy tales

2. Education World: The Educator's Best Friend: www.educationworld.com/a_tsl/archives/031/lesson0003.shtml
   - Fractured fairy tale lesson plans submitted by teachers

3. Lesson Planet: The Search Engine for Teachers: www.lessonplanet.com/search?keywords=fractured+fairy
   - Seventy-five fractured fairy tale lesson plans, sorted by grade level
   - Printable worksheets
   - Fractured fairy tales skits

Appendix

Steps in Binding a Book

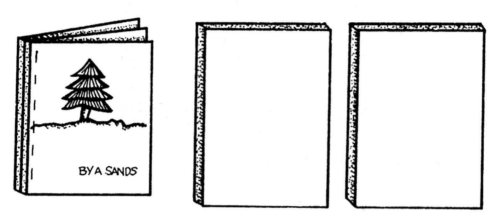

1 Cut two pieces of heavy cardboard slightly larger than the pages of the book.

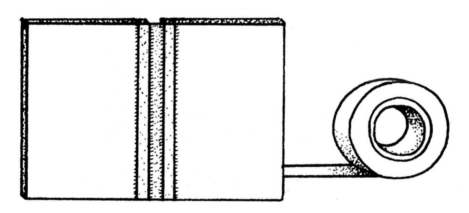

2 With wide masking tape, tape the two pieces of cardboard together with ½" space between.

3 Cut outside cover 1½" larger than the cardboard and stick to cardboard (use thinned white glue if cover material is not self-adhesive.

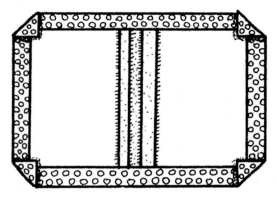

4 Fold corners over first, then the sides.

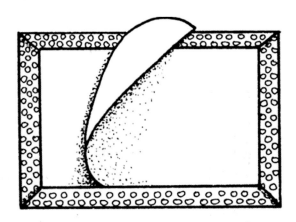

5 Measure and cut inside cover material and apply as shown.

6 Place stapled pages of the book in the center of the cover. Secure with two strips of inside cover material, one at the front of the book and the other at the back.

Songs

She'll Be Comin' 'Round the Mountain"

She'll be comin' 'round the mountain when she comes.

She'll be comin' 'round the mountain when she comes. Toot, toot! *(Pull an imaginary train whistle.)*

She'll be comin' 'round the mountain,

She'll be comin' 'round the mountain,

She'll be comin' 'round the mountain when she comes. Toot, toot! *(Pull an imaginary train whistle.)*

She'll be driving six white horses when she comes. Whoa back! *(Pull back the reins.)*

She'll be driving six white horses when she comes.

She'll be driving six white horses,

She'll be driving six white horses,

She'll be driving six white horses when she comes. Whoa back! *(Pull back the reins.)*

And we'll all go out to meet her when she comes. Hi, babe! *(Wave hand in greeting.)*

And we'll all go out to meet her when she comes.

And we'll all go out to meet her,

And we'll all go out to meet her,

And we'll all go out to meet her when she comes. Hi, babe! *(Wave hand in greeting.)*

We will all have chicken and dumplin's when she comes. Yum, yum! *(Rub tummy.)*

We will all have chicken and dumplin's when she comes.

We will all have chicken and dumplin's,

We will all have chicken and dumplin's,

We will all have chicken and dumplin's when she comes. Yum, yum! *(Rub tummy.)*

She'll be wearing red pajamas when she comes. Scratch, scratch. *(Scratch.)*

She'll be wearing red pajamas when she comes.

She'll be wearing red pajamas,

She'll be wearing red pajamas,

She'll be wearing red pajamas when she comes. Scratch, scratch. *(Scratch.)*

She'll have to sleep with Grandma when she comes. Move over. *(Make pushing motions.)*

She'll have to sleep with Grandma when she comes.

She'll have to sleep with Grandma,

She'll have to sleep with Grandma,

She'll have to sleep with Grandma when she comes. Move over. *(Make pushing motions.)*

We'll have a great big party when she comes. Yahoo! *(Swing arm over head for a lasso.)*

We'll have a great big party when she comes.

We'll have a great big party,

We'll have a great big party,

We'll have a great big party when she comes. Yahoo! *(Swing arm over head for a lasso)*

On the last line of each verse, say the words and perform the actions for that verse and all preceding ones. For example, at the end of the last verse say the words and do the actions for Yahoo; move over; scratch, scratch; yum, yum; hi, babe; whoa back; and toot, toot.

The Little Engine That Could version of "She'll Be Comin 'Round the Mountain"

She'll be on the little blue engine when she comes. Ya-hoo!

She'll be on the little blue engine when she comes. Ya-hoo!

She'll be on the little blue engine,

She'll be on the little blue engine,

She'll be on the little blue engine,

When she comes.

She'll be chugging 'round the mountain, when she comes,

She'll be chugging 'round the mountain, when she comes,

She'll be chugging 'round the mountain,

She'll be chugging 'round the mountain,

She'll be chugging 'round the mountain,

When she comes.

She'll be puffing "I think I can, I think I can, I think I can,"

She'll be puffing "I think I can, I think I can, I think I can,"

She'll be puffing "I think I can, I think I can, I think I can,"

When she comes.

She'll be shouting "I thought I could, I thought I could, I thought I could!"

She'll be shouting "I thought I could, I thought I could, I
thought I could!"
She'll be shouting "I thought I could, I thought could, I
thought could!"
When she's gone!

"Hush, Little Baby"

Hush, little baby, don't say a word,
Mama's gonna show you a mockingbird.
If that mockingbird won't sing,
Mama's gonna show you a diamond ring.
If that diamond ring turns brass,
Mama's gonna show you a looking glass.
If that looking glass gets broke,
Mama's gonna show you a billy goat.
If that billy goat won't pull,
Mama's gonna find you a cart and bull.
If that cart and bull turn over,
Mama's gonna bring you a dog named Rover.
If that dog named Rover won't bark,
Mama's gonna find you a horse and cart.
If that horse and cart fall down,
You'll still be the sweetest little baby in town.

"Lullaby and Good Night (Brahms's Lullaby)"
Lullaby, and good night,
With pink roses bedight,
With lilies o'erspread,
Is my baby's sweet head.
Lay you down now, and rest,
May thy slumber be blessed!
Lay you down now, and rest,
May thy slumber be blessed!

"Rock-a-bye, Baby"

Rock-a-bye, baby, in the tree top,
When the wind blows, the cradle will rock.
When the bough breaks, the cradle will fall,
And down will come baby, cradle and all.

"O, Susanna"

I came from Alabama
With my banjo on my knee,
I'm goin' to Louisiana
My true love for to see;
It rained all night the day I left,
The weather it was dry;
The sun so hot I froze to death;
Susanna, don't you cry.

O, Susanna,
O, don't you cry for me,
I've come from Alabama
With my banjo on my knee.
O, Susanna,
O, don't you cry for me,
'Cause I'm goin' to Louisiana,
My true love for to see.

I had a dream the other night
When ev'rything was still;
I thought I saw Susanna
A-comin' down the hill;
The buckwheat cake was in her mouth,
The tear was in her eye;
Says I, I'm comin' from the south,
Susanna, don't you cry.

O, don't you cry for me,
I've come from Alabama
With my banjo on my knee.
O, Susanna,
O, don't you cry for me,
'Cause I'm goin' to Louisiana,
My true love for to see.

I soon will be in New Orleans,
And then I'll look around,
And when I find Susanna
I'll fall upon the ground.
And if I do not find her,
Then I will surely die,
And when I'm dead and buried,
Susanna, don't you cry.

O, Susanna,
O, don't you cry for me,
I've come from Alabama
With my banjo on my knee.
O, Susanna,
O, don't you cry for me,
'Cause I'm goin' to Louisiana,
My true love for to see.

"The Story of Ibis" by Shirley Raines

(Tune:"Row, Row, Row Your Boat")
Row, row, row your boat
Out to see the whales.
Merrily, merrily, merrily,
There a big whale blows.

Row, row, row your boat
Out to see the whales.
What's that? What's that? What's that?
I-bis is caught.

Row, row, row your boat,
Out to see the whales.
Help her! Help her! Help her!
What are we to do?

Row, row, row your boat
Out to see our whale.
Attach a float, attach a float,
Pull her on home.

Cut, cut, cut the net
Off our dear Ibis.
Feed her well, feed her well,
Feed her well again.

Swim, swim, swim I-bis
Swim out to sea.
Wave goodbye, wave goodbye
So long.
Wave goodbye, wave goodbye, wa-ve,
    wa-ve, wa-ve
Goodbye!

"Over in the Rain Forest"

By Shirley Raines
Over in the rain forest, in their green, green home,
Lived an old mother sloth and her little sloth one.
"Move!" said the mother. "I move," said the one.
So they slowly move for a peek at the sun.

Over in the rain forest, in their green, green home,
Lived an old mother capuchin and her little capuchins two.
"Swing!" said the mother. "We swing," said the two.

So they swung across trees near the sky so blue.

Over in the rain forest, in their green, green home,
Lived an old mother hummingbird and her hummingbirds
    three.
"Hum!" said the mother. "We hum," said the three.
So they hummed near the flowers, the orchids, and a bee.

Over in the rain forest, in their green, green home,
Lived an old mother lizard and her little lizards four.
"Wake!" said the mother. "We wake," said the four.
So they stretched and stretched on the rain forest floor.

"Oh Where, Oh Where Can My Fox Tail Be?"

Oh where, oh where can I get some milk?
Oh where, oh where can it be?
Without the milk my tail is gone,
Oh where, oh where can it be?

Oh where, oh where can I get some grass?
Oh where, oh where can it be?
Without the grass, no milk have I,
Oh where, oh where can it be?

Oh where, oh where can I get some water?
Oh where, oh where can it be?
Without the water, no grass have I,
Oh where, oh where can it be?

Indexes

Index of Authors and Illustrators

Index of Children's Books

Index by Learning Centers or Interest Areas

Index

Index of Authors and Illustrators

Index of Children's Books

Index by Learning Centers or Interest Areas

Index

Y